THE OXFORD SHAKESPEARE

General Editor · Stanley Wells

The Oxford Shakespeare offers new and authoritative editions of Shakespeare's plays in which the early printings have been scrupulously re-examined and interpreted. An introductory essay provides all relevant background information together with an appraisal of critical views and of the play's effects in performance. The detailed commentaries pay particular attention to language and staging. Reprints of sources, music for songs, genealogical tables, maps, etc. are included where necessary; many of the volumes are illustrated, and all contain an index.

N. W. BAWCUTT, the editor of *Measure for Measure* in the Oxford Shakespeare, is Reader in English Literature at the University of Liverpool.

THE OXFORD SHAKESPEARE

Currently available in paperback

The rest of the plays and poems are forthcoming

OXFORD WORLD'S CLASSICS

WILLIAM SHAKESPEARE

Measure for Measure

Edited by
N. W. BAWCUTT

Oxford   New York

OXFORD UNIVERSITY PRESS

Oxford University Press, Great Clarendon Street, Oxford OX2 6DP

Oxford New York

*Athens Auckland Bangkok Bogota Bombay Buenos Aires
Calcutta Cape Town Dar es Salaam Delhi Florence Hong Kong Istanbul
Karachi Kuala Lumpur Madras Madrid Melbourne Mexico City
Nairobi Paris Singapore Taipei Tokyo Toronto Warsaw*

*and associated companies in
Berlin Ibadan*

Oxford is a trade mark of Oxford University Press

© *Oxford University Press 1991*

*First published by the Clarendon Press 1991
First published as a World's Classics paperback 1994
Reissued as an Oxford World's Classics paperback 1998*

*British Library Cataloguing in Publication Data
Data available*

*Library of Congress Cataloging in Publication Data
Shakespeare, William, 1564–1616.
Measure for measure / edited by N. W. Bawcutt
p. cm.—(The Oxford Shakespeare)
Includes index.
I. Bawcutt, N. W. II. Series:
Shakespeare, William, 1564–1616. Works. 1982.
PR2824.A2B39 1991
822.3'3—dc20 90–39513
ISBN 0–19–812908–4 (hbk.)
ISBN 0–19–283422–3 (pbk.)*

1 3 5 7 9 10 8 6 4 2

Printed in Spain by Book Print S.L.

PREFACE

LIKE all editors of Shakespeare I am deeply indebted to my predecessors. I have found J. W. Lever's Arden edition and Mark Eccles's New Variorum particularly valuable. Trevor Howard-Hill's concordance to the play has been useful at all stages of my work. I am grateful to the British Academy for the award of a Fellowship which enabled me to work for three months at the Folger Shakespeare Library. I am also grateful to my wife Priscilla for suggesting numerous improvements, to Dr Susan Brock for her generous help in finding illustrations, and to the General Editor, Stanley Wells, for his efficiency, helpfulness, and heroic patience.

N. W. BAWCUTT

CONTENTS

LIST OF ILLUSTRATIONS

GENERAL INTRODUCTION

Measure for Measure *as a Jacobean Play*

Measure for Measure has been strikingly popular for more than thirty years, both on the stage and in the study, and there have been wide divergences of theatrical and critical interpretation. This shows its continuing power to excite and puzzle us. At the same time, there is much in the play that is deeply rooted in the period at which Shakespeare wrote it, and we need to be aware of its historical background, though this will not necessarily determine our responses today.

The earliest allusion to the play occurs in a set of revels accounts, now in the Public Record Office, for the Christmas entertainments at court during the winter of 1604–5.[1] According

1. The entry for *Measure for Measure* in the Revels Accounts for 1604–5

to this document the play was performed by the King's company in the banqueting hall at Whitehall on St Stephen's Night (i.e. 26 December), 1604. The precise date of composition remains a matter of conjecture. On 1 November of the same year *Othello* had received at court its earliest recorded performance, and between November 1604 and February 1605 there were fourteen performances of plays at court, including Shakespeare's *The Merry Wives of Windsor*, *The Comedy of Errors*, *Love's Labour's Lost*, *Henry V*, and *The Merchant of Venice*, and plays by Jonson, Chapman, and Heywood. Though precise datings are rarely possible, some of these plays had been written ten or more years earlier, so it does not follow that the court performance of *Measure for Measure* was necessarily the first performance. (Also, the players would be

---

[1] PRO AO3/908/13; reprinted in *Collections Volume XIII: Jacobean and Caroline Revels Accounts, 1603–1642*, ed. W. R. Streitberger, The Malone Society (Oxford, 1986), p. 8.

unlikely to risk an untried play at court.) It is possibly relevant that the theatres were closed between 19 March 1603 and 9 April 1604 because of a severe outbreak of plague; no plays could have been performed during that period, but we simply do not know whether or not Shakespeare would have gone on composing plays during such a closure.

Some allusions in the play may have a topical significance that would help to date it, but this kind of material needs to be treated with caution. The play is set in Vienna, as repeated use of the place-name makes clear, and some references—to a peace-conference with the King of Hungary (1.2.1–5), a trip to Poland (1.3.14), and a special mission from the Pope (3.1.474–6)—are presumably intended to give the play a middle-European flavour. But the low-life section, with bawd, pimp, and comic constable, could easily have formed part of a play set in London, and there may well be allusions in the play to contemporary events in England. Some suggestions made so far about allusions are not fully convincing (see, for example, the commentary on 1.2.80–2); the most plausible relates to the opening section of Act 1, scene 2. The discussion between Lucio and the two gentlemen concerning an imminent peace that would deprive soldiers of their occupation, followed immediately by a mention of pirates (surely not very relevant to a Viennese context), seems to allude to King James's attempts in the summer of 1604 to negotiate a peace treaty with Spain. The treaty was signed on 18 August, and on the following day the king took an oath to observe its provisions and issued a royal proclamation to make it publicly known.[1] Privateers from London and the West Country had profited considerably from preying on Spanish shipping, an activity no longer legitimate in peacetime. (In any case, James hated pirates and did his best to suppress them.) If there is an allusion of this kind, the beginning of Act 1, scene 2 must necessarily have been written in the second half of 1604.

In the same scene Mistress Overdone is horrified to learn from her servant Pompey that a proclamation has ordered all the brothels in the suburbs of Vienna to be demolished. This has been related[2] to a proclamation by King James on 16 September

---

[1] No. 42 in *Stuart Royal Proclamations*, ed. J. F. Larkin and P. L. Hughes (Oxford, 1973), i. 91.

[2] Lever, pp. xxxii–xxxiii.

1603,[1] but it has nothing to say about brothels, and its main point is to prohibit new lodgers from residing in houses affected by plague. It does briefly mention pulling down houses, but this must be seen as part of a long though futile campaign by the authorities to prevent any increase in the size of London, and in particular to stop the growth of overcrowded slums which were regarded as breeding-grounds of disease and disorder.[2] James's proclamation refers back to one made by Queen Elizabeth on 22 June 1602, which ordered among other things that no new buildings should be erected except upon the foundations of older buildings, and that any building which flouted this rule should be demolished and the timber sold for the relief of the poor. A letter by John Chamberlain, dated 27 June 1602, indicates that some demolition did take place.[3] But most of the provisions in the 1602 proclamation are derived from a much earlier proclamation of 7 July 1580, and there was a parliamentary act forbidding new building in 1593. In 1596 the Privy Council ordered the Middlesex justices to investigate and suppress all kinds of disorderly houses, including brothels, in the suburbs of London.[4] The first audiences of *Measure for Measure* could easily accept the idea that a zealous magistrate would want to pull down brothels, but we should not restrict the topicality of the idea too narrowly.

The fact that the play had its first recorded performance at court has helped to inspire the speculation that it was deliberately written for court presentation and in particular for King James himself. It is even argued that the Duke is in some sense, differently defined from critic to critic, a portrait of King James, and that the play was intended to give the king advice on the correct behaviour of a ruler. Some of the evidence put forward to support this view is not very convincing. There are a few resemblances between *Measure for Measure* and the king's little treatise, *Basilicon Doron*, written in 1598 to give paternal advice to his young son Prince Henry. Seven copies were privately printed in Edinburgh in 1599, but in 1603 several editions were published in Edinburgh and London, and the book was widely

---

[1] Larkin and Hughes, *Stuart Royal Proclamations*, i. 47–8.

[2] See N. G. Brett-James, *The Growth of Stuart London* (London, 1935), especially chapter 3.

[3] *The Letters of John Chamberlain*, ed. N. E. McClure (Philadelphia, 1939), i. 153.

[4] *Acts of the Privy Council*, ed. J. R. Dasent (London, 1905), xxv. 230–1.

read by Englishmen anxious to gain an insight into the king's way of thinking. Most of the resemblances appear to be coincidental and some consist of commonplaces which Shakespeare had no need to learn from King James. Shakespeare may have read the book and remembered one or two details from it, but there is no case for arguing that he made systematic use of what is in fact a very miscellaneous collection of ideas, or was trying to show the king where he was mistaken.

There are, however, two features in Shakespeare's presentation of the Duke which may be more significant. The first is the Duke's dislike of the type of ruler who parades himself before his subjects because he enjoys popular acclaim (1.1.68–73). This is similar, though not identical, to Angelo's later metaphor describing the paralysing effect of his growing lust for Isabella:

> even so
> The general, subject to a well-wished king,
> Quit their own part, and in obsequious fondness
> Crowd to his presence, where their untaught love
> Must needs appear offence.
>
> (2.4.26–30)

While still in Scotland James had shown a dislike for crowds, possibly because the grim experiences of his youth made him terrified of attempts to kidnap or assassinate him. After his accession his progress southwards to London, beginning on 5 April 1603, drew what by contemporary standards were enormous crowds of English people who jostled to catch a glimpse of the new king. At first James enjoyed the public curiosity, perhaps because it reassured him that he was popular among his new subjects, but by the time he had got to London he had begun to tire of it, and in subsequent years, according to seventeenth-century biographers, he expressed bitter resentment at sightseers, however well-meaning, who thrust themselves into his presence.

The second point is the Duke's repeated references to slander and calumny, which have been related to James's own sensitivity on this issue.[1] An act of 1585 by the Scottish parliament made it treason to slander the king, and in 1596 a second act extended the offence to cover remarks made about the king's parents and

[1] See Ernest Schanzer, *The Problem Plays of Shakespeare* (London, 1963), p. 125.

4

ancestors. There were at least three executions in Scotland under the provisions of these acts, and James asked Burghley to punish Edmund Spenser for his portrayal of Mary Queen of Scots in *The Faerie Queene*, 5.9.38–50. James's claim to the English throne depended upon his legitimate descent from his great-grandmother Margaret Tudor, sister to Henry VIII and wife of the Scottish king James IV, but it was a common theme of contemptuous gossip that he was in fact the bastard son of his mother by David Rizzio. Slander of royalty, however, was also a serious offence in England, and in February 1601 a lawyer's clerk named Waterhouse was hanged at Smithfield for making libels against the queen.[1] Furthermore, slander of anyone in authority was dangerous: in the early part of Act 5 Isabella and Mariana seem at risk of severe punishment for apparently slandering Angelo.[2]

These connections between the play and the king have some plausibility, but if they are genuine they raise puzzling questions. Thomas Tyrwhitt, the earliest scholar to note the references to crowds, suggested that Shakespeare's intention was 'to flatter that unkingly weakness of James the first',[3] and this bluntly raises the central issue: was Shakespeare's purpose flattery, and if so, why did he base it on these particular aspects of the king's personality, which hardly seem an impressive foundation for it? (It is true that Shakespeare disliked riotous mobs, and portrayed them unsympathetically in several plays, but that is not the point at issue in *Measure for Measure*.) Is it likely that James would have been flattered by even a partial identification of the Duke as himself? In December 1604 the king's company performed a play about the Gowrie conspiracy of 1600, which could hardly have avoided putting the king on stage, but it was so thoroughly suppressed that we know very little about it. Shakespeare's only indubitable topical allusion is to the Earl of Essex in the chorus to Act 5 of *Henry V*, and there may be a flattering reference to Queen Elizabeth in *A Midsummer Night's Dream*, 2.1.155–64; both are incidental digressions done with tact and delicacy. It would be best to be sceptical about excessive claims for a royal presence in *Measure for Measure*.

---

[1] *Calendar of State Papers (Domestic)*, 1601–3, ed. M. A. E. Green (London, 1870), p. 88.

[2] Other references in the play to slander are discussed below, pp. 55–6.

[3] Thomas Tyrwhitt, *Observations and Conjectures upon some Passages of Shakespeare* (Oxford, 1766), p. 36.

On the question of the play's status as a tract directed at King James, it seems inherently implausible that a mere playwright would have the impertinence to act as schoolmaster to the king. The job of the king's company of actors, as set out in their patent, was to provide the king with 'solace and pleasure'; it was hard enough for the Privy Council to give him advice. In the first two years of James's reign there poured from the presses a flood of panegyrical poems, congratulatory addresses, descriptions of welcoming entertainments, sermons before the king, and the like. Most of them express simple delight at the accession of the king, and any political ideas they contain are the most bland and inoffensive commonplaces. As one anonymous pamphleteer put it:

> My muse dares undertake for to disclose
> Nothing but what the meanest reader knows.[1]

Some writers mention James's reputation as a scholar in tones which suggest that his learning made them even more diffident about presuming to address him. Finally, there is no evidence that James himself regarded *Measure for Measure* as anything out of the ordinary. He saw *The Merchant of Venice*, written between 1596 and 1598, on 10 February 1605, and liked it enough to request a second performance, which took place two days later. There was no repeat performance of *Measure for Measure*.

There are other ways in which the play belongs to its age, and some of the obsolete customs referred to may baffle the twentieth-century reader. One of these, vital to the plot, is the 'contract', or 'pre-contract'. It had some resemblance to the modern 'engagement' between a couple who intend to marry later, but had a much stronger legal force. As Richard Greenham remarked: 'although it be a degree under marriage, yet it is more than a determined purpose, yea more than a simple promise'.[2] In earlier centuries it had been a valid form of marriage for a couple simply to accept each other as husband and wife, though theologians believed that they ought subsequently to be publicly married in church after the banns had been called. It was not even oblig-atory to have witnesses to the contract, so that if a couple who had contracted privately later quarrelled it was impossible for an

---

[1] *Queen Elizabeth's Loss, and King James his Welcome* (London, 1603), A3^v (STC 21497).

[2] *A Treatise of Contract*, in *Works* (London, 1599), p. 288.

outsider to know precisely what had gone on between them. It is not surprising that the overwhelming mass of medieval marriage-litigation was concerned not with decrees of nullity but with attempts by one party to enforce a contract that the other party now repudiated.[1] The continuing coexistence of contract and marriage frequently created legal problems, but the anomalies were not removed until 1752, when Lord Hardwicke's Marriage Bill established that only a church wedding, made under certain specific conditions, was legally valid.

The problem was compounded by the fact that there were two versions of the contract, *de praesenti* and *de futuro*. Perhaps it would be best to let an Elizabethan lawyer define the difference:

First and principally spousals be either *de futuro*, of that which is to come, or else *de praesenti*, of that which is present. Spousals *de futuro* are a mutual promise or covenant of marriage to be had afterwards, as when the man saith to the woman, 'I will take thee to my wife', and she then answereth, 'I will take thee to my husband'. Spousals *de praesenti* are a mutual promise or contract of present matrimony, as when the man doth say to the woman, 'I do take thee to my wife', and she then answereth, 'I do take thee to my husband'.[2]

A *de praesenti* contract had almost the force of marriage, though the couple did not have the full legal status of husband and wife; it was indissoluble, and could annul a subsequent marriage by one of the parties, even if celebrated publicly in church and then consummated. The *de futuro* form was more conditional, and could be broken off by mutual consent, though it was made binding if the couple had intercourse. This at any rate was the theory, but it may be doubted whether the practice was equally neat. No set verbal forms existed for these two types of contract, and there was obviously much room for dispute in deciding which category a particular contract came into.

The device used by Claudio and Julietta of secretly contracting themselves but not marrying, in case they lose her dowry by alienating her family, is paralleled by an incident affecting Thomas Russell, one of the overseers of Shakespeare's will.[3] In

---

[1] See R. M. Helmholz, *Marriage Litigation in Medieval England* (Cambridge, 1974), p. 26.

[2] Henry Swinburne, *A Treatise of Spousals* (London, 1686), p. 8.

[3] The story is told in detail by Leslie Hotson, *I, William Shakespeare* (London, 1937), pp. 124–210.

1599 he wished to marry a rich widow, Anne Digges, but by her former husband's will she would have lost much of her property if she remarried. The couple therefore contracted themselves, and lived together as man and wife. In 1603 they were able to make arrangements which freed Anne Digges from the penalties of the will, and the couple married on 26 August 1603. Presumably they felt that the contract made their cohabitation legitimate, but it was clearly not fully equivalent to marriage. This ambiguous status helps to explain the paradoxes of Act 5 by which Mariana, who regards her contract to Angelo as still valid, can admit that she has never been married and yet considers herself and Angelo as wife and husband.[1]

Something must also be said of Elizabethan attempts to control sexuality through the law. Probably to most members of a modern audience the idea of sentencing a young man to death for making his fiancée pregnant is so utterly preposterous that Angelo must seem a kind of monster even to think of it. They are entitled to their opinion, but it does not follow that an Elizabethan (or to be strictly accurate, Jacobean) audience would have had precisely the same reaction. This does not mean for a moment that there was a single uniform 'Elizabethan' attitude to sexuality to which Shakespeare was obliged to conform. Official theory and popular practice were frequently at variance: the moralists and theologians took sexual offences very seriously, but complained bitterly that far too many people regarded them as trivial and undeserving of punishment. Philip Stubbes was scandalized by arguments that God approved of copulation because he had equipped man, as well as all his other creatures, with the organs of generation and told him to increase and multiply. For Stubbes this was legitimate only within the confines of holy matrimony, and all sexuality outside marriage was 'damnable, pestiferous, and execrable'.[2] Stubbes was an extremist, but very few even of the more moderate Elizabethans would have believed, and none would have had the audacity to put into print, the position

---

[1] It may also throw light on the play to cite a case tried in the ecclesiastical court in York in 1422, as given in Helmholz, op. cit., pp. 32–3, where the circumstances parallel Angelo's behaviour to Mariana, as described at 3.1.210–32. In this case, however, it was the girl who tried to repudiate a contract made before witnesses because her partner, a merchant, lost most of his money while abroad on a business venture.

[2] Philip Stubbes, *The Anatomy of Abuses*, Part I (London, 1583), G7^v–8^v.

increasingly popular in the twentieth century that sexuality is a purely private matter which the State should not attempt to regulate.

It does seem, indeed, that there was increasing pressure in the late sixteenth and early seventeenth centuries for sexual offences to be treated more rigorously. In the Old Testament adultery had been punished by death, and there were frequent assertions by the severer moralists that this was clearly the correct punishment, and several attempts were made to introduce parliamentary bills to alter the law. None succeeded until 1650, after the triumph of Puritanism, when a bill was passed which made adultery a felony punishable by death.[1] (It did not, apparently, have much impact, and lapsed after ten years.) The Puritans had no monopoly of this kind of moral rigour: in Sir Thomas More's *Utopia* adultery is punished on the first offence by slavery and on the second by death. How far Shakespeare was aware of this trend can only be conjectured. In one of his mad speeches (4.5.107–28) King Lear rejects the death penalty for adultery and uses the kind of naturalistic argument ('The wren goes to't, and the small gilded fly | Does lecher in my sight') that so horrified Stubbes, but it may be significant that the speech as a whole presents a nightmare vision of a world in which all restraints on sexuality have broken down.

Claudio's offence, ante-nuptial fornication, was easily recognizable to a contemporary audience, and it would normally have been dealt with by the Church or consistory court which met at intervals in most parishes. (These courts handled so many sexual offences that they were nicknamed the 'bawdy courts'.) In such matters there was an overlapping jurisdiction among the various Elizabethan courts, but we could perhaps say that the minor, personal offences were handled by the bawdy courts, those with social implications, like prostitution and bastardy, by the justices of the peace, and the more outrageous ones, such as flagrant adulteries by people of higher social standing, by the Church commissioners who sat at London and various major towns (the so-called Court of High Commission, abolished in 1641). The Church courts were entitled to investigate any offensive

[1] See Keith Thomas, 'The Puritans and Adultery: The Act of 1650 Reconsidered', in *Puritans and Revolutionaries*, ed. D. Pennington and K. Thomas (Oxford, 1978), pp. 257–82.

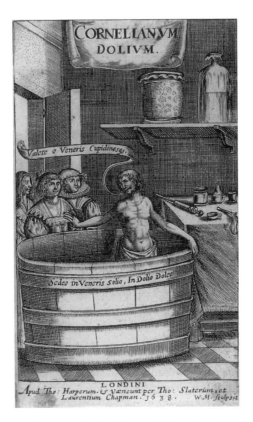

CORNELIANVM DOLIVM.

Valete ó Veneris Cupidinesqs,

Sedeo in Veneris Solio, In Dolio Dolco

LONDINI
Apud Tho: Harperum. & Vaeneunt per Tho: Slaterum, et
Laurentium Chapman. 1638. W.M. sculpsit

2. Title-page of *Cornelianum Dolium* by 'T.R.', 1638, showing the sweating-tub used to treat venereal disease (see 1.2.81 and 3.1.323)

behaviour, even if impelled to do so merely by local gossip or hearsay. Constables, like Elbow in Act 2, scene 1, and Act 3, could bring offenders before a magistrate, and they even had power to break into houses where they suspected the presence of illicit sexuality, a power which they sometimes used in the crudest way. Church and State thus provided an elaborate machinery for the punishment of various sexual misdemeanours, in a way which the twentieth century would find intolerable.

Those accused of ante-nuptial fornication could not escape

punishment simply by getting married; there are cases where a couple were 'presented', to use the technical term, because the early birth of a child proved that conception had taken place before marriage. The existence of a contract did not automatically remove the offence, though it might mitigate the punishment. (Thomas Russell and Anne Digges seem lucky to have got away with their arrangement; perhaps they carefully avoided any outward cause of scandal, and they were reasonably well off.) Offenders were not, of course, sentenced to death; normally they had to undergo penance and public humiliation by standing, sometimes in a white sheet, for a certain period of time before the congregation or in the local market-place. (Presumably the way in which Claudio is 'shown to the world', 1.2.115, is intended as a form of penance or humiliation.) Fornication which resulted in a bastard usually received a whipping. Severity of punishment varied from place to place and court to court. In Bury St Edmunds in 1578 a group of Puritan magistrates drew up a penal code by which the penalty for fornication was to be

tied to the post for that purpose appointed (having her hair cut off if it be a woman) and so remain tied to the post for the space of one whole day and a night, and that day to be the Lord's day, and after on the market day to be whipped, receiving thirty stripes well laid on till the blood come, the constable seeing the execution thereof.[1]

This seems harsh enough, but Puritan moralists poured scorn on the traditional punishments for fornication of penance and whipping as ridiculously lenient. The offence of ante-nuptial fornication was not legally abolished in England until 1787; by then it had become largely a dead letter, though in Scotland Robert Burns had to do penance for getting Jean Armour pregnant as late as 1786.

The conclusion appears to be that a spectator of *Measure for Measure* in the early seventeenth century lived in a society that attempted to control sexuality in all its manifestations, where radical voices took a fundamentalist religious line that urged a far more rigorous control than actually existed. (It is a nice irony that *Measure for Measure* contains the first use recorded in *OED* of the word 'permissive' in its modern sense.) In such a context Angelo's

[1] Quoted from Patrick Collinson, *The Religion of Protestants: The Church in English Society 1559–1625* (Oxford, 1982), pp. 158–9.

behaviour in condemning Claudio to death for fornication would probably seem painfully plausible rather than so extreme as to be absurd. As the following section on sources will make clear, the story of sexual blackmail which lies at the centre of the play was used by many other writers of the sixteenth century, and several of them were concerned with the social control of sexuality and the punishment of sexual offences, though the degree of severity they advocated varied widely.

Sources

The main plot of *Measure for Measure* derives ultimately from a story widely popular throughout Western Europe during the sixteenth century. It was a moral exemplum rather than a folk-tale, and some of the earliest examples of its use occur in theologians and historians. It was known to Luther and Melancthon, and is often found in a kind of treatise popular with Protestant clergymen, in which harsh moral lessons are drawn from lurid anecdotes of sin and punishment. (A good English example is Thomas Beard's *The Theatre of God's Judgements*, London, 1597.) The story also had a literary appeal, and formed the foundation of several narrative poems, plays, and short stories. Many of these versions cannot be shown to have any direct relationship to *Measure for Measure*, and it would be tedious to list them in detail.[1] We could, however, summarize the most popular form of the story in the following way, as a starting-point to a discussion of Shakespeare's treatment of the theme.

A man is in prison under sentence of death, either as a prisoner of war or because he has committed a crime which renders him liable to execution. His beautiful wife goes to an official, civil or military, to plead for her husband's pardon and freedom. The official is attracted by her, and offers to release her husband if she will spend the night with him. (In several versions a sum of money is offered by the wife or demanded by the official.) Very

---

[1] Most earlier editions of the play, and the standard discussions of Shakespeare's sources, do not fully indicate how widely the story was known, and need to be supplemented by John Hazel Smith, 'Charles the Bold and the German Background of the "Monstrous Ransom" Story', *PQ* 51 (1972), 380–93. Some additional details are given in Eccles, pp. 387–90.

reluctantly the wife agrees and carries out her side of the bargain, sometimes after obtaining her husband's agreement. Despite his promise the official orders the husband to be hurriedly executed and returns his body to his wife. She complains to a higher level of authority; the overlord, duke or emperor, is horrified at the official's treachery and decides on the appropriate punishment. The official is forced to marry her and also to make financial restitution, in some versions endowing her with all his property. He is then executed.

It cannot be established precisely how the story originated, and to what degree it is history rather than fiction. In one important set of versions the higher authority is Charles the Bold, Duke of Burgundy from 1467 to 1477; in another he is described as 'Gonzaga Duke of Ferrara', and the events take place in Como in 1547. One German writer, Andreas Hondorff, gave both versions consecutively, as though he regarded them as two distinct stories (*Theatrum Historicum*, Frankfurt, 1575, p. 476). As we should expect, the writers of plays and short stories add many kinds of independent variations to the story, some of which will be considered later, and they give names and motives to the characters in their own distinctive fashion.

Most modern readers will probably see the story as one of unrelieved painfulness, and some of the authors concerned emphasize what seems like gratuitous cruelty in the way it unfolds. In several versions the official sends the husband's body back to his wife and then claims that he has carried out his promise to release him, a grim joke that Shakespeare uses in *Measure for Measure*, 4.3.113–14. In Lupton's *The Second Part ... of ... Too Good to be True* (1581) the official is punished by a betrayal similar to the one he had inflicted on his victim: he is deliberately allowed to assume that by marrying the woman he has redeemed his crime, but on emerging from the church after his wedding he is stopped and led off to execution. The woman at the centre of the story is in an impossible position; we cannot expect her to settle down comfortably in a marriage to her blackmailer and the executioner of her first husband, yet we find it difficult to sympathize when Lupton makes her gloat exultingly over his death.

Whatever the twentieth-century reader may feel, Protestant theologians of the sixteenth century had no difficulty whatever in accepting the story. Luther was delighted by the 'princely way' in which Charles the Bold dealt with the problem:

No pope, no jurist, no lawbook could have given him such a decision. It sprang from untrammeled reason, above the law in all the books, and is so excellent that everyone must approve of it and find the justice of it written in his own heart.[1]

Beard, who borrowed the Gonzaga version from Hondorff's *Theatrum Historicum*, was equally laudatory: 'O noble justice, and comparable to the worthiest deeds of antiquity, and deserving to be held in perpetual remembrance!'[2] It may indeed have been the rigour with which justice was carried out that aroused their enthusiasm: Beard told another story, borrowed from a German moralist named Albert Krantz and also found in Hondorff, of a man executed for rape despite the fact that he had subsequently married the woman, who no longer wished to press charges against him. Beard explicitly rejected the idea that marriage could atone for sexual offences:

A notable example for them that after they have committed filthiness with a maid think it no sin, but competent amends, if they take her in marriage whom they abused before in fornication.[3]

Hondorff linked the *Measure for Measure* story with one in which a young nobleman of the court of Charles the Bold raped a peasant girl while out hunting. Charles forced the nobleman to marry the girl and then had him executed, despite the protests of his courtiers, who considered that to turn a woodcutter's daughter into a countess was an ample reparation for her injuries.

Some versions of the *Measure for Measure* story bring it closer to these rape anecdotes in portraying the supreme authority-figure as carrying out justice with inflexible rigour, regardless of the wishes of those involved. In his history of the duchy of Burgundy a Flemish writer, Pontus Heuter, claimed that after Charles the Bold had forced the official to marry his victim, the duke asked her whether she was fully satisfied with the reparation done to her. Even though she said that she was, the duke exclaimed, 'but

[1] Martin Luther, *Temporal Authority: To What Extent It Should Be Obeyed* (1523), from *Works*, general editor H. T. Lehmann, vol. 45 (Philadelphia, 1962), p. 129.

[2] Thomas Beard, *The Theatre of God's Judgements* (London, 1597), p. 314.

[3] Ibid., p. 313.

I am not yet satisfied', and ordered the official to be executed in the same cell where the husband had perished. Not surprisingly, the woman was shattered by her experiences and died two years later.[1] In all the versions where the suffering couple are husband and wife, the only sense in which there is 'measure for measure' is an Old Testament one, an eye for an eye and a tooth for a tooth: a brutal crime receives an equally brutal punishment.

Three writers, of whom the last and greatest is Shakespeare, made radical innovations in their handling of the story. The earliest is the Italian, Giovanni Baptista Giraldi Cinthio, whose *Hecatommithi*, first published in 1565, is a collection of a hundred stories divided into ten sections or 'decades'. As a whole the collection is very miscellaneous: some tales are of sordid or brutal crimes, and among the love stories some deal with extremes of romantic fidelity while others are comic or even obscene. This collection provided the source for *Othello* (Decade 3, novella 7), and several other Elizabethan and Jacobean dramatists borrowed plots from it. The two stories used by Shakespeare were not translated into English during his lifetime, though there was a French translation of the whole collection by Gabriel Chappuys which appeared in two parts, 1583–4. In the case of *Measure for Measure*, the French version omitted several sentences of the Italian, and in certain points of detail seems slightly further from Shakespeare than the original.

The narrative related to *Measure for Measure* occurs as the fifth novella of the eighth decade. Cinthio usually had a common theme linking together the narratives within a section, and in the eighth decade it was ingratitude: the first four stories are all of appalling treachery and cruelty shown by children or servants towards their kindly benefactors. The narrator of the fifth novella, a woman named Fulvia, argues that kings should punish ingratitude as severely as more obvious crimes like murder, but her story is not simply one of an exemplary punishment inflicted on a corrupt official by his overlord, as in the Protestant moralists mentioned earlier. In this case the goodness and courtesy of a woman have a redemptive quality, and events conclude in forgiveness and reconciliation. It is possible, though the point is not explicitly made, that Fulvia intended her portrayal of a

---

[1] Pontus Heuter, *Rerum Burgundicarum Libri Sex* (Antwerp, 1584), pp. 165–7.

woman of noble character to counterbalance the immediately preceding narrative, in which a woman behaves with repulsive brutality.

Cinthio altered the story in various ways, the most important of which was to turn the heroine from the wife to the sister of the condemned man. In one way this simplifies matters: instead of being in a triangular sexual relationship between her husband and would-be seducer, the girl is a young virgin who is free to marry if she wishes. (Indeed, it is made fairly clear that if the official had married her and freed her brother she would not have felt undue resentment at the loss of her virginity.) The official's conduct is made to seem deeply repellent: he dangles the prospect of marriage in front of the girl with no serious intention of marrying her, and secretly orders her brother to be executed before he gets into bed with her. Presumably Cinthio intended the official's callous behaviour to make the girl's generosity at the end of the tale appear even more striking: once she has become the official's wife she cannot bear to think of herself as responsible for his death, and successfully pleads for his pardon.

As in earlier writers the girl is the central figure of the story, but Cinthio gave her a fuller personality than his predecessors had done. She is both beautiful and intelligent; she has been taught philosophy by an old man acting as a tutor to herself and her brother, and presents very skilfully the arguments for her brother's pardon. In begging her to give in to the official's demands, the brother tells her that she is refined and attractive and has a wonderful way of talking (*sei gentilesca, et avvenente, hai una mirabile maniera di favellare*), a description that may have inspired Claudio's portrait of Isabella (1.2.182–4). She responds passionately to events, but can control her feelings when necessary (as when she successfully conceals from the official her bitter resentment at his betrayal), and at several points she allows wiser or nobler second thoughts to overrule her initial response. Despite a number of obvious differences, Cinthio's heroine is closer to Shakespeare's Isabella than any of the women in other sixteenth-century versions.

Cinthio made the girl's brother a boy of 16; his offence is rape, punishable by death whether or not the man is willing to marry his victim, but his action was provoked by a violent love he could not control rather than brutality, and he would be only too glad to marry the girl. In these circumstances, it is implied, mercy would be appropriate, and the official is put in a position where he orders another man to be executed for an offence similar to one that he himself is about to commit. Cinthio thus began the process, which Shakespeare later carried to an extreme, of introducing symmetrical patterns into a somewhat disconnected narrative. Cinthio also opened his story with a distinctive episode in which the official is appointed to his post by the overlord (in this case the Emperor Maximilian) and told to uphold justice at all costs, even against the Emperor himself. This was obviously the model for Shakespeare's opening scene in *Measure for Measure*, though Shakespeare, unlike Cinthio, did not give Angelo the option of turning down the post if he felt inadequate to it. This episode helps to link the beginning to the end of the story: the overlord will naturally be interested in the conduct of an official he has deliberately and personally appointed to his post.

At some time before his death in 1573 Cinthio turned his story into a five-act play called *Epitia*, published in 1583 by his son Celso Giraldi, who made it clear in dedicating the play to the Duchess of Ferrara that it had remained unacted in manuscript until that date. Cinthio revised the plot in a way that made it very different from *Measure for Measure*, and the detailed verbal resemblances that scholars have detected between the two plays may be no more than coincidences. Since, however, there is a faint possibility that Shakespeare did read *Epitia*, which has some interest and artistic value of its own, it deserves a brief account.

As a neo-classical dramatist Cinthio set the action within a single day, that immediately following the night in which Epitia gave herself to the official (it is a happy coincidence that the Emperor chanced to be in the neighbourhood on that day). There are therefore no interviews between Epitia and the official, or between Epitia and her brother, who never appears on stage. Furthermore, Cinthio added several supplementary characters not in his novella, in a way which rather dilutes the intensity of the action. There is a *podestà* (a kind of judge or magistrate) who was responsible for sentencing the brother to death for rape and is single-mindedly determined that justice shall be done and the appropriate sentence carried out. The official is given a secretary who pleads with the *podestà* for mercy to the brother. Additional female characters include an older sister for the official and an aunt for Epitia. Perhaps with some surprise the audience learns that during the events which preceded the opening of the play Epitia gave up in despair when the official refused to pardon her brother, and it was the official's sister who suggested that Epitia should sleep with the official, in return for which he promised to marry her and free her brother. After he has broken his word and given orders for the execution to go ahead, Epitia can think only of vengeance, and it is her aunt who suggests that she should go to the Emperor. An obvious result of these changes is that in the play Epitia and the official are much more subordinate characters, and much less directly responsible for their behaviour, than in the novella.

When the play opens the brother is in prison under sentence of death, but the atmosphere is not sombre. The *podestà* grumbles because justice looks like being thwarted, but all the other characters rejoice because a happy solution has been found to a potentially tragic situation. Epitia expresses no anguish at the sacrifice of her virginity, and no one else condemns her for having made the sacrifice. (Most of the characters in the play seem to know what has happened.) There is no suggestion that the official has resorted to sexual blackmail; on the contrary, remarks made on the power female beauty has over men convey some impression that Epitia has seduced him. In this version the official is not a cold-blooded hypocrite: at first quite happy to carry out his bargain with Epitia, he changes his mind through fear that the *podestà* will denounce him to the Emperor for failing to fulfil his duty. He is thus torn between love and duty, somewhat like a hero in Corneille, but he has after all made a promise, and most of the other characters, including his sister and the Emperor, are outraged by his breach of faith. He is condemned to marry and then to be executed, but at the end of the play Cinthio made some important changes from his earlier version. Epitia is pleased that the official is about to die, even though he is her husband, and refuses to intercede for him even when the other women beg her to. Then, at the last moment, a new character is introduced: a captain of the guard, a kindly man similar to Shakespeare's provost, who took pity on the brother and saved his life, substituting a justly executed criminal who fortunately closely resembled him. Only after the captain has begged her to save the life of the official is Epitia willing to plead for him. She is quite unlike the noble heroine of the novella, and the play ends with a rather trite moral that despite the strange reversals and uncertainties of fortune man must place his faith in divine providence.

Cinthio's novella was borrowed by George Whetstone as the basis of his two-part play *Promos and Cassandra*, published in 1578 but probably never performed. In his dedication Whetstone rebuked contemporary English dramatists for failing to observe critical decorum in various ways, but his own play has none of the neo-classical austerity of *Epitia*. He made no attempt to observe the unities, and added an elaborate sub-plot, full of independent scenes of low-life trickery and deception. His dramaturgy was crude and amateurish: most of Cinthio's events were used up in the first part of the play, and the second part, which roughly corresponds to Shakespeare's fifth act, had to be padded out with much extraneous matter. Whetstone's verse is clumsy (he had no gift for memorable poetry), and his character-portrayal completely lacks subtlety. Yet there does emerge from the play a genuine sympathy for those oppressed by corrupt officials and excessively harsh laws, and even the rogues are sometimes treated with a comic tolerance that is faintly Shakespearian.

Whetstone added a number of distinctive features to his treatment of the story. Promos, corresponding to Angelo, is a grey-haired old man who suddenly becomes infatuated with Cassandra. There is no preliminary interview between Promos and the king who appoints him, which strengthens the case for Shakespeare's having read Cinthio's *Hecatommithi*. Promos has a corrupt subordinate called Phallax, and it is he who suggests to Promos that he can blackmail Cassandra. Phallax himself blackmails a beautiful prostitute called Lamia who is brought to him for punishment together with her comic servant Rosko: in return for his protection she must yield him sexual favours. She willingly accepts the arrangement, and Whetstone may have intended the incident as a deliberate contrast to Cassandra's behaviour in the main plot. Shakespeare borrowed the woman and her servant, but gave her a much smaller part and transformed her to an elderly procuress, Mistress Overdone.

The brother's role is significantly enlarged. His gaoler takes pity on him and allows him to escape, substituting the head of a man recently executed for the brother's head. This is strikingly similar to Cinthio's device in *Epitia*, but the two writers must have hit on the idea independently. (It is after all a fairly obvious way of keeping the brother alive.) Whetstone went a stage further: wandering about the countryside in disguise, the brother encounters a rustic who tells him that the official is about to be executed. He goes off to witness the execution, but is so moved by his sister's distress at the imminent death of her new husband that he bravely decides to reveal himself to the king, despite the risk involved, in the hope that his survival will influence the king to pardon Promos. The king, of course, pardons both men. Unlike Shakespeare, Whetstone seems to have wanted to balance the brother against the sister, each taking a risk for the sake of the other.

Certain innovations in *Promos and Cassandra* clearly lead on to *Measure for Measure*. The brother's condemnation is based on the revival of a harsh old law which previous judges had allowed to fall into abeyance. His offence is not very clearly stated: Promos insists on regarding it as rape, but from what the other characters say it seems to be a case of a girl giving way to the demands of her ardent lover. The girl herself appears on stage, in the blue gown of a penitent, lamenting her misfortune. The brother urges his sister to plead with Promos for mercy, not as in Cinthio's *Hecatommithi* where she goes of her own accord. In Part 2 of *Promos and Cassandra* the king ceremonially enters the city rather like Shakespeare's Duke in Act 5 of *Measure for Measure*; the king already knows of Promos's wickedness, but pretends to be pleased with him.

Four years later Whetstone published the story as a prose narrative in his *Heptameron of Civil Discourses* (1582), using his own play as a source. (A marginal note in the *Heptameron* made it clear that so far the play had not been performed.) The prose version is only a few pages long, and much of the play, including the low-life sub-plot, was omitted. There are a few shifts of emphasis—here the brother is more reluctant than his counterpart in the play to urge his sister to submit to Promos—but they are very briefly touched on and are unlikely to have influenced Shakespeare. One or two features in other parts of the *Heptameron* may remind us of *Measure for Measure*, but not so clearly as to suggest indebtedness on Shakespeare's part. There is a crude version of the bed-trick, which Whetstone borrowed from Boccac-

cio's *Decameron*, Day 8, Novel 4, and one of Whetstone's characters, named Lucia Bella, is determined to be a nun but is won over
to acceptance of marriage by the end of the book.

Another relatively detailed version of the *Measure for Measure*
story that Shakespeare could easily have read occurs in the
second part of Thomas Lupton's *Siuqila. Too Good to be True* (Part
1, 1580; Part 2, 1581). Siuqila (Aliquis, 'Somebody') from
Ailgna (Anglia, 'England') meets Omen (Nemo, 'No-one') from
Mauqsun (Nusquam, 'Nowhere'), and the book consists entirely
of dialogues in which the two men compare the morals and laws
of their respective countries, much to the detriment of Ailgna.
Mauqsun is a Puritan Utopia in which immorality is almost non-
existent, partly because the inhabitants are virtuous by nature
and partly because the rare acts of misbehaviour that do occur
are punished with terrifying rigour. Adulterers, for example, are
stoned to death, and anyone attempting to defend them is
deprived of half his property. No girl ever becomes pregnant
before her marriage, and Omen believes that if she did the other
girls would tear her to pieces in their righteous indignation. In a
case that occurred many years ago the couple were obliged to go
about for a year dressed in goat-skins, 'with the hairy side
outward'. The story related to *Measure for Measure* is told by
Siuqila himself, and set vaguely in an unnamed foreign country,
not in Mauqsun. Lupton seems not to have known of Cinthio or
Whetstone, and used the older version in which the woman is the
wife of the condemned man. Lupton describes the interviews
between the wife and the official, a corrupt judge, in some detail,
but the story remains a grim tale of treachery which meets its
merited punishment. Lupton's book as a whole gives a vivid
picture of a State governed by 'strict statutes and most biting
laws', but it is hard to believe that Shakespeare could have read it
with much enjoyment.

How extensively did Shakespeare study the varying forms of
the story used in *Measure for Measure*? He certainly knew *Promos
and Cassandra*, and it is highly probable that he took account of
Cinthio's *Hecatommithi*. He may have read Cinthio's *Epitia*,
though it can hardly have been easily accessible to him,[1] and

---

[1] *Epitia*, printed in 1583, appears never to have been subsequently reprinted.
Hecatommithi, first printed in 1565, went into at least five further editions before
the end of the century.

Whetstone's *Heptameron*, though readily available, had little fresh to offer him. His knowledge of the other versions, in which the condemned man is the woman's husband, not her brother, is even more problematical. When, for example, the duke condemns Angelo, he awards all his property to Mariana as a dowry (5.1.423–6). There is nothing similar to this in Cinthio or Whetstone, but in some of the husband-and-wife versions the official's possessions go to the wife after the official has been executed. But Angelo had rejected Mariana precisely because of her lack of a dowry, and Shakespeare may have added this small touch because he found it ironically appropriate, not because he came across it somewhere in his reading. It would be an odd assumption that Cinthio and Whetstone were capable of inventing fresh variations on the story, but Shakespeare was not.

It is not easy to determine precisely what potentialities Shakespeare saw in the story as he first encountered it, or to assess the purposes, psychological and ethical, behind the modifications he introduced. Even so, we can perhaps manage to isolate some of the distinctive features of his own version and to put forward tentative explanations for them. On the most general level, he seems to have been concerned to shape the narrative in a more coherent manner than his predecessors, partly by making the various sections of the plot more closely related to each other than they had been. In the earliest versions of the story there had been some concern for symmetry: the execution of the official balances the execution of the husband, though a second marriage is hardly an equivalent, at least in the eyes of a modern reader, to a seduction which comes close to rape. Cinthio and Whetstone added fresh parallelisms: they both, for example, made the brother's offence a matter of sexuality, so that the official condemns another man to death for behaviour which is no worse than his own. When the brother is rescued from death it becomes easier to rescue the official as well.

Shakespeare adopted this pattern and extended it. He provided a fresh link between Claudio and Angelo by making them both contracted to marry a woman, though Angelo has long since repudiated his contract to Mariana. Much scholarly effort has gone into determining whether these contracts were *de praesenti* or *de futuro*, but the way they are described in the play suggests that Shakespeare was not concerned to establish distinctions of this kind. But there is a difference between the two contracts which critics neglect. Angelo's contract is mentioned on four separate occasions; at the end of the play it is referred to twice in public, and is finally acknowledged by Angelo himself. Claudio tells Lucio of his contract to Julietta in 1.2, but we never hear of it again, and no one else in the play appears to know about it. The version of events that Lucio gives to Isabella is simply, 'he hath got his friend with child' (1.4.29). Isabella seems to think that Claudio has irresponsibly seduced Julietta, and her attitude has important consequences which must be considered later. The Duke's last words to Claudio are, 'she, Claudio, that you wronged, look you restore' (5.1.528); there is no hint of 'say, wast thou e'er contracted to this woman?' (5.1.376).

Both Cinthio and Whetstone rescued the brother by substituting for him the corpse of a recently executed criminal. Shakespeare seized on the concept of substitution, and made it ramify throughout the play. In its literal form, one person takes the place of another. In its more metaphorical form the characters are urged to imagine themselves in someone else's place, in order to achieve a more sympathetic understanding of his behaviour.[1] The original substitution is duplicated: Barnardine refuses to be executed, so a fresh substitute, Ragozine, has to be found. Angelo is presented not simply as a senior official appointed by the Duke, but as completely taking over the Duke's functions during his absence, with 'absolute power and place' (1.3.13). The word 'substitute' is used four times in *Measure for Measure*, always with reference to Angelo.

Above all, Mariana goes to bed with Angelo in place of Isabella. This use of the 'bed-trick' makes *Measure for Measure* unique compared to its predecessors: in this work alone the blackmailed girl does not in fact yield to the official, though she pretends to. Shakespeare also used the bed-trick in *All's Well that Ends Well*, and here the device is an integral part of the plot as Shakespeare found it in Boccaccio's *Decameron*, Day 3, Novel 9. Because of this it is usually assumed that *All's Well that Ends Well* is the earlier of the two plays, and that Shakespeare borrowed from himself when he came to write *Measure for Measure*. In both plays the girl is contracted or actually married to the man she sleeps with, and

---

[1] Most strikingly at 2.1.8–16 and 2.2.64–70 and 138–43; other relevant passages are at 2.4.99–104, 3.1.110–17, 378–82, and 519–20, and 5.1.109–13.

the trick is seen not as a culpable deception but as a means of creating good out of evil, of making the man involved right an old wrong rather than commit a fresh one. Alone among the heroines of the blackmail story, Isabella is shown to us as a postulant to a religious order, though she has not yet taken any vows. As a potential bride of Christ, Isabella would naturally be deeply reluctant to surrender her virginity to Angelo, but as I shall argue later Shakespeare could easily have had other motives for giving her this rather specialized status.

Shakespeare gave his overlord, the Duke, a more extended and elaborate role than in any earlier version. He made the Duke deliberately appoint Angelo, like Cinthio in his *Hecatommithi*, and gave him a ceremonial re-entry in Act 5, such as Whetstone gave to the king in *Promos and Cassandra*. But Shakespeare alone provided the Duke with a friar's disguise which enables him to observe the action unrecognized. There seems to have been a vogue for disguised rulers in plays roughly contemporary with *Measure for Measure*, such as Middleton's *The Phoenix* and Marston's *The Malcontent*, but the device is common enough on the stage, and had already been used by Shakespeare in *Henry V*, so there is little point in looking for a particular source.

The Duke's continuing presence helps to hold the play together, but it also has less happy consequences. If Shakespeare was going to work the bed-trick, he needed a substitute for Isabella, but he could hardly make Isabella herself suggest the device, and still less name a possible candidate. It was easy enough to make the Duke do so, but the result was to diminish Isabella's significance: she is no longer the independent and resourceful heroine of Cinthio's novella, who single-handedly determines the course of events. The Duke's presence also leads to what is, in terms of narrative structure, the weakest moment in the play. When Isabella visits the prison at 4.3.103 she expects to hear that her brother has been pardoned, but if her plea for Angelo's life in Act 5 is to be fully effective she must be convinced that her brother is dead. In earlier versions where the brother was rescued it was a private arrangement between the brother and the gaoler, both of whom were anxious to conceal what had happened. In Shakespeare's play the Duke has organized the rescue and knows the full truth, but is forced by the exigencies of the plot to lie to Isabella and make a feeble excuse for doing so:

> I will keep her ignorant of her good,
> To make her heavenly comforts of despair
> When it is least expected.

$$(4.3.106-8)$$

If my argument is correct this weakness must be debited to Shakespeare's plot-arrangement, not to the Duke's personal character.

Shakespeare took over from Whetstone a sub-plot involving low-life characters, but made a number of significant modifications. Whetstone's equivalent of Angelo has other crimes to expiate apart from blackmailing a virgin into sexual submission, and his subordinates are brutal and corrupt. Angelo's offence in *Measure for Measure* is serious enough, but appears to be an isolated lapse, and the other senior officials, Escalus and the Provost, are conscientious and humane. Elbow, the constable, is comically inefficient but not corrupt. *Measure for Measure* does not present a Viennese society riddled with evil. The murder committed by Barnardine, the only serious crime referred to, took place long ago and is not described in detail, as though Shakespeare did not want it to have a very active force in the play. Shakespeare stresses the youthfulness of Claudio, Isabella, and Julietta, and most of the offences in the play relate to youthful excess and intemperance (see, for example, Pompey's list of prisoners at the opening of 4.3), or to those, like Pompey and Mistress Overdone, who pander to libertines like Lucio.

The Play in Performance

The popularity of *Measure for Measure* in the theatre has been remarkably fluctuating. To put it briefly, comparative neglect in the seventeenth century was followed by fairly regular performances in the eighteenth century, culminating in the famous partnership of John Philip Kemble as the Duke and Mrs Siddons as Isabella between 1794 and 1812. But for more than a century afterwards there were no more than brief intermittent revivals, none of which managed to restore the play to popularity on the stage. In the past thirty or forty years, however, there has been a striking revival of interest, and *Measure for Measure* is now among the most frequently performed of Shakespeare's plays.[1]

---

[1] No comprehensive survey of the play's stage-history has been written; the fullest list of productions up to 1977 is in Eccles, pp. 467–77. An excellent

[*cont. on p. 26*]

There are no records of production between 1604 and the closing of the theatres in 1642, and during the Restoration the play survived only in the form of adaptations by other dramatists. On 18 February 1662 Samuel Pepys saw a performance of Sir William Davenant's *The Law against Lovers*, based on *Measure for Measure*; he thought it 'a good play and well-performed', and was impressed by 'the little girl', a very minor character added by Davenant, who at one point dances a saraband with castanets.[1] Davenant omitted the low-life scenes, and crudely stitched in the characters of Beatrice, Benedick, and Balthazar from *Much Ado About Nothing*, making Benedick Angelo's brother. Many of the longer speeches, such as the Duke's on death in Act 3, were clumsily abbreviated or omitted.

The first half of Davenant's play makes some attempt to follow the structure of *Measure for Measure*, but increasingly diverges from Act 3 onwards. Isabella tells Claudio that she does not intend to yield to Angelo, but Claudio eventually accepts her decision and the couple do not quarrel. The Duke, in disguise as a friar, has a brief and pointless discussion with Isabella, since he does not propose the substitution of Mariana, who is omitted by Davenant. Several unsuccessful attempts are made to free Claudio and Julietta from prison by means of trickery and disguise. At the end of Act 4 there is a third interview between Angelo and Isabella, written in stilted rhyming couplets. Angelo reveals that he never intended to execute Claudio, and merely wanted to test Isabella as a prospective wife. She remains unconvinced. In Act 5 Benedick raises an insurrection against the prison in order to free Claudio, and the resulting complications are sorted out only by the sudden re-emergence of the Duke as himself. At the end Isabella and Angelo and Beatrice and Benedick are about to marry, and the Duke proposes to enter a monastery. The effect of Davenant's alterations is to reduce Shakespeare's play to a meaningless jumble.

A second adaptation, *Measure for Measure, or Beauty the Best*

discussion of productions between 1950 and 1970 by Jane Williamson, 'The Duke and Isabella on the Modern Stage', is in *The Triple Bond*, ed. Joseph Price (1975), pp. 149–69. For some later versions see chapter 2 of Ralph Berry, *Changing Styles in Shakespeare* (1981).

[1] *The Diary of Samuel Pepys*, ed. Robert Latham and William Matthews, vol. 3 (1970), p. 32. What may have been the première took place on 15 February 1662; another performance is recorded on 17 December of the same year.

Advocate, was made by Charles Gildon; the date of the earliest performance is not known, but it was probably in the first two or three months of 1700. Gildon was clearly influenced by Davenant—he introduced Balthazar, though not Beatrice and Benedick, and omitted all the low-life scenes—but was much more faithful to Shakespeare. At the same time he made a number of small changes which destroy some of Shakespeare's effects. Claudio and Julietta are in fact married, but need time to produce a witness. Not surprisingly Gildon's Julietta, unlike Shakespeare's, expresses no penitence for what she has done. There is a prison interview between Claudio and Isabella which includes a version of Isabella's outburst at 3.1.139–50, but Claudio then explains that Isabella has misunderstood him: he does indeed want to live, but not at the expense of his sister's honour. Isabella is forced to apologize. The Duke's role is severely abridged; he does not appear until the end of Act 2, where he informs the audience that Angelo and Mariana were secretly married, though Angelo now repudiates the marriage. Gildon's purpose, apparently, was to make the bed-trick respectable (at least, Isabella will not consent to the substitution until she is reassured that the couple are truly man and wife). The oddest feature of Gildon's version, as printed in 1700, is that it includes a performance of Purcell's opera *Dido and Aeneas*, with music and dancing, divided into four sections or 'Entertainments'. A performance also took place on 26 February 1706, but with Motteux's *Acis and Galatea* as the interpolated opera.

Fortunately these adaptations proved to be short-lived, and the next production, in 1720, returned to Shakespeare's text in a remarkably authentic form (more so, indeed, than the stage-versions of the late nineteenth and early twentieth centuries). Up to the end of the eighteenth century *Measure for Measure* was performed at regular intervals, though less frequently in the second half of the century. Several leading actors and actresses distinguished themselves in the roles of the Duke and Isabella: James Quin played the Duke regularly from 1720 to 1750, while Isabella was played by Mrs Cibber from 1737 to 1758 and by Mrs Yates from 1771 to 1782. The most famous Isabella, Mrs Siddons, began playing the part in London in 1783, to be joined by her brother, John Kemble, in 1794. Kemble gave the Duke a statuesque dignity, and Mrs Siddons played Isabella's

3. Mrs Yates as Isabella (from Bell's edition, 1773)

4. Mrs Siddons as Isabella

5. Liston as Pompey (from Oxberry's edition, 1822)

major scenes with tragic intensity, though she did not, apparently, project the unconscious youthful charm that Claudio attributes to his sister at 1.2.180–2 (Mrs Siddons was 40 in 1795). The impact of the play did not depend exclusively on its major roles; during the season of 1811–12, when Mrs Siddons made her last appearances as Isabella, the role of Barnardine was played by John Emery with striking effect:

When I saw Emery crawl from his den with the straws sticking in his clotted hair and filthy garments, growling out his remonstrance at being disturbed from his sleep, I absolutely started! I had read the play often, and the character was familiar to me as that of a depraved, abandoned wretch; but here was a real, sombre splendour thrown upon it by the power of genius.[1]

The role of Pompey the clown attracted the leading comic actors of the time, 'Dicky' Suett in 1794–9, and Liston in 1811 and 1816.

The acting-editions, which indicate the cuts made in performance, give an impression of what was actually seen and heard by the eighteenth-century audiences. The earliest, published by Tonson in 1722, was used for the 1720 revival with Quin as the Duke and Mrs Seymour as Isabella. Bell's edition, first published in 1773, with notes by Francis Gentleman, follows the text used in 1771, with Bensley as the Duke and Mrs Yates as Isabella. The text was further revised for the production of 1783 in which Smith played the Duke and Mrs Siddons Isabella, and this version was published in 1784. Kemble adapted the play for his own productions beginning in 1794; it was published in this form in 1795, and reprinted, with revisions, in 1803 and 1815. Kemble's version is important because it was used for productions during the next fifty years, and was taken over by several compilers of drama-anthologies (Mrs Inchbald, 1808; William Oxberry, 1822; John Cumberland, ?1826). Oxberry and Cumberland inserted stage-directions taken from contemporary prompt-books.

On the whole the cutting became more severe as the century progressed, though later editions occasionally restored deletions made in earlier ones. The major cuts in 1722 were the first hundred lines of 1.2, so that it began at line 115, and the interrogation of Elbow, Froth, and Pompey (2.1.39–273). These comic scenes were not restored until 1795, though in a heavily

[1] William Robson, *The Old Play-goer* (1846), pp. 78–9.

expurgated form. Apart from this the cuts in 1722 were fairly light, and were mainly of textual obscurities and obsolete phrases, though there were certain deletions which persisted throughout the eighteenth century: Lucio's tender description of Julietta's pregnancy (1.4.39–44) was omitted, and Isabella was not allowed to address her brother as 'you beast' (3.1.139) or to talk of Angelo's 'concupiscible intemperate lust' (5.1.99). Mariana's scene at the moated grange (4.1) vanished gradually: lines 7–15 in 1722, lines 1–23 in 1773, and the whole scene from 1784 onwards. The two very short scenes which conclude Act 4 were discarded from 1773 on. Kemble deleted 2.3, with the result that Julietta disappeared from the play. In the Folio this scene helps to separate the two interviews between Angelo and Isabella; Kemble got over the problem by inserting at this point the interrogation of Elbow, Froth, and Pompey, but omitted Angelo and gave his speeches to Escalus. He rearranged the beginning of the play so that the Duke's dialogue with Friar Thomas (1.3) came immediately after the opening scene. Kemble also gutted a number of long speeches: the Duke's first address to Angelo had received various cuts in 1773 and 1784, but Kemble omitted nearly two-thirds of it (lines 30–43).

The early acting-editions gave their own answers to some of the problems that face producers of the play. In the 1773 version (but not the others) Claudio explicitly asks Isabella's pardon at 3.1.174 ('Pardon, dearest Isabel'); in Cumberland's text he kisses her hand. Kemble made Claudio and Isabella embrace when Claudio reveals himself at the end of the play, and in Oxberry and Cumberland she exclaims, 'Oh, my dear brother!' The Duke's final speech was clearly felt to be insufficiently decisive, and all editions except 1784 add a newly written conclusion. Kemble omitted the Duke's first tentative proposal to Isabella at 5.1.493–6 and the last eight lines of his final speech, substituting for them a rousing finale of his own:

> For thee, sweet saint,—if, for a brother sav'd,
> From that most holy shrine thou wert devote to,
> Thou deign to spare some portion of thy love,
> Thy Duke, thy Friar, tempts thee from thy vow:
>> (*Isabel is falling on her knees, the Duke*
>> *prevents her—kisses her hand, and proceeds*
>> *with his speech.*)

> In its right orb let thy true spirit shine,
> Blessing both prince, and people:—thus we'll reign,
> Rich in possession of their hearts, and, warn'd
> By the abuse of delegated trust,
> Engrave this royal maxim on the mind,
> To rule ourselves, before we rule mankind.
> (*Flourish of drums and trumpets.*)

Kemble had already made the opening of Act 5 highly ceremonious: the Duke enters to the sound of drums and trumpets, and there are nearly thirty attendants on stage (soldiers and gentlemen). Angelo and Escalus then kneel and deliver their commissions to him.

The success of Kemble and Mrs Siddons was unable to establish the play securely in the theatrical repertory. Other actors and actresses came forward to play the Duke and Isabella—Charles Young and Eliza O'Neill in 1816, Macready and Margaret Bunn in 1824—but they disappointed those who could remember Kemble and Mrs Siddons. This sense that the great performers of the play's central roles all belonged to the past no doubt helped to cause a decline in its popularity; another important factor was an increasing distaste for its overt sexuality. (Miss O'Neill's biographer felt that, excellent though her performance had been, she had rather wasted her talents in a piece 'disgraced by much coarse ribaldry and obscene wit'.[1]) This was not an entirely new development. Gentleman regarded the cause of Claudio's predicament as 'indecent and therefore blameable',[2] and the adaptations of Dávenant and Gildon suggest that even during the Restoration sexual blackmail and the bed-trick were regarded with some embarrassment. Acting-editions from 1773 onwards were increasingly heavily bowdlerized: Julietta's pregnancy was merely hinted at, and eventually she was deleted from the play, while the arrangements for Mariana's substitution in Angelo's bed, spelt out in detail several times by Shakespeare, were so abbreviated that an audience which did not know the play might well have been baffled about what was going on.

Measure for Measure is inescapably about sexuality, and this approach undermined its central structure. Its vocabulary is explicitly sexual: there are, for example, eleven references to a woman being 'with child' (no other Shakespeare play has more

---

[1] Charles Inigo Jones, *Memoirs of Miss O'Neill* (1816), p. 83.
[2] Bell's edition of 1773, p. 21.

than three), and Gentleman, in a note on 4.3.165–6, commented with exasperation, 'there is too much child-getting in this piece'. When Samuel Phelps prepared his prompt-copy for a revival in 1846,[1] he based it on Cumberland's text, which is already heavily bowdlerized. To his credit he restored a little of the comic dialogue omitted by Cumberland, and reverted to the Folio order of the opening scenes, but when he came to the few remaining instances of 'with child' he substituted a more decorous paraphrase: 'with child, perhaps' at 1.2.154 turned into 'like to become a mother mayhap'. It is hardly surprising that to Victorian taste there was 'no other play of Shakespeare's in which so much of the dialogue is absolutely unspeakable before a modern audience'.[2] Despite his bowdlerization Phelps was evidently committed to the play, which he performed twenty-five times between 1846 and 1857, but it is significant that whereas there were fifteen performances in the 1846–7 season, there were only two in the 1856–7 season. During the next fifty years the only major commercial production in London was at the Haymarket Theatre in 1876 and 1878, where the play served mainly as a vehicle for Adelaide Neilson as Isabella.

At the turn of the century William Poel used *Measure for Measure* as part of his campaign to break away from heavy-handed Victorian methods of production, in which the use of elaborate and realistic stage-sets caused long delays between one scene and the next while the scenery was being shifted, and lack of time necessitated severe cuts in the text. He directed the Shakespeare Reading Society in a costume recital in London in 1891, followed two years later by three performances at the Royalty Theatre. In 1908 he produced the play for Miss Annie Horniman's professional company at the Gaiety Theatre, Manchester, which also gave two performances at the old Memorial Theatre at Stratford-upon-Avon. In 1893 and 1908 Poel used what was intended to be a replica of the Elizabethan Fortune Theatre, but it was set behind a conventional proscenium arch and there was no sense of actors coming forward into the centre of the audience. The costumes were Elizabethan in style, but there were no sets or scenery, and the only break in performance was a single ten-minute interval.

---

[1] Now in the Folger Shakespeare Library.
[2] William Archer, *The Theatrical 'World' for 1893* (1894), p. 269.

6. The setting of Poel's production, 1893

7. The setting of the National Theatre production, 1981

Theoretically the text should have been uncut, but in fact it was heavily bowdlerized. Poel had strong and rather idiosyncratic beliefs about the speaking of verse, and spent hours trying to instil into his actors what he felt to be the correct rhythmical stresses. He favoured a much more rapid delivery than had been customary in the middle of the nineteenth century, and reviewers complained that because of this the words were occasionally unintelligible. Poel was indifferent, however, about the speaking of prose, and left the performers of comic roles to their own devices. He did not see the play as painful or problematic and felt that the Duke should be presented as a kindly and cheerful man anxious to make sure that no real harm is done. He insisted that Isabella should wear secular costume because she had not yet taken her vows as a nun.[1] But the final result was impressive, particularly in 1908 when Poel had a talented professional company at his disposal, and his pioneering approach undoubtedly played an important part in transforming modern approaches to the staging of Shakespeare.

Even so, during the first half of the present century the play received only sporadic performances. In 1906 Oscar Asche prepared a heavily cut and rearranged text for a production at the Adelphi Theatre in London, which he published in the same year. Asche himself was a sombre Angelo, and Lily Brayton, heavily costumed in a nun's robes and wimple, was a beautiful and soulful Isabella. There were intermittent revivals by the Shakespearian repertory companies—four productions at the Old Vic in London between 1918 and 1937, and five at Stratford-upon-Avon between 1923 and 1947. Some of these were memorable, especially at the Old Vic in 1933, when Charles Laughton played Angelo, Flora Robson Isabella, Roger Livesey the Duke, and James Mason Claudio. Laughton in particular was formidably sinister: the producer Tyrone Guthrie later described him as 'not angelic, but a cunning oleaginous monster, whose cruelty and lubricity could have surprised no one, least of all himself'.[2] Yet the excellent cast failed to draw in audiences, despite pleas by Sir John Gielgud and T. S. Eliot in letters to *The Times* (8 and 14 December 1933).

The production which did most to establish the play in the

---

[1] See Robert Speaight, *William Poel and the Elizabethan Revival* (1954), pp. 90–3.

[2] Tyrone Guthrie, *A Life in the Theatre* (1960), p. 110.

8. Lily Brayton as Isabella (Adelphi Theatre, London, 1906)

current repertory was undoubtedly Peter Brook's at Stratford-upon-Avon in 1950. Brook saw the play as containing, 'almost schematically', two kinds of theatre which he termed the Holy and the Rough:

They are opposed and they co-exist. In *Measure for Measure* we have a base world, a very real world in which the action is firmly rooted. This is the disgusting, stinking world of medieval Vienna. The darkness of this world is absolutely necessary to the meaning of the play: Isabella's plea for grace has far more meaning in this Dostoevskian setting than it would in lyrical comedy's never-never land. When this play is prettily staged, it is meaningless—it demands an absolutely convincing roughness and dirt. Also, when so much of the play is religious in thought, the loud humour of the brothel is important as a device, because it is alienating and humanising.[1]

---

[1] Peter Brook, *The Empty Space* (1977), p. 88. Perhaps it should be pointed out that no scene in the play actually takes place in a brothel, though some recent productions set the beginning of 1.2 in a brothel. In 1987 at Stratford-upon-Avon
[*cont. on p. 36*]

9. Sir John Gielgud as Angelo, Barbara Jefford as
Isabella (Shakespeare Memorial Theatre, 1950)

Brook emphasized the 'rough' by introducing extras into the
outdoor scenes—peasants, cripples, beggars, and whores—in
costumes which reminded several reviewers of Brueghel's paint-
ings. (The reference to 'the generous and gravest citizens',
4.6.13, was discreetly omitted: none were seen here.) The prison
was made grimmer by elaborate props—a block, a weapons rack,
a torture machine—and when Pompey, at the beginning of 4.3,
enumerated the former customers of Mistress Overdone who were
now prison inmates, they came vividly to life and processed
across the stage.

The 'holy' scenes made an effective contrast. Sir John Gielgud,
in his first appearance at Stratford, presented Angelo as a man

the setting was a street, as the text suggests, but it was full of urban squalor,
including middle-aged men who vanished into an underground lavatory, apparently for homosexual assignations. Though producers frequently introduce young
prostitutes into the prison there is no textual warrant for doing so, and Pompey's
account of the inmates at 4.3 gives no hint that there are any.

who genuinely believed in his own integrity, and was horrified when it proved to be flawed. He conveyed with great power and subtlety the impact made on him by Isabella at their first encounter.[1] She was played by a 19-year-old actress, Barbara Jefford. While some reviewers felt her to be lacking in experience and forcefulness, for others her youthful ardour gave her performance an authenticity it would otherwise have lacked. At 5.1.444 occurred one of the most famous pauses in modern theatre; she was required by Brook to stand silent for as long as she thought the audience could bear before dropping on her knees to plead for Angelo.[2] For Brook this was 'a silence in which all the invisible elements of the evening came together, a silence in which the abstract notion of mercy became concrete for that moment to those present'.[3] The final note was one of reconciliation, with the characters in pairs making their way upstage, hand in hand.

Brook evidently intended the Duke, played by Harry Andrews, to dominate the play as a benevolent presence. To achieve this effect he cut the Duke's part severely, softening and simplifying it.[4] Omitted were his concern for his own reputation at 1.3.41–3 and 3.1.402–6, his probing of Julietta's motives at 2.3.30–4, and his harsh rebuke to Pompey at 3.1.287–98. Any suggestion of deviousness was left out—the 'sacred vow' of 4.3.142 and the 'strange fever' of 5.1.152. There were substantial modifications to Act 5. Isabella was not told why he had failed to intervene to rescue Claudio, and Mariana was not informed of his prudential motives for marrying her to Angelo. Barnardine did not appear to receive his pardon, as though Brook did not want to remind the audience of one of the Duke's failures. Angelo's speech at lines 477–80 was inserted immediately after Mariana's 'Merely, my lord' at line 455, so that the Duke's 'Your suit's unprofitable' was a reply to Angelo's plea for his death, not to Isabella's plea for his

---

[1] See the account by Gwen Watford in Ronald Hayman, *John Gielgud* (1971), p. 170.

[2] The only pauses I have encountered in earlier stage-versions occur in Samuel Phelps's prompt-copy. After Isabella's 'Dar'st thou die?' at 3.1.78 is written 'Pause. Claudio averts his face', and after 'O Isabel', 3.1.117, 'Despairingly. A Pause'. Clearly the assumption is that Claudio is being tested rather than his sister.

[3] *The Empty Space*, p. 89.

[4] The prompt-copy is in the Shakespeare Centre Library, Stratford-upon-Avon.

life.[1] The reviewers, however, seem not to have noticed this, and clearly the production as a whole was deeply memorable.

It would be impossible to give a detailed account of every production in the past forty or so years. The period has been very much one of 'directorial' theatre, in which directors have been expected to stamp their individual outlook on the play, and reviewers have sometimes been disappointed if they have not done so. Not surprisingly, approaches have been much more experimental than in the past. The play has been brought forward into modern times, frequently to Vienna in the late nineteenth or earlier twentieth century. In 1981 two productions carried this to an extreme. At the Royal Exchange Theatre, Manchester, the setting was a rather confusing mixture of what appeared to be the France of the *belle époque* (the opening of 1.2 was placed in an extremely elegant brothel) and India (Lucio was played by Zia Mohyeddin and Alfred Burke presented the Duke as a Buddhist monk rather than a Christian friar). At the National Theatre in London events took place on a Caribbean island in post-colonial times, with a mixed cast of black and white actors.[2]

Some general tendencies can be discerned in all this variety. The low-life scenes, which had shocked earlier centuries,[3] offered no problem at all; these were presented with great enthusiasm and often with the addition of various kinds of stage-business. It was the serious scenes (what Peter Brook termed the 'holy') which had become more difficult to accept: now the most embarrassing line in the play was not a bawdy joke but Isabella's defiant 'More than our brother is our chastity' (2.4.186). The couplet forming 2.4.185–6 seems to have been omitted from most stage-versions between 1787 and the early twentieth century, so we cannot know how the great actresses of the past would have handled the line. Few actresses in recent times have spoken it as though they believed in it and at the same time expected the audience to sympathize with them. When it was delivered with conviction, it usually indicated spiritual pride or

[1] The device may have been borrowed from Frank McMullan's Stratford production of 1946; it was used again by Anthony Quayle at Stratford in 1956.

[2] See Stanley Wells, '*Measure for Measure* in Manchester and London', *Critical Quarterly*, 23 (1981), 5–13.

[3] But only in respect of their explicit sexuality; critics like Johnson and Hazlitt admired the comic elements in the play, and Lucio and Pompey were frequently great successes on the stage.

sexual repression in Isabella. On other occasions the actress playing Isabella tried in some way to detach herself from the line, as if she believed it but found the belief unbearably painful. Barbara Jefford played Isabella at Stratford in 1950, and

When she came to the perilous words she turned, from speaking full to the audience, to hide her face passionately against the wall behind her, as if herself ashamed that her intellect could find no more adequate expression of her heart's certainty.[1]

At the Old Vic in 1957 Miss Jefford provoked differing responses. Kenneth Tynan thought that she uttered the line 'as if it were the most anguishing thought that had ever crossed her mind',[2] while Mary Clarke felt that in this version of the play she had been genuinely tempted by Angelo, 'and the hysterical, almost theatrical cry was uttered in order to re-arm herself with a conviction she had been in danger of losing'.[3] At Stratford in 1962 Judi Dench spoke the line 'in an agonized whisper, as if appalled that the truth should be so hard'.[4]

In the closing scene the Duke makes two fairly tentative proposals of marriage to Isabella, but the text gives her no explicit response. In the past actresses playing Isabella looked pleased at the Duke's attentions and seemed to welcome them. Indeed, Adelaide Neilson was rebuked by one Victorian critic for her over-ready reaction to the Duke's 'Give me your hand and say you will be mine' (5.1.495): 'it would be better, instead of smiling a gratified response, to assume a sweet and timid doubt and dismay'.[5] Doubt and dismay, though not sweet or timid, became the keynote of the 1970s. At Stratford in 1970 John Barton made his Isabella (Estelle Kohler) brusquely ignore the Duke's proposals, and at the end of the play she was left alone on the stage to gaze out at the audience in obvious shock and bewilderment. Jonathan Miller directed a touring production, in modern dress, for the National Theatre in 1973, and put it on again at Greenwich in 1975. His Isabellas (Gillian Barge and Penelope Wilton) were made to be sexually unattractive, and at the

[1] Richard David, 'Shakespeare's Comedies and the Modern Stage', *Shakespeare Survey 4* (Cambridge, 1951), pp. 136–7.

[2] *Observer*, 27 Nov. 1957.

[3] Mary Clarke, *Shakespeare at the Old Vic*, vol. 5 (1958), unpaginated.

[4] Robert Speaight, *Shakespeare on the Stage* (1973), p. 285.

[5] Joseph Knight, *Theatrical Notes* (1893), p. 113.

conclusion they decisively rejected the Duke, retreating from the stage 'in undisguised horror'.[1] In the late 1970s, however, the trend was reversed. Strong-minded Isabellas (Paola Dionisotti at Stratford in 1978 and Helen Mirren at the Riverside Theatre, London, in 1979) quickly and decisively accepted the Duke. Juliet Stevenson at Stratford in 1983 made an impact similar to Barbara Jefford in 1950: sensitive and vulnerable, she spoke her lines with transparent honesty. There was a sense of steadily ripening intimacy between her and the Duke, and their final union came as no surprise. Yet in the most recent Stratford production to be considered here, in 1987, there was a shift back to the seventies, and when the Duke proposed to Isabella, played by Josette Simon, she merely stared at him 'in what appeared to be incredulous distaste at the sheer crassness of his timing'.[2]

The presentation of the Duke has shown a similar pattern to that of Isabella. In the 1960s he tended to be a God-like figure in complete control of the action (though perhaps somewhat sinister precisely because of this). At Stratford in 1970 Sebastian Shaw presented him in a very different light:

Certainly no God figure, he was an aging, spectacled Duke, a genial but rather smug and slightly eccentric fellow who was constantly surprised and foiled in his efforts to manipulate the complicated individuals and circumstances he encountered.[3]

The most subversive production in recent times was undoubtedly Keith Hack's at Stratford in 1974. The whole of Vienna was seedy and corrupt, and its figures of authority deeply questionable, none more so than the Duke himself, who emerged as a cynical and lecherous manipulator, even at times a melodramatic villain. At the beginning of Act 5 he descended from the flies on a bar labelled 'Deus ex machina'. Most reviewers loathed what they regarded as a travesty of the play.[4] Four years later at Stratford the pendulum swung back and Michael Pennington gave the

---

[1] Benedict Nightingale, 'Vienna and its Discontents', *New Statesman*, 30 Nov. 1973.

[2] Keith Brown, 'Forms of Tyranny', *Times Literary Supplement*, 20–26 Nov. 1987.

[3] Jane Williamson, 'The Duke and Isabella on the Modern Stage', p. 168.

[4] For a more sympathetic approach see Peter Thomson, 'The Smallest Season: The Royal Shakespeare Company at Stratford in 1974', *Shakespeare Survey 28* (Cambridge, 1975), pp. 146–8.

Duke a quiet dignity and thoughtfulness. In the Stratford production of 1983 Adrian Noble set the play in the eighteenth century of the *ancien régime*, but his Duke (Daniel Massey) was no despot. Dignified, even solemn, he responded intensely to events and became increasingly human as the action progressed.[1] But the most recent Duke at Stratford, Roger Allam, 1987, was an altogether smaller figure; in the opening scene his hand shook as he signed papers before going away, as though the burden of office was simply too much for him. It has to be said that the Duke's role is clearly an extremely difficult one, and no modern actor has been able to achieve a performance of recognized classical status.

The BBC television production, broadcast on 18 February 1979 as part of a complete version of all Shakespeare's plays, was generally regarded as one of the best of a somewhat uneven series. Produced by Cedric Messina and directed by Desmond Davis, it used the ability of the camera to close in on characters as a means of creating an intimate approach which reminded us how often in the first four acts there are no more than two speakers on stage at the same time. The confrontations between Angelo and Isabella were remarkably powerful: Tim Pigott-Smith's Angelo was arrogantly efficient until overcome by lust, and Kate Nelligan played Isabella as a strong-minded and intelligent young woman who passionately believed in the virtue of chastity. (In 2.2 the sense of intimacy was reinforced by sending off the Provost at line 25, so that he was absent from the rest of the scene, and showing Lucio for only a few seconds at a time, when he made his interjections.) Kenneth Colley as the Duke was quietly spoken and introspective, playing him as an even-tempered figure who did not seem noticeably burdened by his power and resorted to trickery only because the unexpected twists of the plot forced him to. In contrast to the rest of the play, Act 5 was more theatrical, a kind of play within the play observed by a large audience of stage-extras. Isabella did not hesitate to kneel before the Duke at Mariana's appeal; her pause came later, at line 540, when the Duke held out his hand after his second proposal. She looked at him for a few seconds and then decisively grasped it.

---

[1] At 4.1.54, for instance, he smiled and shrugged his shoulders when Isabella looked surprised at being expected to tell Mariana the proposed arrangements for tricking Angelo.

Outside the British Isles the play has had a rather limited stage-history. North American productions began in New York in 1818, but remained intermittent until the past thirty years, when it began to appear with some regularity at local Shakespeare festivals (for example, Stratford, Ontario, and Stratford, Connecticut). The play was first staged in France in 1908 under Lugné-Poë's direction, in a poor translation, at the Cirque d'Été in Paris; in 1978 Peter Brook directed his own French company at the Bouffes-du-Nord theatre, in a completely new production using a prose translation. In Communist countries the emphasis has been more explicitly political than elsewhere: Brecht adapted the play for his Berliner Ensemble in 1952 so that it became an attack on a corrupt and class-ridden society. A Chinese translation, put on at Peking in the spring of 1981, seems to have fascinated an audience which had recently experienced the Cultural Revolution.[1]

The Play

Measure for Measure is classed as a comedy in the First Folio, and it ends in forgiveness and reconciliation, but much in the play is hardly comic in any conventional sense. Two of its most famous speeches are on death ('Be absolute for death', 3.1.5 ff., and 'Ay, but to die, and go we know not where', 3.1.121 ff.), and the title is ultimately biblical (Matt. 7: 2), not a throwaway phrase like *Much Ado About Nothing*. Its most powerful scenes exhibit the desperate attempts of a young woman to rescue her brother from execution for a crime which most modern readers would hardly regard as a crime at all, let alone one deserving so severe a punishment. It contains many observations—some memorably detachable—about law and theology, so that critics are tempted, understandably but in my view wrongly, to see it as a kind of morality play, or an intellectual treatise in dramatic form. It ends with four marriages in prospect, but they seem far more contrived and problematic than the four marriages which conclude *As You Like It*. Partly because of this the play has aroused varying and contradictory responses, and two characters in particular, the

[1] See Carolyn Wakeman, '*Measure for Measure* on the Chinese Stage', *Shakespeare Quarterly*, 33 (1982), 499–502.

Duke and Isabella, have provoked reactions ranging from whole-hearted approval to violent hostility.

In 1896 F. S. Boas grouped together *Measure for Measure*, *All's Well that Ends Well*, *Troilus and Cressida*, and *Hamlet*, and labelled them 'problem plays'.[1] The term became widely current, though its precise meaning and appropriateness or otherwise to the plays as a group has been much debated. The universal assumption has been that the 'problems' in question are all ethical and moral, and *Measure for Measure* has been exhaustively discussed in these terms, often with a further assumption that at any point in the play Shakespeare was free to make the characters behave in any way he wished, so that their actions can always be attributed to them as individuals and interpreted as evidence of their innermost natures. But it could be argued that Shakespeare's elaborations of an existing story sometimes led to difficulties of plot-arrangement which were not adequately resolved, and resulted in confusions for which the characters involved need not be held responsible. One has already been mentioned, the Duke's speech at 4.3.104–8 explaining to the audience why he does not intend to reveal to Isabella that her brother is still alive.[2]

The problems of *Measure for Measure* are thus artistic as well as moral, and occasionally it may be possible to see Shakespeare altering his presentation of the characters in order to cope with a specific difficulty. At 1.3.45–8 the Duke asks Friar Thomas to give him instruction in the correct way to behave as a friar, as though this is the first time he has acted in the role, but at 4.1.8–9 and 52 Mariana gives the impression that she has known him as a friar for some time, certainly for longer than the day or two that has elapsed since the play began. The discrepancy may hint at some kind of deviousness in the Duke, though if he has disguised himself as a friar in the distant past it is hard to see why he should bother to lie to Friar Thomas. The explanation, however, may simply be that in 4.1 the Duke is about to ask Mariana to do something that she might find very questionable from a complete stranger. Shakespeare did not want to put elaborate speeches of exposition and persuasion into the Duke's mouth, and improvised a long-standing relationship of trust between Mariana and

[1] F. S. Boas, *Shakespere and his Predecessors* (London, 1896), p. 345.
[2] See above, pp. 24–5.

the Duke in order to carry through this part of the plot more easily.[1]

A similar problem arises with a more important incident, the sudden revelation half-way through the play that in the past Angelo had contracted himself to Mariana, but broke off the contract and abandoned her when she lost her dowry. The intention behind this revelation, which is not found in any of the sources, is to some extent clear enough: it makes Angelo much more like Claudio than he had seemed to be at first, in that both men have entered into contracts, and both have allowed financial considerations to influence their sexual behaviour. Angelo can now be made to do precisely what Claudio did, go to bed with a woman to whom he is contracted but not married.

This new information, though, has to come from the Duke, who seems to be the only person apart from Angelo and Mariana who knows about it. (Lucio never mentions it, although he delights in being outrageously rude about Angelo.) Is the Duke's concealment of his knowledge up to this point intended to be taken into account when we judge his own character and his relation to Angelo? Are we supposed to go back to the beginning of the play and re-read the opening scene with this new fact in mind? My own feeling is that the opposite is true, and that the explanation is once again a matter of dramaturgy. Shakespeare wanted the audience to be ignorant of Angelo's past for the first two acts, and in particular during his interviews with Isabella. An audience aware that Angelo had dubious secrets in his past would probably expect him to lapse again, and there would be a loss of uncertainty and surprise. The revelation centres on Angelo, and the fact that it comes via the Duke is relatively unimportant.

An editorial introduction cannot discuss the whole play in detail, and I propose to concentrate on a few central issues.[2] The

[1] In this connection it is odd that the Duke has clearly failed (see 4.1.47–8) to carry out his promise to Isabella at 3.1.256–7 that he will 'frame and make fit' Mariana to act as her substitute. If he had done so it might have simplified the action in 4.1, and done away with the need for the Duke to make a clumsy speech at lines 58–63, during the temporary absence of Isabella and Mariana. But the anomaly seems to be an oversight on Shakespeare's part, or a foul-papers confusion not sorted out, which need not be explained realistically (the Duke did not have time to do it) or seen as an indication that the Duke is unreliable.

[2] I have discussed the relationship between the Duke and Angelo in more detail in ' "He who the sword of heaven will bear"; the Duke versus Angelo in *Measure for Measure*', *Shakespeare Survey 37* (Cambridge, 1984), pp. 89–97.

play is a complicated work of art, and its aim is to present a series of vivid dramatic situations, not merely to act as a vehicle for political and moral ideas which as some critics describe them sound like the most banal of platitudes. The play itself seems to resist neat interpretations. There is at times a kind of recalcitrance built into the characters, who stubbornly refuse to do what is confidently expected of them. Angelo does not free Claudio, and Barnardine is determined not to die; it is a fortunate and implausible coincidence, which owes nothing to conscious plotting, that a young man rather like Claudio happened to die from fever that very morning. A further stroke of luck is that he was 'a most notorious pirate' (4.3.68), so that cutting off his head does not seem like desecrating a corpse.

The outcome of events is sometimes problematic or open-ended. The enquiry in 2.1 never finally establishes what did happen to Elbow's wife when she ventured into Mistress Overdone's establishment. There are places where characters remain silent, or fail to respond, in a puzzling way. This particularly applies to the last fifty lines, where we should normally expect a clear and unambiguous resolution of events. Barnardine makes no response to his pardon, nor Angelo to his, though there is apparently 'a quickening in his eye' (5.1.498) when he realizes that Claudio has not been executed. Julietta and Isabella are given nothing to say or do when Claudio suddenly reappears as if from the dead, and Isabella makes no reply to the Duke's tentative proposals. In most of these cases Shakespeare may have felt that the character's attitude was so obvious that it did not need to be made explicit, but modern readers and audiences find it increasingly difficult to take anything for granted about Isabella's final response to the Duke, and the way the actress treats it is a vital factor in establishing the impact made on the audience by the play as a whole.

To stress that *Measure for Measure* is a work of art and of the theatre is not for a moment to deny that it is 'about' important issues like mercy and justice. The play is full of striking themes and concepts, but they are not part of a logical structure intended to eliminate inconsistencies and to work rigorously towards a definable conclusion ('Shakespeare is showing us that ...'). The best analogy would be musical: themes can be introduced and then counterpointed in a wide variety of ways, and given contrasting harmonies, but they do not cancel each other out, and the final meaning is the total pattern created, not just a part of it. *Measure for Measure* incorporates a wide range of moods and tones, comic and tragic, and it would be wrong to concentrate too exclusively on a single one of these as the essence of the play. There is much debate and argument, but the arguments are always in a dramatic context, spoken by individual characters who have their own interests to pursue, who wish to persuade or accuse other people or defend themselves against attack.

Measure for Measure is much concerned with the law (indeed the word itself occurs more frequently in this play than in any other by Shakespeare). But it is not a legal treatise, and the way law is presented is difficult to define. In one sense it is not realistic at all: the nearest approach to a full-scale 'trial scene' is in Act 5, but I assume that no Jacobean court of law would have operated quite so chaotically, with the presiding figure switching between his role as a judge and his role, in the disguise of a friar, as a witness, and with other witnesses appearing muffled and then suddenly and dramatically revealing their identities. Yet at the same time the whole thing is not mere fantasy or fairy-tale, and in the first three acts Claudio's predicament needs to appear, as indeed it does, grimly plausible.

The very term 'law' is probed and questioned. It is usually qualified by adjectives implying that Viennese law is harsh by its very nature—'strict statutes and most biting laws' (1.3.19), 'the hideous law' (1.4.63), 'the angry law' (3.1.204)—but there is also a series of striking, sometimes faintly ludicrous, images suggesting that the law can be despised and ineffective. It is like 'an o'ergrown lion in a cave | That goes not out to prey' (1.3.22–3) or the 'threatening twigs of birch' (1.3.24) which become 'more mocked than feared' because 'fond fathers' cannot bear to use them on their children. If the law is not applied effectively it will be like the motionless scarecrow that the birds of prey regard as 'their perch and not their terror' (2.1.4), or will 'Stand like the forfeits in a barber's shop, | As much in mock as mark' (5.1.323–4). A different sort of contempt is shown by Angelo's apparent ability to 'bite the law by the nose | When he would force it' (3.1.111–12). Furthermore, the law's operations are intermittent and unpredictable; it can be 'drowsy' (1.2.168) or even 'sleep' (see 2.2.91), but then awaken with appalling consequences.

The result of all this is to build up a paradoxical double image: the law can frequently be ignored with impunity, but it may suddenly inflict savage punishment, with a kind of arbitrariness that is half accepted and half resented, as in the opening speeches of Claudio. Many of the characters in the play make their way rather nervously past the law, 'As mice by lions' (1.4.64), hoping not to be noticed by it. There is little sense of the law as just and equitable, carefully allocating graded sentences which are appropriate to particular cases. Punishment tends to be exemplary; those who are unlucky enough to get caught are treated severely in order to act as a deterrent to others.

In the opening scene the Duke tells Angelo that from now on 'Mortality and mercy in Vienna | Live in thy tongue and heart' (1.1.45–6), and these two extremes, execution or pardon, seem to be all that Viennese law can offer. By the end of the play four characters have been condemned to death—Claudio, Barnardine, Angelo, and Lucio—but only in the last few minutes of the action are they suddenly freed from danger. Reflecting on it afterwards we may feel that Angelo deserved some kind of punishment, and that Friar Peter will have a hard job persuading Barnardine to repent. Such speculations are inevitable but not very helpful. The alternative extremes have already been established, and the final pardon for all concerned is not merely a stock comic device. It is therefore hard to agree with those critics who discern in the play an educative process in which characters such as Angelo, Isabella, and the Duke himself, learn that justice must be tempered with mercy, that the ideal is some sort of middle way or compromise. There is no question of carefully tuned degrees of severity or mildness; the choice is between harsh punishment or forgiveness.

It is, we could say, a matter of life and death, and the two words resonate throughout the play, sometimes in unexpected contexts, as when Isabella expresses her indignation at Angelo's treatment of Mariana:

What a merit were it in death to take this poor maid from the world! What corruption in this life, that it will let this man live! (3.1.233–5)

The more exalted characters wish to live and die by religious or aristocratic codes which will preserve their honour. Most of the other characters are more concerned with living in the basic sense of making a living, managing to survive; they are aware of morality, but sacrifice it when necessary, like the pirate who ignores the commandment against stealing because it would force him to give up his job. These two attitudes are not totally separate: Pompey describes himself as 'a poor fellow that would live' (2.1.212), but the phrase could apply equally to Claudio. In Act 3, the Duke uses curiously similar arguments to both men. To Claudio he stresses that our physical needs are 'nursed by baseness' (3.1.15) or 'issue out of dust' (21), and that we do not accumulate money until we are too old and feeble to enjoy it: 'What's in this | That bears the name of life?' (38–9). To Pompey he is more outspoken:

> The evil that thou causest to be done,
> That is thy means to live. Do thou but think
> What 'tis to cram a maw, or clothe a back
> From such a filthy vice; say to thyself,
> From their abominable and beastly touches
> I drink, I eat, array myself, and live.
> Canst thou believe thy living is a life,
> So stinkingly depending?

$$(3.1.287–94)$$

Claudio is impressed, though his resolution soon crumbles; Pompey characteristically tries to wriggle out of the Duke's condemnation.

There are complex cross-linkages between death, money, and sexuality. Both Claudio and Angelo are affected by the dowries their potential wives might bring them; both are condemned to death for having given way to their sexual drive. Mariana is told that she can have Angelo's estate, after his execution, to 'buy ... a better husband' (5.1.426), but the idea appals her: 'I crave no other nor no better man' (427). In the world of Pompey and Mistress Overdone the connections are much cruder; in Elbow's unexpectedly powerful formulation, they 'buy and sell men and women like beasts' (3.1.271). Pompey, who enjoys an argument, tries to assert that of the 'two usuries'—prostitution and money-lending—the 'merrier' is unjustly suppressed while the 'worser' is allowed legal privileges (3.1.274–8). But he has no deep convictions, and will happily alter his trade in order to get by. It is appropriate, however, that he should change from an 'unlawful bawd' to a 'lawful hangman' (4.2.14–15), and he offers death to

10. Claudio and Julietta going to prison (Shakespeare Memorial Theatre, 1950)

his new clients as cheerfully as he had previously offered sexuality to his old ones.

Claudio's offence is appropriate to the pattern of extreme alternatives that has just been described. It can be regarded as a serious moral lapse; Isabella, Angelo, and the Duke see it in this way, and the climax of Julietta's brief role comes when her noble penitence silences the Duke's interrogation:

> I do repent me as it is an evil,
> And take the shame with joy.
>
> (2.3.35–6)

In the same scene, however, the Provost portrays Claudio as

> a young man
> More fit to do another such offence
> Than die for this.
>
> (13–15)

In conversation with Isabella Lucio describes the impregnation of Julietta as the human equivalent of the processes that lead in nature to crops and harvest (1.4.40–4), but elsewhere he speaks of Claudio's deed as 'a game of tick-tack' (1.2.188) or 'filling a

49

bottle with a tundish' (3.1.430). The sexual act can thus be a trivial amusement, or an essential renewal of life, or a brutal oppression (if Angelo has his way with Isabella), or a deadly sin (see 3.1.112–17). The play does not invite us to single out one of these attitudes and treat it as definitive.

This approach to the play may help us to deal with one of the commonest criticisms made against it. For many readers *Measure for Measure* splits apart in the middle, half-way through Act 3, a change clearly marked by the shift from powerful blank verse in the opening section to a mannered and artificial kind of prose which begins at line 156. Dramatic debate and conflict, of a power and intensity which would be appropriate for great tragedy, give way to intrigue and manipulation; the Duke takes over and Claudio, Isabella, and Angelo have very little to do, making only brief appearances. It would have been better, some critics feel, for them to work out their destiny unhindered by the Duke, even if the results had been disastrous. A happy ending is provided, but it is not artistically convincing, and in any case, as Coleridge and others argued, Angelo's offence was so repulsive that he ought not to have been forgiven.

I have tried to state the case as powerfully as possible, and it would be foolish to brush it aside as negligible. Those who would have preferred the play to be exclusively in the mode of some of its most impressive scenes—2.2, 2.4, and the opening of 3.1—are entitled to their opinion, though it might be pointed out that they seem to wish that Shakespeare had used Lupton as his source and not followed Cinthio and Whetstone in enlarging and redeeming what was originally a rather sordid anecdote. At the same time it is inherently improbable that at 3.1.155 Shakespeare suddenly lost his ability to write great verse or equally abruptly became bored with the story and decided to botch up a contrived and feeble ending. We ought to look at the play as impartially as we can to see if a more sympathetic reading is possible.

The Duke's entry at 3.1.155 occurs at the bleakest point in the play, where events as Shakespeare has shaped them have reached an impasse from which no escape seems possible. Isabella, Claudio, and Angelo are locked into obsessions and compulsions which sweep them along regardless of whatever degree of uneasiness or shame they may experience. Isabella clearly cannot bear the idea of giving herself sexually to Angelo; Claudio knows that an honourable young man should not expect this sacrifice from his sister, and ought to be resolute in the face of death, but when it comes to the point his urge to live overwhelms him. There seem to be only two possibilities here, one of which is that Isabella will storm off leaving her brother to an ignominious execution, deliberately made as painful as possible by a resentful and frustrated Angelo (2.4.164–70). The second possibility, adopted by Shakespeare, is that another character, in the form of the Duke, will intervene to break the deadlock.

The shift to prose is so striking that it is hard to see it as accidental. To modern taste the style of the discussion between the Duke and Isabella may seem cold and formal, but this is not necessarily the correct response. We may prefer the joky, subversive colloquialism of Lucio or Pompey, which Shakespeare had no difficulty in writing throughout the play, but that tone would not have been appropriate for this particular episode. After the violent, even hysterical, quarrel between brother and sister has led to a rupture between them, the formal solemnity is deliberate, and the highly structured and articulated prose indicates a movement away from the chaotic emotionalism of the preceding part of the scene to a calmer, more balanced exploration of what can be done to rescue Claudio and Isabella. The Duke's stylized, even faintly ritualistic, manner gives him an authority which leads the young people to trust him, though at the same time the sudden revelation of new information about Angelo's past comes as a shock both to Isabella and to the audience.

The move from verse to prose at 3.1.156 is only the first of several transitions in Act 3. After Isabella's exit at line 269 the play reverts to a cruder form of legal activity. Angelo does not appear, but his enforcement of law against sexual misconduct continues with the arrest of Pompey and Mistress Overdone. The structure of the scene could be described as operatic: the Duke remains continuously present while two trios of characters—first Elbow, Pompey, and Lucio, then Escalus, the Provost, and Mistress Overdone—appear to him in turn. After each trio he has a verse-soliloquy of response (lines 442–6 and 515–36). There are considerable fluctuations of tone and style, from Lucio's surrealist sexual fantasy in prose at lines 370–4, to the Duke's moral indignation in verse at lines 286–94 and 442–6. There is even a reversion, at lines 478–514, to the gnomic, formal style of the Duke's discussion with Isabella; for a brief while Escalus speaks in this manner, though he does not do so normally, and this might suggest that his comments on the Duke are author-itative and prove that Lucio is an irresponsible liar.

The act concludes with a soliloquy by the Duke in rhyming couplets. There is nothing similar to this elsewhere in the play, and its strangeness and occasional obscurity made critics in the past suggest that it was spurious, though there is no reason to doubt its authenticity. In it the Duke combines two functions, one of a chorus commenting on events so far, and one of an active participant who can determine what will happen from now on:

> With Angelo tonight shall lie
> His old betrothèd, but despisèd;
> So disguise shall by the disguisèd
> Pay with falsehood false exacting,
> And perform an old contracting.
>
> (532–6)

It is a decisive turning-point. Shakespeare tells the audience what to expect with an explicitness paralleled at few other places in the canon. Yet there are still more surprises in store. The speech is followed by another striking change of tone, the song for Mariana which opens Act 4 and is the sole example of lyricism in the play. This sequence of rapid modulations is carried out with audacious self-confidence, and it suggests that a kaleidoscopic effect was deliberately intended by the dramatist.

The Duke's character and role in the play have aroused violent controversy, but here again the problem can be regarded as basically artistic. Before putting together all he says and does, and making moral or psychological judgements derived from this assembled material, we ought to ask more searching questions: how far is he intended to be a fully rounded 'character', and how successfully has he been integrated into the structure of the play? In most earlier versions of the source-story the equivalent of the Duke has to appear only in the final stages of the plot and act as the ultimate arbiter of justice. He needs to be shrewd and benevolent, but his role is a simple one and there is no call for psychological complexity. Even if he also appears at the beginning of the story, as in Cinthio's *Hecatommithi*, and appoints the Angelo-figure to his post, his role is still straightforwardly that of the good ruler who has done his best to act responsibly. He can hardly be blamed if the person appointed suddenly and unexpectedly begins to misbehave, and at the end does all he can to put things right.

Shakespeare strikingly enlarged the Duke's role, most noticeably by making him pretend to go away but in fact remain behind in disguise, observing the action and intervening to take charge of the plot half-way through the play. As a result he has by far the largest role in terms of the number of lines he is given to speak; in this respect he is comparable to tragic figures like Hamlet and Macbeth, but unlike them he does not seem to be at the emotional centre of the play. His destiny is not at stake, and he risks little more than personal embarrassment. At any time he could reveal himself and resume power, though this would obviously bring the play to an end. As a manipulator of the action he can be compared to Prospero, but Prospero has already suffered exile and the loss of his dukedom, and his future and that of his daughter depend upon a successful outcome for his plotting. It is even possible that Shakespeare arranged for the Duke to fall in love with Isabella partly to make him more intimately concerned in events and less of a detached observer.

The Duke has been summarized in various ways—as an emblem of divine providence, as an ideal ruler, as a cold-hearted manipulator, and as a ridiculous old busybody—but these are all extremist views which tend to cancel each other out. For Angelo's virtue to be tested as rigorously as possible, he must be given the impression that his power is absolute and unchallengeable. This requires the Duke to hand over power completely, and in effect to vanish; he must be given motives for doing so, but few critics have found the Duke's motives very plausible. One of these, the restoration of firm rule to Vienna after a period of laxity, gradually slips from sight as the play progresses, and does not figure at all in the final resolution. Furthermore, no one in the play apart from the negligible Friar Thomas has any idea why the Duke has gone and where he has gone to, which on realistic grounds hardly seems to be responsible behaviour from a head of state.

In the second half of the play the Duke has to be present to arrange events in which other people are tried and tested; he is essentially a functional character, but his constant presence gives

11. Barrie Ingham as the Duke, Francesca Annis as Isabella (Royal Shakespeare Theatre, 1974)

12. Daniel Massey as the Duke, Juliet Stevenson as Isabella (Royal Shakespeare Theatre, 1983)

him a disproportionate significance. Even at the end of the play there are puzzles about his role: evidently most of Act 5 is stage-managed by the Duke, but it is not clear whether certain events—his unmasking by Lucio, and Mariana's appeal to Isabella to plead for Angelo—occurred by chance or were a deliberate part of his original scheme. Perhaps the fundamental problem is that the Duke's various activities had to be arranged so as to fit in with a complex plot deriving from a story which originally had very little room for him: character derives from plot, not the other way round, and the result is a lack of coherence. The Duke remains a collection of attributes which fail to coalesce.

One aspect of the Duke's character can perhaps be defended against recent criticism. He has been rebuked for being excessively sensitive to spiteful gossip, but his relationship to Lucio should not be judged entirely by the standards of the twentieth century, when royalty has to tolerate public mockery. Lucio's impudence, and the embarrassment he causes the Duke, are amusing, but the Duke's anger is not merely the result of a pompous self-importance. The Duke's complaint that virtue attracts calumny is a stock Shakespearian idea (see 3.1.443–4 n.), and Shakespeare seems to sympathize with the unjustified sufferings of virtue. Ordinary Elizabethans bitterly resented sexual slander from their neighbours, and went to law about it, as Elbow threatens to do when Pompey asserts that Mrs Elbow was 'respected' before her marriage (2.1.166–71). It is clear that Angelo slandered Mariana in order to facilitate breaking off his contract ('pretending in her discoveries of dishonour', 3.1.228–9). The theme recurs in Act 5: Isabella is arrested for her 'scandalous breath' (5.1.123) against Angelo, and the Duke's accusations at 5.1.318–24 provoke an outburst from Escalus, 'Slander to the state! Away with him to prison.'

Clearly, then, a concern with slander is not exclusive to the Duke; it extends throughout the play, and can be linked to another key term, 'seeming', in the sense of 'hypocrisy, false pretence of virtue'. Is the 'well-seeming' (3.1.224) Angelo quite as 'strait in virtue' (2.1.9) as he appears to be? Reputation has important consequences: when Isabella tries to blackmail Angelo into pardoning Claudio, he calmly replies that his 'unsoiled name' (2.4.156) will overweigh her accusations, and she will merely blacken herself, an assertion apparently borne out at the beginning of Act 5. It is Lucio who most aggressively challenges the apparently virtuous—the Duke, both as himself and as a friar, and Angelo—but he is a self-confessed liar (4.3.165–9) and possibly an informer (3.1.455–6), and it is hard to see him as speaking with any authority. His accusations against the Duke as a friar are ludicrous (see 5.1.336 n.), though they might have done serious damage, and he continues to claim that Angelo is sexually frigid after the audience has seen how untrue that is. His remarks about the Duke are the products of irresponsible malice; in the end they do no harm and we may feel that they ought to have been ignored, but we should perhaps remember that in a roughly contemporary play, *Othello*, sexual slander has horrifying consequences.

Like the Duke, Isabella has aroused contradictory responses. Shakespeare's version of the sexual blackmail story is the only one in which the heroine refuses to surrender herself to save the man under sentence of death; it is also the only version in which she is a postulant to a religious order, though it is clear that she has not yet taken her vows, and is free to leave the convent if she wishes. No other Shakespearian heroine has a situation resembling Isabella's, and our reaction to her will inevitably be conditioned by our personal convictions about sexuality and female behaviour. It hardly seems necessary, however, either to celebrate her as a miracle of chastity or to sneer at her as cold and priggish. She is a young woman of exceptional strength of character who has to cope with an unexpected series of extremely painful crises and challenges, and for this alone she surely deserves our sympathy, even if we do not wholeheartedly approve of every aspect of her behaviour.

Shakespeare's motives in making Isabella a postulant can only be guessed at, but it need not have been done crudely in order to make the surrender of her virginity impossible, or to make Angelo assume that he could gain access to her only by blackmailing her. In earlier versions of the story the man in authority lusts after an attractive young woman who needs his help. Shakespeare characteristically makes the relationship much more subtle. Though Angelo behaves with deplorable hypocrisy, he is not to be defined simply as a hypocrite; his austerity matters deeply to him, and we may believe his assertions that he was immune to the conventional kinds of female enticement. He is excited by Isabella

13. Charles Laughton as Angelo, Flora Robson as Isabella (Old Vic, 1933)

partly because he recognizes her as a kindred spirit: both of them impose severe restraints on a temperament which is not easily stirred, and may therefore appear cold to an outsider, but which can break out with explosive violence when it is finally aroused. Angelo's soliloquy at the end of 2.2 has a tragic intensity: he is genuinely disgusted at what has happened to him, though his disgust does not enable him to break free of his obsession, and he repeatedly stresses the horrible paradox that it is precisely her genuine virtue and modesty that have triggered off his desire:

> O cunning enemy, that to catch a saint
> With saints dost bait thy hook!
>
> (2.2.183–4)

Only a woman like Isabella could have had this devastating effect upon him.

Isabella has been condemned because in pleading for Claudio she makes no attempt to use what might seem to be the strongest argument in his favour, his contract to Julietta. Yet later on, in a way which has been regarded as hypocritical, she welcomes the

Duke's proposal to put Mariana in her place, a proposal justified and made acceptable because of the contract between Mariana and Angelo, which Mariana still endorses so wholeheartedly that she regards herself as Angelo's wife. The simplest answer is that Isabella knows nothing about Claudio's contract. Her only information about her brother's position comes from what Lucio says in 1.4, and he makes no mention of the contract. Isabella's suggestion that Claudio should marry Julietta is brushed aside by Lucio: Claudio can do nothing to save himself. He has been sentenced and the warrant for his execution prepared; the only hope is for Isabella to appeal personally to Angelo, to induce him to exercise his prerogative of pardon. Lucio offers her no arguments to use, though lines 80–3 suggest that he expects her to rely on a female emotionalism that men find difficult to resist.

There is another reason, perhaps more important, for Isabella's failure to make use of the contract. Her strategies in 2.2, as shaped by the dramatist, are vitally important to the development of the plot. Angelo's proud self-assurance must be made to crumble, but this can come about only through a radical challenge to his own perception of himself. Escalus makes a very tentative attempt to do so at the beginning of 2.1, but his arguments are not powerful enough to cause Angelo any strong discomfort. The real test comes in 2.2, and it is essential that the person on trial should not be Claudio, but Angelo. If the point at issue had been the degree of Claudio's guilt, and the mitigating circumstances that might or might not be urged in his favour, such as his contract, Angelo would have coped with this easily, perhaps even enjoying an argument on the legal niceties involved. What actually happens is different and unexpected. Isabella does not 'weep', as Lucio expects her to (1.4.81). She does not condone her brother's guilt, and is prepared to give up at the first rebuff, so that Lucio has to bring her back for a second try. But then she seems as it were to ignite, and as she becomes increasingly indignant at Angelo's rigid legalism she launches into a scathing attack on his authority which leaves him shaken and bewildered ('What dost thou, or what art thou, Angelo?', 2.2.176). Ironically, her arguments are only too successful: Angelo is forced to examine himself as a human being under his trappings of power, and discovers that he is like Claudio in having a sexual appetite he cannot control.

In 3.1 Isabella has to inform her brother that there is a way to save his life, but that it involves a price she refuses to pay. We may rebuke her for this if we wish, and it is true that all her predecessors in the blackmail story paid the same price, however reluctantly. But she has consistently been shown as taking sexuality very seriously, and her refusal is passionate: she simply is the kind of woman who could not bear to bring herself to do it. The echo of *Hamlet* at line 101 may be merely a verbal coincidence, but it helps to emphasize the fact that for Claudio as well as Isabella the deed she is being asked to perform is one of the seven deadly sins. (Claudio's assertions that it cannot be so bad if Angelo is prepared to do it, and that it becomes no sin if she is compelled to do it to save his life, are self-interested special pleading that Isabella totally ignores.) Her furious outburst at the end of her discussion with Claudio, including the wish that he should turn out to be the result of adultery on the part of their mother, has offended many critics. This is understandable, but something must be allowed for her anger and distress at her discovery that two men whom she had assumed to be honourable, first Angelo and then her brother, are prepared in different ways to exploit her sexually.

In the second half of the play Isabella has little to do or say. The one point at which the audience's attention is exclusively focused on her occurs towards the end of Act 5, when Mariana begs her to intercede on Angelo's behalf. She is still under the impression that her brother is dead, though 5.1.400 suggests that she is now much more reconciled to the idea of his death than at 4.3.115–20. The audience is not certain how she will respond, and the suspense can be highly dramatic, as in Peter Brook's 1950 production. It is distressing to find so magnanimous a critic as Dr Johnson regarding her willingness to intercede as partly motivated by vanity, and her arguments as ludicrously inadequate. The mere fact of her willingness is surely intended to be highly to her credit, and on the spur of the moment she has to devise the best arguments she can. (What arguments would Johnson have expected her to use?) It is often assumed that the Duke has arranged this episode as a test of Isabella's fitness to be his future wife, but there is nothing in the text to put this beyond question.

The play concludes with a single elaborate scene occupying the whole of Act 5. The audience knows that the outcome will not be disastrous, but there are many unexpected twists in the plot. To judge from 1.1.68–73 we might have assumed that the Duke will return to his dukedom as quietly and inconspicuously as he left it; instead, he enters to the sound of trumpets in a ceremonial procession. This could be an inconsistency, or it could result from the need to conduct Angelo's trial in as public a manner as possible, so that he can be 'shown to the world' (see 1.2.115) as Claudio had been. His final pardon by the Duke may or may not be an affront to justice, as Johnson and Coleridge thought it was; at any rate it is clear that to so reserved a man, intensely proud of his reputation for austerity, complete exposure as a liar and hypocrite, not to say murderer, comes as a shattering blow. He pleads for immediate execution, and his reply to Escalus, at lines 477–80, shows that he has no interest in his wife's desperate attempts to rescue him. Only when it is clear that Claudio is alive, and that Angelo has been rescued from the worst effects of his crime, is there 'a quickening in his eye' (line 498), as though the will to live has begun to assert itself.

His punishment is made worse by being delayed; for two-thirds of the scene it looks as though he will be able to evade detection, largely because the Duke pretends to be heavily biased in his favour, even praising him in the opening lines of the scene as though he was a fit subject to be immortalized by a Renaissance sonneteer. The Duke may seem to be playing a sadistic game with Angelo, who has already been subjected to a kind of psychological warfare in the form of the Duke's puzzling and contradictory letters, but it is right that Angelo should undergo the torturing suspense that he inflicted on Isabella. Unlike Isabella he has a guilty secret, and his refusal to reveal it, even though he is given several opportunities to do so, only serves to deepen his eventual humiliation.

For the good characters it might seem at first that things are going badly wrong. Isabella's accusation against Angelo appears to backfire on herself; she is treated first as a madwoman, then as an accomplice in a political intrigue to discredit Angelo, and is led off in ignominious arrest. Mariana's statement, though it challenges Isabella's, is regarded as merely another slander, and Angelo is allowed to supervise the investigation of charges into his own behaviour. (This is presumably a deliberate device of the

Duke to allow Angelo to incriminate himself further, since the Duke in his disguise as a friar bitterly criticizes the injustice of it at lines 301–4.) Even after the true identity of 'Friar Lodowick' has been revealed there is no simple 'unfolding' of the truth. Isabella is still given the impression that her brother is dead, the plea by the two women for Angelo is rejected, and the Provost is discharged for failing to carry out his duties, though this is patently a cue for him to make the final revelation that Claudio and Barnardine are still alive.

The final scene brings together the stylistic effects established in earlier parts of the play, from a passionate simplicity ('I crave no other nor no better man') to an elaborate use of rhetorical figures, reminiscent of the Duke's prose in Act 3, and sometimes in a cryptic, riddling manner which helps to heighten the problematic nature of events:

> Who thinks he knows that he ne'er knew my body,
> But knows, he thinks, that he knows Isabel's.
>
> (202–3)

Lucio is at hand to give the crudest interpretation to the riddles:

DUKE Why, you are nothing then: neither maid, widow, nor wife?
LUCIO My lord, she may be a punk, for many of them are neither maid, widow, nor wife. (177–80)

There is powerful irony, clearly evident in several of the Duke's speeches, but also found in remarks by Angelo and Lucio, at lines 236–40 and 264–6, where they have insights which turn out to be truer and more far-reaching than they themselves realize.

Act 5 also ties up some of the strands of imagery used elsewhere in the play, sometimes by turning a metaphor into a literal event. Clothing, for example, usually has a moral significance—the 'English kersey' contrasted with the 'French velvet' (1.2.27–34), the 'idle plume' of the foppish gallant (2.4.11), the usurer's 'furred gown', with 'fox on lambskins' (3.1.276–7)—and those in positions of power, 'Dressed in a little brief authority' (2.2.120), can use the trappings of power to hide corruption:

> O place, O form,
> How often dost thou with thy case, thy habit,
> Wrench awe from fools and tie the wiser souls
> To thy false seeming!
>
> (2.4.12–15)

In the final scene Angelo's 'false seeming' is nakedly exposed, and three characters—Mariana, the Duke in his friar's disguise, and Claudio—enter with their faces covered by clothing and then dramatically revealed, though in their case to establish truth and reality, not falsehood. The first two are urged to show their faces (see lines 168–70 and 352–5), and there seems to be a sense here, in contrast to *Macbeth*, that the face is a reliable index to the mind, despite the fact that Pompey has already used the idea to defend Froth against Elbow's accusations (2.1.140–52).

The conclusion is comic, not tragic; those condemned to death are pardoned, and several of them are married off, or about to be. Yet it is no conventional 'happy ending'. Even Barnardine, the murderer, is forgiven, but there is nothing to suggest that the stubbornly assertive figure of 4.3 now intends to reform. Mariana is no doubt delighted to be united at last to the man she loves; Angelo's own feelings on the matter are kept from us. Lucio is not to be hanged or whipped, but he must marry Kate Keepdown, the mother of his child. This would be a third case, after Angelo and Claudio, of a man's fulfilling his contract, since he had promised to marry her (3.1.457), but Lucio can only see his marriage as worse than the most barbaric forms of execution, and it has to be justified as an appropriate punishment for 'slandering a prince' (527). Claudio and Julietta are the only young lovers with a mutual relationship, but their marriage will have to grow from a painfully inauspicious beginning.

The Duke's proposals to Isabella at the end of the play come as a surprise, especially as in 1.3 he had claimed to have a 'complete bosom' which could not be pierced by the 'dribbling dart of love'. Critics who are outraged by his behaviour are entitled to their opinion; even so, we should try to see as clearly as possible what actually takes place. His first proposal, at lines 493–6, is tentative, and he does not persist when he realizes that this is not the appropriate time. His last speech to her, at lines 538–40:

> I have a motion much imports your good,
> Whereto if you'll a willing ear incline,
> What's mine is yours, and what is yours is mine.

is even more tentative: not a proposal, but a statement that he intends to make a proposal, which she is free to accept or reject. This is hardly dictatorial, and it might be argued that Isabella is not shown as responding to it precisely because at this stage no response is called for. He has courteously let her know his intentions and given her time to think it over. If this is so, the play is strikingly open-ended: the stage empties, and the audience never discovers Isabella's final response.

TEXTUAL INTRODUCTION

THE earliest text of *Measure for Measure* is in the First Folio, where it is the fourth play, occupying two complete quires or gatherings, F and G, pages 61–84. The pattern of type-distribution in these two quires is extremely complicated and hard to interpret, and Hinman's attempt to determine the compositors at work in this section of the Folio has been substantially modified by subsequent investigation.[1] The fidelity of the Folio text to Shakespeare's original play has been questioned, most vividly by Dr Johnson:

> There is perhaps not one of Shakespeare's plays more darkened than this by the peculiarities of its author and the unskilfulness of its editors, by distortions of phrase or negligence of transcription.[2]

Recent criticism has been far less hostile, and although there are verbal cruces (though not as many as used to be thought) and a number of muddles or contradictions in the plot-arrangements, together with some possible signs of revision which will be discussed later, the greater part of the text is perfectly acceptable. There is, in other words, a series of specific local problems, but no pervasive corruption or contamination.

It is highly probable that the manuscript from which the compositors worked was prepared by the professional scribe Ralph Crane, as the Folio text exhibits a number of Crane's distinguishing characteristics. These include distinctive spellings and heavy punctuation, with a frequent use of colons and, to a lesser extent, semicolons, as well as a fondness for parentheses, hyphens, and what has been called the 'Jonsonian elision', where an apostrophe indicates that an elision is to be made but the elided word is written out in full. (Examples in *Measure for Measure* are 'I'haue' at 3.1.4 and 'pray'thee' at

---

[1] Charlton Hinman, *The Printing and Proof-reading of the First Folio of Shakespeare* (Oxford, 1963), ii. 376–87; T. H. Howard-Hill, 'The Compositors of Shakespeare's Folio Comedies', *SB* 26 (1973), 61–106; John S. O'Connor, 'Compositors D and F of the Shakespeare First Folio', *SB* 28 (1975), 81–117; and Paul Werstine, 'Cases and Compositors in the Shakespeare First Folio Comedies', *SB* 35 (1982), 206–34.

[2] *Johnson on Shakespeare*, edited by Arthur Sherbo, Yale Edition of the Works of Samuel Johnson, vi (New Haven and London, 1968), p. 174.

1.2.61.)[1] Crane was a conscientious professional who rarely made errors through carelessness, but unlike a modern scholar he felt no obligation to transcribe the manuscript in front of him with minute fidelity. In his transcripts of Middleton's *A Game at Chess*, for example, which we can compare with a copy of the play in Middleton's own hand, he frequently though not invariably inserted contractions and altered word-forms, changing ''tis' to 'it's', 'my' to 'mine', and 'has' to 'hath'. His intervention can hardly be described as helpful, as it added an extra stage in the transmission of the text which makes it harder for us to recover the original readings.

We shall never know precisely how far Crane modified the play as it passed through his hands. He certainly imposed his own system of spelling and punctuation, and may have done a certain amount of tidying-up and rearrangement. A possible example is the way '*within*' speeches are indicated at 1.4.6 and 4.3.23 and 103. At 1.4.6 F has the following:

Lucio within.
Luc. Hoa? peace be in this place.

The other two follow the same pattern, which Greg describes as 'unusual and perhaps confined to this play'.[2] It has not been noted that Crane has two examples of this layout in his play-manuscripts, on fol. 20ᵛ of *Sir John van Olden Barnavelt* (MSR, lines 2045–6) and on page 82 of the version of Middleton's *A Game at Chess* now in the Folger Shakespeare Library (Archdall MS V.a.231). In his manuscripts the direction is in the right margin, but Crane normally put stage-directions in the right margin, and the compositor would naturally centre it. If Crane did no more than make minor adjustments of this kind, his intervention would not matter unduly, but we cannot be certain. In the circumstances it seems best to give Crane the benefit of the doubt and assume that he was reasonably faithful to his copy.

It would be very helpful if we could decide what kind of manuscript, foul papers or prompt-copy, Crane was working

---

[1] For lists of examples see Lever, Introduction, pp. xi–xii; T. H. Howard-Hill, *Ralph Crane and Some Shakespeare First Folio Comedies* (Charlottesville, 1972), pp. 99–102 and 127–8; and Eccles, pp. 293–4.

[2] W. W. Greg, *The Shakespeare First Folio* (Oxford, 1955), p. 354.

from, but the evidence does not point decisively in one direction. As they stand in the Folio the stage-directions have none of the characteristics of prompt-copy, and their deficiencies would indicate foul papers. The present edition contains 23 exits not in F; it is true that prompt-copies sometimes omit exits, and in most cases it is clear enough what action is necessary, but even so the number is high (about the same as for *All's Well that Ends Well*, an obvious foul-papers text), and one particular case, that for Isabella in the middle of Act 5, is decidedly problematic, as though Shakespeare had not fully sorted out what to do with her (see the note on 5.1.126 in Appendix A). More importantly, entrances are omitted: for Lucio at 1.4.15, and for a servant at 2.2.17. If the Provost goes out at 5.1.254, as seems probable, he should already be on stage, but he is not included in the entry-list at the beginning of the act. Between 3.1.47 and 3.1.182 F has no stage-directions of any kind, though the Duke and Provost go out and come in again; Claudio says 'Let me ask my sister pardon' (line 174), but no provision is made for him to do so, and producers have coped with this in various ways. It is hard to believe that prompt-copy would not have given some indication to the actors of what they were supposed to do.

There are no striking variations in the names given to characters, but some peculiarities of nomenclature point to a foul-papers origin. Two characters, '*Frier Thomas*' and '*Francisca a Nun*', are given names at the beginning of the scenes in which they make their only appearances (1.3 and 1.4), but the names are never spoken, as though Shakespeare provisionally named them but then decided that it was not necessary to use the names. At 4.3.135 the Duke suddenly mentions 'Friar *Peter*', who appears as a speaking character and is named again by Isabella at 4.6.8. It is sometimes suggested that the two friars are the same person (Shakespeare having forgotten at 4.3 that he had earlier named him differently), but this seems unlikely: Friar Thomas is treated with respect as someone to whom the Duke feels obliged to explain himself, whereas Friar Peter is curtly ordered to run around with letters and messages. There is also some tendency in the play towards generic rather than specific names—Duke, Provost—which is more characteristic of foul papers than of prompt copy. It is true that the Duke is named as Vincentio in 'The names of all the Actors' at the end of the Folio text, but the name is never used, and there is some doubt about the origin and authenticity of the cast-list. (There are seven cast-lists in the First Folio, four of them in plays thought to derive from Crane transcripts.) In stage-directions and speech-prefixes Mistress Overdone is always simply '*Bawd*' and Pompey is '*Clown*', though his real name is repeatedly used. (It is also odd that he should first be referred to as '*Thomas* Tapster'; see 1.2.111 n.)[1]

Some features in the play, on the other hand, could be held to indicate that the text we have is not a straightforward transcript of foul papers, and that revision was carried out by someone other than Shakespeare. The most striking single piece of evidence is the Duke's speech at 4.1.58–63. A soliloquy is needed while Isabella persuades Mariana to act as her substitute, but five and a half lines give Isabella very little time to explain the proposed arrangements, and the sentiments expressed hardly seem very appropriate to the occasion. Warburton in 1747 pointed out the similarity of these lines to the Duke's earlier speech at 3.1.442–5, and plausibly suggested that they had been transferred from the earlier scene to the later, presumably to cover a deficiency in the manuscript.[2] Shakespeare himself would not have needed to resort to so crude an expedient; at the same time, if the agent was the book-keeper getting the text ready for performance, he would have needed to do a great deal more to bring it to a state where it could be acted.

Another characteristic of the play that might indicate revision is the absence of oaths and profanity. A parliamentary act of May 1606 forbade the use of God's name on the stage; not a single instance occurs in *Measure for Measure*. There are, however, forty-four examples of 'heaven', 'heavens', or 'heaven's', and it has been argued that some of these, notably at 2.4.4–5 ('Heauen in my mouth, | As if I did but onely chew his name') are substitutions for 'God'. Similarly, ' 'Saue' at 2.2.25 and 165 may

[1] For additional brief indications of foul-papers origin see the notes on 4.2.100 and 120.

[2] An alternative possibility is that this speech was originally placed at the end of Act 3, while the Duke's couplet speech, now 3.1.515–36, was originally spoken here, and that a reviser switched them round. But the 'O place and greatness' lines would be just as inappropriate at the end of Act 3 as in their present position, and it is hard to see what point or benefit there could be in substituting one for another.

68

originally have read 'God save', and in his edition Nosworthy emends 'heaven' to 'God' at 2.4.4 and 45 and inserts 'God' before both instances of 'Save'.

We should not be too dogmatic on the issue. There may have been originally more oaths in the play than there are now, but we have no early quarto to prove this beyond question. 'Heaven' is not necessarily a substitute for 'God': in Jonson's poem 'An Elegy' (' 'Tis true, I'm broke!', *The Underwood*, no. 38) 'God' and 'Heaven' are used interchangeably, and in lines 64–5 'Heaven' is followed by 'he' (referring to God) in a very similar way to 'heaven' and 'his' in *Measure for Measure*, 2.4.4–5. The abbreviation 'Save' can be found in plays printed before 1606, such as Marston's *The Malcontent*, 1604 (see 2.2.164 n.). Even if there was censorship in *Measure for Measure*, we need to ask who did it and when. One Folio play, *1 Henry IV*, seems to have been censored in readiness for publication.[1] It is possible that the censor in *Measure for Measure* was Crane and that he did his work while preparing the transcript on which the Folio text was based. All the Folio plays which are thought to derive from Crane have been drastically purged of oaths, and the 1623 text of Webster's *The Duchess of Malfi*, now thought to be based on a Crane transcript, has noticeably fewer oaths than *The White Devil*, printed in 1612.[2] (Both plays were written later than 1606.) If Crane was responsible for censoring *Measure for Measure*, he must have been working from uncensored foul papers.

It has sometimes been asserted that Mariana's song at the beginning of 4.1 was not written by Shakespeare but was inserted into the play after his death in 1616.[3] A two-stanza version was published in 1639, in the first quarto of *Rollo, Duke of Normandy, or The Bloody Brother*, attributed on the title-page to 'B.J.F.'. A second quarto was published in 1640; this is generally held to be

---

[1] The Folio text of *1 Henry IV* derives from a copy of Q5 (1613), slightly revised and censored. The uncensored text continued to be published in quarto, the censored in folio. If there was no difficulty about publishing the uncensored quarto text, it is hard to explain why censorship was thought necessary for the folio.

[2] See G. P. V. Akrigg, 'The Name of God and *The Duchess of Malfi*', *N & Q*, 27 May 1950, 231–3. Akrigg concludes that 'Crane was the censor who removed "God" from *The Duchess of Malfi*'.

[3] The earliest critic to make this assertion seems to have been Boswell, in the 1821 Variorum edition of Shakespeare.

textually superior to the first quarto, and in this version the second stanza reads as follows:[1]

> Hide, O hide those hills of snow
> That thy frozen bosom bears,
> On whose tops the pinks that grow
> Are yet of those that April wears;
> But first set my poor heart free,
> Bound in those icy chains by thee.

Rollo is a collaborative play, and there has been much debate about the participants in this collaboration and their respective shares, but all modern scholars agree that the scene (5.2) in which the song appears was written by John Fletcher. Also in 1640 the whole poem was published in John Benson's collection, *Poems written by Will. Shakespeare, Gent.*, in a form not deriving from those found in *Rollo*.

A musical setting was composed by Dr John Wilson (1595–1674), and first published in 1652 in John Playford's *Select Musical Airs and Dialogues* (London, two editions in 1652 and 1653). Playford also included the song in collections published in 1659 and 1669. Obviously this setting was not available in 1604; it may have been intended for use in *Rollo*, though there is no evidence to make this completely certain. As no earlier setting survives, it is impossible to determine whether Wilson's setting was completely fresh or to some extent derived from an earlier one. There also exist, in manuscript collections which appear to date from the middle seventeenth century, five copies of the words and music, and four of the words alone. There is thus a grand total of sixteen versions of the two-stanza poem, seven printed and nine in manuscript. Many minor textual variants occur, some of them evidently corruptions, but they cannot be arranged into a clear pattern which would enable us to construct a stemma.

What is the relationship between the single-stanza poem, found only in *Measure for Measure*, and the two-stanza poem found in *Rollo* and elsewhere? Out of several possibilities the most plausible are as follows:

1. Shakespeare wrote the first stanza for use in *Measure for*

---

[1] The text given here is modernized from J. D. Jump's edition of *Rollo* (Liverpool, 1948).

Measure, with a setting which has now vanished. Fletcher decided to borrow it for *Rollo*, adding a stanza which makes the poem unmistakably addressed by a man to a woman. A new or revised setting was prepared, possibly the one by John Wilson of which several copies survive.

2. Fletcher wrote the whole poem; the original version of *Measure for Measure* did not contain a song, but in a late Jacobean revival it was thought appropriate for one to be inserted. Only the first stanza, which in isolation could be regarded as addressed by a woman to a man, was used.

There is remarkably little evidence to decide the point. The version in *Measure for Measure* is textually unique in two readings, 'but' in line 6 (all other texts read 'though'), and the repetitions in lines 5 and 6 ('bring again, bring again'; 'sealed in vain, sealed in vain'). The first appears to be a corruption, an accidental repetition of 'But' in line 5 by a scribe or compositor. The second may be more significant: if the song was a success in *Rollo* and was then transferred to *Measure for Measure*, there would be no point in making this duplication, which is not the kind of thing that scribes or compositors would bother to do, and cannot be sung in Wilson's setting.

The song is not strikingly more appropriate to one play than the other. *Measure for Measure* is not a lyrical comedy, and this is its only song; if it were omitted the play might have a more consistent tone, but most critics regard the song as artistically successful in its context. In 5.2 of *Rollo* Edith is trying to lure Rollo, who has killed her father, into a kind of sexual ambush, where she will pretend to love him and then kill him when he is off his guard. It hardly seems very sensible in the situation for her boy to sing a song in which a man complains of female treachery. A cautious conclusion would be that the presence of the song in *Rollo* raises doubts about its authenticity in *Measure for Measure*, but there is no decisive evidence for Fletcher's authorship of both stanzas.

A further aspect of the play needs to be taken into account, though its significance is ambiguous. Certain plot-confusions or inconsistencies exist which can be interpreted and accounted for in a variety of ways. Dover Wilson, for example, assumed as a general rule in his earlier editions of Shakespeare's plays that loose ends in the plot indicated revisions by someone other than the original author. In his 1922 edition of *Measure for Measure* he constructed an extremely complicated scheme in which the play had been drastically abridged and then subsequently expanded by a second dramatist. But this was before scholars had realized that the texts of some of Shakespeare's plays, such as *Much Ado About Nothing* and *Timon of Athens*, are based on authorial foul papers which had not been tidied up for theatrical use, and that the confusions are first thoughts which have not been sorted out rather than the bungles of an incompetent reviser. At the same time it is clear that some Elizabethan and Jacobean plays were revised, by the author or someone else, and no doubt the result could be something of a patchwork. Each case needs to be considered on its merits, and it must be remembered that some even of Shakespeare's most fully worked out masterpieces contain one or two minor inconsistencies.

Act 1, scene 2, has a number of problematic features. We are given what some scholars regard as two separate accounts of Claudio's arrest, at lines 58–79 and 83–91. In the first of these Mistress Overdone is aware of his arrest and the reasons for it, but is baffled by Pompey's remarks at lines 83–91, which can hardly refer to anyone other than Claudio. Julietta has an entrance and is named in the text at line 114, but she remains mute and the discussion between Lucio and Claudio takes no account of her presence. The two gentlemen who accompany Lucio are also mute in the second half of the scene. Lucio already knows the facts, but asks Claudio why he is restrained and what his offence is. Finally, the scene is full of references to current events, and though this is not necessarily a textual problem it might be helpful and relevant if we could work out whether or not they are topical allusions which can be dated.

The last two points can be dealt with fairly summarily. It has already been suggested that some lines in the scene could be topical allusions,[1] but there is no need to extend the search for allusions further than strictly necessary. The king of Hungary is mentioned in the opening lines of Whetstone's *Promos and Cassandra*, and his name is brought in so that the first gentleman can make a play on words (see the notes on lines 2 and 4–5). Mistress Overdone's list of reasons for being 'custom-shrunk' is

---

[1] See above, pp. 2–5.

not specific enough to be datable (see lines 80–2 n.). Lucio's assumed ignorance of Claudio's misfortune shows tactfulness towards him, and in any case Lucio was not completely persuaded by Mistress Overdone's account and wanted to 'learn the truth of it' (line 79). The device also has a dramatic function in providing an opportunity for Claudio to tell Lucio, and through him the audience, his own feelings about his predicament and the nature of his relationship with Julietta.

The double account of Claudio's arrest need not indicate revision. Mistress Overdone's speeches at lines 58–71 prove that she knows the full details of Claudio's situation. It is important that this information should be disclosed to the audience, so that it can judge how the other characters in the scene respond to his danger. (And Claudio's own speech at lines 119–22 has its full power only if we already know that he has been sentenced to death.) Mistress Overdone is sympathetic to Claudio, but clearly assumes that she can do nothing about his fate. Lucio and the two gentlemen are concerned, and rush out to investigate. Pompey, however, treats the whole affair with casual brutality. His reference to 'yonder man' puzzles Mistress Overdone, who is not shown as particularly quick-witted, but her attempts at clarification are met by cryptic and bawdy jokes about 'doing' a woman and 'groping for trouts in a peculiar river'. The latter phrase is vivid, but has never been satisfactorily explained; it seems to imply that Pompey regards Claudio as a skilful seducer of other men's wives. Mistress Overdone's baffled reply, 'What, is there a maid with child by him?', suggests a dim awareness that he is really talking about Claudio, but after another joke he is bored with the topic and turns to something else. Seen in this light the two accounts are complementary rather than contradictory.

Julietta and the two gentlemen who are friends of Lucio are brought in at lines 110–22,[1] but they are given nothing to say before they go off again at the end of the scene. This, however, is only part of a wider problem. Julietta makes her third appearance at 5.1.480; she says nothing, but Claudio and Barnardine, who enter at the same time, also remain silent. Varrius enters at

---

[1] F has a comprehensive entry for all the fresh characters who participate in the last section of the scene, after line 114, which has been split into two separate entries in the present edition.

4.5.10, when the Duke twice addresses him by name, and also at the beginning of Act 5, but never speaks. The anonymous 'Justice', whose entrance at the beginning of 2.1 has the air of a last-minute addition,[1] has only three speeches, totalling ten words, at the end of the scene. There may not necessarily be a common explanation for all these examples, though it does seem that mute characters are more characteristic of foul-papers texts like *Much Ado About Nothing* than of prompt copy. The dramatist introduces a character as part of his first thoughts for the scene, but then finds that he or she is not needed in the dialogue. This may account for Julietta and the two gentlemen in the second half of 1.2.[2] Varrius is not a great problem, and it may be that at the end of 2.1 Shakespeare needed someone for Escalus to talk to, invented the justice, and then went back to the beginning of the scene to tack on an entrance for him. The silences in Act 5 are as much a critical as a textual problem, and have already been briefly discussed in the critical introduction.

Other confusions exist but are relatively insignificant. Claudio says that the laws have not been enforced for nineteen years (1.2.166), whereas the Duke gives the number as fourteen (1.3.21); the inconsistency can be interpreted in various ways (see 1.2.166 n.), though none of them involves the hand of a reviser. The Duke's arrangements to return to Vienna are confused (see 4.3.90 n. in Appendix A), but some at least of this confusion is deliberately created by the Duke, and modern audiences do not seem to be bothered by it. The time-scheme of the play is not strictly consistent, but this is characteristic of Shakespeare's plays, and need not be attributed to a reviser.[3]

A general conclusion about the Folio text of *Measure for Measure* must necessarily be tentative. Many of its characteristics are most easily explicable as originating from a foul-papers manuscript. There are some signs of revision, but not sufficiently

---

[1] F reads *Enter Angelo, Escalus, and seruants, Iustice*.

[2] 1.2.113–14 resembles 5.1.249–50 of *Much Ado About Nothing*, 'Here, here comes Master Signor Leonato and the sexton too', followed (in Q though not in F) by an entrance for the sexton, who then has nothing to say.

[3] The problem is fully discussed by Lever, Introduction, pp. xiv–xvii. Bernard Beckerman argues that the use of dramatic, not realistic, time, particularly the continued repetition of 'tomorrow', is brilliantly effective (see 'A Shakespeare Experiment: The Dramaturgy of *Measure for Measure*', in *The Elizabethan Theatre II*, edited by David Galloway, London, 1970, pp. 108–10).

thoroughgoing to render the play ready for production. Censorship may have occurred, but it could have been done by Crane in readiness for publication. I propose to treat the play as basically a foul-papers text; the editorial implications will be discussed in the note on editorial procedures.

EDITORIAL PROCEDURES

THERE is only one authoritative text of *Measure for Measure*, that found in the First Folio, and the present edition is necessarily based on it. My approach to the substantive readings has been conservative: I have tried wherever possible to explain F rather than emend it. For example, F readings such as 'weeds' (1.3.20), 'enshield' (2.4.80), and 'delighted' (3.1.124) were frequently treated in the past as corruptions needing alteration, but it is possible to interpret them in a way which makes emendation quite unnecessary. Even when explanation is not possible, as with 'prenzie' at 3.1.95 and 98, F is retained because no emendation made so far seems convincing. F's punctuation, however, is regarded as deriving from Crane and has been drastically modified and simplified, with the omission of hundreds of colons and medial commas.

Contractions are more problematical, since Crane's practices were varied and even contradictory. The 'Jonsonian elisions' at 1.2.61, 3.1.4 and 470, and 4.3.147 were inserted by Crane and have been altered to the standard contracted form. Elsewhere it is hard to be certain whether contractions derive from Crane or from the manuscript he was copying. (There are at least twenty places in his transcripts of *A Game at Chess* where Crane uses contractions when Middleton himself, in the Trinity manuscript, writes 'the', 'to', 'in the', and 'of the' in full.) I have decided to expand F's contractions of 'the' and 'to', for a variety of reasons: they may have been inserted by Crane, they are not used consistently (why have 't'affect' in 1.1.4, but 'to unfold' in the preceding line?), and in a modernized text it seems inconsistent to retain totally archaic forms like 'th'hopefull' (1.1.60) or 'th'wall' (1.2.165). But it is also true that occasionally Crane writes out in full contractions in his copy-text, and possibly 'it is', in such lines as 1.2.70 and 2.1.73, is Crane's rewriting of a Shakespearian ' 'tis', and 'never' should be 'ne'er' at (for example) 2.2.113 and 5.1.224. I have not thought it right to emend, but the reader should be alert to these possibilities.

If F is to be regarded as basically a foul-papers text, one part of the editor's job is to turn it into prompt-copy. F is noticeably deficient in stage-directions, and many have been added in the hope that they will aid the reader to visualize the action. But it is not the editor's responsibility to resolve issues which the text leaves problematic, and though Isabella has been provided with an exit at 5.1.126 no attempt has been made to determine whether or not Claudio asks her pardon at 3.1.174–6, or what she does at the end of the play when she discovers that Claudio is still alive and that the Duke wants to marry her. Certain generic names used in speech-prefixes and stage-directions have been altered ('*Bawde*' to '*Mistress Overdone*' and '*Clowne*' to '*Pompey*') because the characters are given these names in the spoken text, but I have not changed '*Duke*' to '*Vincentio*' because this name is never used in the play itself. I have assumed that Claudio's sister is named 'Isabella', often shortened to 'Isabel'; by the same logic his partner is 'Julietta', though the name more commonly occurs in the form 'Juliet'.

The textual collation is intended to be economical, and is confined to alterations of F made in the present edition, though it does include a few plausible emendations which have not been accepted. For the sake of simplicity readings which derive from *The Law Against Lovers* have been credited to Davenant, though of course he is not strictly speaking an editor of Shakespeare. Added stage-directions are assigned to the earliest editor to use them, though in many cases the wording has been silently modified. Certain alterations and insertions are wholly the work of modern editors, and have not been recorded in detail in the textual collation. These include asides and indications that a speech is addressed to a particular character, the use of 'an' for 'and' where it is equivalent to modern 'if', as at 2.1.154, and dashes indicating interrupted speech or a parenthesis (except at 2.4.88–90, where the meaning of the lines is determined by the way the parenthesis is arranged).

References to other plays by Shakespeare follow the text and line-numbering of the Oxford edition of the *Complete Works*, edited by Stanley Wells and Gary Taylor (1986). The following abbreviations are used in the collations, commentary, and appendices. The place of publication is London unless otherwise specified.

F	The First Folio, 1623
F2	The Second Folio, 1632
F3	The Third Folio, 1663
F4	The Fourth Folio, 1685
Alexander	Peter Alexander, *Complete Works* (1951)
Bald	*Measure for Measure*, ed. R. C. Bald, in *Works*, 'The Pelican Text Revised' (Baltimore, 1969)
Capell	Edward Capell, *Comedies, Histories, and Tragedies*, 10 vols. (1767–8)
Clark	W. G. Clark and W. A. Wright, *Works*, The Cambridge Shakespeare, 9 vols. (Cambridge, 1863–6)
Collier	John Payne Collier, *Works*, 8 vols. (1842–4)
Davenant	William Davenant, *The Law Against Lovers*, in *Works*, Part II (1673)
Dyce	Alexander Dyce, *Works*, 6 vols. (1857)
Evans	G. Blakemore Evans, *The Riverside Shakespeare* (Boston, 1974)
Hanmer	Thomas Hanmer, *Works*, 6 vols. (Oxford, 1743–4)
Hudson	H. N. Hudson, *Works*, 11 vols. (Boston, 1851–6)
Johnson	Samuel Johnson, *Plays*, 8 vols. (1765)
Keightley	Thomas Keightley, *Plays*, 6 vols. (1864)
Knight	Charles Knight, *Works*, Pictorial Edition, 8 vols. (1838–43)
Leisi	Ernst Leisi, *Measure for Measure: An Old-Spelling and Old-Meaning Edition* (Heidelberg, 1964)
Lever	J. W. Lever, *Measure for Measure*, New Arden Shakespeare (1965)
Malone	Edmond Malone, *Plays and Poems*, 10 vols. (1790)
Neilson	W. A. Neilson, *Works* (Boston, 1906)
Nosworthy	J. M. Nosworthy, *Measure for Measure*, New Penguin Shakespeare (Harmondsworth, 1969)
Oxford	Stanley Wells and Gary Taylor, *Complete Works*, The Oxford Shakespeare (Oxford, 1986)
Pope	Alexander Pope, *Works*, 6 vols. (1723–5)

Rann	Joseph Rann, *Dramatic Works*, 6 vols. (Oxford, 1786–94)
Ridley	M. R. Ridley, *Measure for Measure*, The New Temple Shakespeare (1935)
Rowe	Nicholas Rowe, *Works*, 6 vols. (1709)
Steevens	George Steevens and Isaac Reed, *Plays*, 15 vols. (1793)
Theobald	Lewis Theobald, *Works*, 7 vols. (1733)
Warburton	William Warburton, *Works*, 8 vols. (1747)
White	R. G. White, *Works*, 12 vols. (Boston, 1857–66)
Wilson	John Dover Wilson, *Measure for Measure*, The New Shakespeare (Cambridge, 1922)
Winny	James Winny, *Measure for Measure*, Hutchinson English Texts (1959)

OTHER WORKS

Abbott	E. A. Abbott, *A Shakespearian Grammar*, 3rd edn. (1870)
Bullough, *Sources*	Geoffrey Bullough, *Narrative and Dramatic Sources of Shakespeare*, vol. 2 (1958)
EETS	Publications of the Early English Text Society
Mason	J. Monck Mason in *Plays*, ed. Isaac Reed (1803)
MSR	Malone Society Reprints
N & Q	*Notes and Queries*
OED	*Oxford English Dictionary*, 20 vols. (Oxford, 1989)
PQ	*Philological Quarterly*
PRO	The Public Record Office (London)
RES	*Review of English Studies*
SB	*Studies in Bibliography*
Smith	Charles G. Smith, *Shakespeare's Proverb Lore* (Cambridge, Mass., 1963)
SQ	*Shakespeare Quarterly*
STC	*A Short-Title Catalogue of Books Printed in England, Scotland, & Ireland 1475–1640*, ed. A. W. Pollard and G. R. Redgrave, 2nd edn. ed. Katharine Pantzer, 2 vols. (1976, 1986)

Tilley	M. P. Tilley, *A Dictionary of the Proverbs in England in the Sixteenth and Seventeenth Centuries* (Ann Arbor, 1950)
Tilley/Dent	R. W. Dent, *Shakespeare's Proverbial Language: An Index* (Berkeley, 1981)
Whiting	B. J. Whiting, *Proverbs, Sentences, and Proverbial Phrases from English Writings Mainly Before 1500* (Cambridge, Mass., 1968)

Measure for Measure

THE PERSONS OF THE PLAY

THE DUKE, Vincentio
ANGELO, the deputy
ESCALUS, an ancient lord
CLAUDIO, a young gentleman
LUCIO, a fantastic
Two other like gentlemen
PROVOST
THOMAS ⎫
        ⎬ two friars
PETER ⎭
ELBOW, a simple constable   10
FROTH, a foolish gentleman
CLOWN, named Pompey
ABHORSON, an executioner
BARNARDINE, a dissolute prisoner
ISABELLA, sister to Claudio
MARIANA, betrothed to Angelo
JULIETTA, beloved of Claudio
FRANCISCA, a nun
MISTRESS OVERDONE, a bawd
[JUSTICE   20
BOY, servant of Mariana
VARRIUS, friend of the Duke
Lords, Attendants, Officers, Servants, Citizens]

The scene: Vienna

Persons of the Play] Names of all the Actors, *at end in* F

5 **fantastic** someone who is odd or extravagant in speech and dress
6 **like** similar

85

Measure for Measure

1.1   *Enter Duke, Escalus, Lords, and Attendants*

DUKE   Escalus.

ESCALUS   My lord.

DUKE

Of government the properties to unfold
Would seem in me to affect speech and discourse,
Since I am put to know that your own science
Exceeds in that the lists of all advice
My strength can give you. Then no more remains
But that to your sufficiency …

             … as your worth is able,
And let them work. The nature of our people,   10
Our city's institutions, and the terms
For common justice, you're as pregnant in
As art and practice hath enrichèd any
That we remember. There is our commission,
From which we would not have you warp.

      He gives Escalus a paper

                           Call hither,
I say, bid come before us Angelo.   *Exit an Attendant*
What figure of us think you he will bear?

1.1.0.1 *and Attendants*] CAPELL; *not in* F   8–9 But … able] This edition ; *one line in* F   8 that]
F ; this OXFORD   15 *He … paper*] OXFORD; *not in* F   16 *Exit an Attendant*] CAPELL; *not in* F

1.1.3 **properties** distinctive attributes or qualities
    unfold open up, explain
4 **seem … discourse** give the impression that I enjoy making long speeches
5 **put** not 'compelled', as in *OED* v¹ 28b, but simply 'given to know, informed'; compare 'I am made to understand' at 3.1.495–6
    science knowledge
6 **that** i.e. the nature of government
    lists limits
7 **strength** power of mind
7–10 **Then no more … work** For a discussion of these lines see Appendix A.
11 **institutions** established laws and customs
    terms technical vocabulary of the law

12 **common** general, applicable to the whole community
    pregnant well-informed, fertile in ideas
13 **art and practice** skill or learning combined with practical experience
    enrichèd used here figuratively, with no financial implication
15 **warp** deviate (and thus become twisted or corrupt)
17 **figure … bear** The first of the play's many references to the stamping of an impression, as with a coin or seal. But it cannot refer simply to the image of the Duke as it might appear on a coin, since the Duke is asking a question about something he considers problematical, and he presumably means, 'What appearance will

For you must know, we have with special soul
Elected him our absence to supply,
Lent him our terror, dressed him with our love,   20
And given his deputation all the organs
Of our own power. What think you of it?

ESCALUS

If any in Vienna be of worth
To undergo such ample grace and honour,
It is Lord Angelo.

Enter Angelo

DUKE   Look where he comes.

ANGELO

Always obedient to your grace's will,
I come to know your pleasure.

DUKE   Angelo,
There is a kind of character in thy life
That to the observer doth thy history
Fully unfold. Thyself and thy belongings   30
Are not thine own so proper as to waste
Thyself upon thy virtues, they on thee.
Heaven doth with us as we with torches do,

Angelo present as my substitute? In what
way will he represent me?'

18 **you must know** not 'you know already'
but 'I want you to know'
with special soul 'Special' often has a
legal flavour ('referring to a particular
matter or person') and 'soul' is the
rational soul making decisions (compare
l. 67 below, 'As to your soul seems good',
and *Hamlet* 3.2.61, 'Since my dear soul
was mistress of her choice'). The phrase
thus means 'with my mind giving this
matter particular and individual attention', and anticipates the 'leavened and
preparèd choice' of l. 52.

19 **Elected** chosen
supply make up for, make good

20 **terror** awe-inspiring ability to punish
dressed him with our love Lever glosses
as 'adorned him with the outward signs
of our love', but 'terror' and 'love' seem
to be antithetical, so that 'our love'
would mean 'our power to give favour
and reward (as opposed to punishment)'.

21 **deputation** appointment as deputy
organs instruments

24 **undergo** sustain

28 **character** The word is most frequently
used in Shakespeare to mean 'letter of the
alphabet' or 'writing', and by extension,
'distinctive personal handwriting', as at
4.2.190 below. Here it seems to mean
'external sign indicating what is within',
in the way that her pregnancy 'with
character too gross is writ on Juliet'
(1.2.153): Angelo's outward appearance
indicates the kind of man he is and has
been.

29 **history** personal history, life-story

30 **belongings** attributes, endowments (the
sense 'possessions' did not come into
being until after 1800)

31 **Are not . . . proper** do not belong to you in
such an exclusively private way
waste consume, use up

32 Angelo must not spend his time simply
cherishing his own virtues, and using
them for purely personal ends.

33–41 Shakespeare seems to have written
these lines with three New Testament
parables at the back of his mind: (1) the
candlestick (e.g. Matthew 5: 15), (2) the
woman with an issue of blood (the ver-

88

Not light them for themselves; for if our virtues
Did not go forth of us, 'twere all alike
As if we had them not. Spirits are not finely touched
But to fine issues, nor nature never lends
The smallest scruple of her excellence
But, like a thrifty goddess, she determines
Herself the glory of a creditor,   40
Both thanks and use. But I do bend my speech
To one that can my part in him advertise.
Hold therefore, Angelo.
        ⌈*He offers Angelo a paper*⌉
In our remove, be thou at full ourself:
Mortality and mercy in Vienna
Live in thy tongue and heart. Old Escalus,
Though first in question, is thy secondary.
Take thy commission.
ANGELO   Now, good my lord,
Let there be some more test made of my mettle,

43.1 *He ... paper*] This edition; *not in* F

sion in Luke 8: 43–8 contains the words
'issue', 'touched', 'virtue', and 'gone out
of me'), (3) the talents (Matthew 25:
14–30). But they are influences rather
than allusions, and with the second
Shakespeare uses the vocabulary with an
entirely different set of meanings. In
addition, the idea that virtue must show
itself in action is a commonplace of
classical writing on ethics (e.g. Aristotle,
Nicomachean Ethics 1.8).

35 **go forth of us** manifest themselves actively
all alike all the same, as though
36–7 **Spirits ... fine issues** This is usually
regarded as another image of coining,
with 'touched' referring to the tests applied to precious metals. But 'issue' as the
act of putting coins into circulation is a
19th-c. usage, and 'issues' here means
'consequences' (compare *Kinsmen*
1.3.61–3, 'the elements | That ... do
effect | Rare issues by their operance').
'Touched' means 'emotionally aroused,
affected', as elsewhere in the play
(2.2.54, 71). We cannot claim, says the
Duke, to have deeply sensitive souls unless we prove it by noble actions.
38 **The ... excellence** the most minute

amount of her noblest qualities
39 **determines** ordains, decrees (like a judge
in a lawsuit)
41 **thanks and use** the person to whom
Nature has lent must show gratitude and
also pay interest on the loan (compare
Sonnet 4)
bend direct
42 **my part in him advertise** make publicly
known what I bestow on him (the part of
him that comes from me). 'Advertise' is
stressed on the second syllable.
43 **Hold** In Shakespearian English this can
mean 'take what I am about to offer you';
the Duke holds out Angelo's commission.
Angelo hesitates, however, and the Duke
has to repeat his command at l. 48.
44 **remove** absence
at full fully, completely
45 **Mortality** the power of sentencing to
death
46 It is hard to see why editors repeatedly
assert that 'tongue' refers back exclusively to 'mortality' and 'heart' to
'mercy', since both are necessary whatever verdict is pronounced.
47 **in question** under consideration
secondary subordinate, second in rank
49 **mettle** In the 16th c. 'mettle' and 'metal'
were interchangeable spellings of the

Before so noble and so great a figure   50
Be stamped upon it.
DUKE   No more evasion.
We have with a leavened and preparèd choice
Proceeded to you, therefore take your honours.
        Angelo takes his commission
Our haste from hence is of so quick condition
That it prefers itself, and leaves unquestioned
Matters of needful value. We shall write to you,
As time and our concernings shall importune,
How it goes with us, and do look to know
What doth befall you here. So fare you well.
To the hopeful execution do I leave you   60
Of your commissions.
ANGELO   Yet give leave, my lord,
That we may bring you something on the way.
DUKE
My haste may not admit it.
Nor need you, on mine honour, have to do
With any scruple: your scope is as mine own,
So to enforce or qualify the laws
As to your soul seems good. Give me your hand;
I'll privily away. I love the people,
But do not like to stage me to their eyes.
Though it do well, I do not relish well   70

---

52 a leavened] F; leavened NOSWORTHY   53.1 *Angelo ... commission*] OXFORD; *not in* F

same word, which could mean 'temperament or disposition' as well as 'metal' in
the modern sense. As both meanings are
present I have retained the Folio spelling.

50 **figure** design or image (of the sort put on
  a coin)
51 **evasion** excuse made to escape responsibility
52 **leavened** matured (as with bread-dough
  left to rise)
54 **so quick condition** such an urgent nature
55 **prefers itself** gives itself precedence over
  other matters
  unquestioned unexamined, unconsidered
56 **of needful value** both necessary and
  important
57 **concernings** concerns, affairs of importance

57 **importune** urge
58 **look** expect
62 **bring** accompany
  something somewhat, a little
63 **admit** permit
64 **have to do** concern yourself
65 **scruple** doubt, hesitation
  scope freedom of action
66 **qualify** mitigate
68 **privily** secretly, privately
69 **stage me** flaunt myself in public, like an
  actor who wishes for applause. Used by
  Shakespeare as a verb only here and in
  Antony 5.2.213; in both plays the tone is
  contemptuous. See the Introduction,
  p. 4.
70 **do well** is appropriate
  relish enjoy

Their loud applause and aves vehement,
Nor do I think the man of safe discretion
That does affect it. Once more fare you well.

ANGELO

The heavens give safety to your purposes!

ESCALUS

Lead forth and bring you back in happiness!

DUKE I thank you; fare you well.   *Exit*

ESCALUS

I shall desire you, sir, to give me leave
To have free speech with you, and it concerns me
To look into the bottom of my place.
A power I have, but of what strength and nature   80
I am not yet instructed.

ANGELO

'Tis so with me. Let us withdraw together,
And we may soon our satisfaction have
Touching that point.

ESCALUS   I'll wait upon your honour.

                                                        Exeunt

I.2   *Enter Lucio and two other Gentlemen*

LUCIO If the Duke with the other dukes come not to
composition with the King of Hungary, why then all the
dukes fall upon the king.

FIRST GENTLEMAN Heaven grant us its peace, but not the
King of Hungary's!

76 *Exit*] F2; *after l.75* in F

71 **aves** shouts of welcome
72 **safe discretion** reliable judgement
73 **affect** like
75 A continuation of Angelo's prayer in the
   preceding line, with 'The heavens' as an
   implied subject.
   in happiness with a successful outcome
   to your affairs
78 **concerns me** is important to me
79 **bottom** depths, furthest extent
83 **satisfaction** removal of doubt or uncertainty
I.2 The textual problems associated with
   this scene are discussed in the Introduction, pp. 72–4.
 1–5 These lines may contain topical allusions (see the Introduction, p. 2) or

may simply be intended to give a general
sense of young gallants talking about
politics. The audience later discovers that
Lucio's air of having inside information
about current events should be viewed
with scepticism (see 3.1.392–7).
2 **composition** agreement over a truce or
   peace-treaty
   the King of Hungary The opening speech
   of Whetstone's *Promos and Cassandra*
   refers to 'our liege, the King of Hungary'.
   The name may have been introduced to
   allow for the joke in the next speech.
3 **fall upon** will attack
4–5 **Heaven grant ... the King of Hungary's!** The First Gentleman wants 'the
   peace of God', as in Philippians 4: 7

SECOND GENTLEMAN Amen.

LUCIO Thou conclud'st like the sanctimonious pirate, that went to sea with the ten commandments but scraped one out of the table.

SECOND GENTLEMAN 'Thou shalt not steal'?   10

LUCIO Ay, that he razed.

FIRST GENTLEMAN Why, 'twas a commandment to command the captain and all the rest from their functions: they put forth to steal. There's not a soldier of us all that in the thanksgiving before meat do relish the petition well that prays for peace.

SECOND GENTLEMAN I never heard any soldier dislike it.

LUCIO I believe thee, for I think thou never wast where grace was said.

SECOND GENTLEMAN No? A dozen times at least.   20

FIRST GENTLEMAN What, in metre?

LUCIO In any proportion or in any language.

FIRST GENTLEMAN I think, or in any religion.

LUCIO Ay, why not? Grace is grace, despite of all controversy; as, for example, thou thyself art a wicked villain, despite of all grace.

(glossed as 'peace of conscience' in the Geneva marginalia) but he does not want the war to end and deprive him of his job as a soldier. 'Hungarian' was used jokingly at the time to refer to a hungry or needy person (see *OED*), so the King of Hungary's peace would be one which made the gentleman go hungry.

4 **its** This usage is very rare in Shakespeare, whose normal possessive form is 'his'. Abbott, 228, says that the use here is for the sake of emphasis.

7 **sanctimonious** making a show of sanctity (*OED*'s earliest example of this ironic usage)

9 **table** a wooden board or panel on which the commandments were painted (a normal item of church furnishings at the time)

11 **razed** erased, scraped off

13 **from their functions** to give up their trade or occupation

15–16 **thanksgiving ... peace** Several 16th-c. graces to be spoken before meals concluded with a petition for peace.

17 **dislike** express dislike for

21 **in metre** perhaps referring to a grace in some kind of doggerel verse, not intended to be taken seriously

22 **In any proportion** in any shape or form, of any kind whatever

23 **think** think so (Abbott 64)

24–6 Lucio's logic is not easy to follow. Perhaps 'why not' refers back to the increasing exaggeration of the previous three lines, culminating in 'any religion': 'why shouldn't we talk in this way, because a grace before food will continue to be a grace however much we argue about it?' But 'grace' can allude to God's grace or mercy (see the similar punning in *1 Henry IV* 1.2.16–21), so that Lucio is also asserting that God's grace exists despite all the theological controversies about its nature and operation. Probably 'as' means 'in the same way as', and ll. 25–6 invert the argument: just as grace exists despite human frailty, shown in disputes, so human frailty, shown in the gentleman's wickedness, exists despite the availability of God's grace.

FIRST GENTLEMAN Well, there went but a pair of shears
between us.

LUCIO I grant, as there may between the lists and the
velvet. Thou art the list.   30

FIRST GENTLEMAN And thou the velvet. Thou art good
velvet; thou'rt a three-piled piece, I warrant thee. I had
as lief be a list of an English kersey, as be piled as thou
art piled for a French velvet. Do I speak feelingly now?

LUCIO I think thou dost, and indeed with most painful
feeling of thy speech. I will, out of thine own confession,
learn to begin thy health, but whilst I live forget to drink
after thee.

FIRST GENTLEMAN I think I have done myself wrong, have I
not?   40

SECOND GENTLEMAN Yes, that thou hast, whether thou art
tainted or free.

Enter Mistress Overdone

LUCIO Behold, behold, where Madam Mitigation comes! I

1.2.42.1 *Mistress Overdone*] DYCE; *Bawde* F (*and throughout the play*)

27–8 **there went ... us** a stock proverbial
phrase (Tilley P36): the two men were
cut from the same piece of cloth, are
identical

29–30 **lists ... list** The 'list' of a cloth is the
plain edge or selvage, often trimmed
away when the cloth is being cut.

32 **three-piled** with a pile of treble thickness,
of high quality

32–3 **had as lief** would as willingly

33 **kersey** a coarse woollen cloth, whose
name may derive from the village of
Kersey in Suffolk

33–4 **piled as thou art piled** A play of words
on 'piled', said of cloth having a pile or
nap, and 'pilled', equivalent to 'peeled',
'deprived of hair, bald' (an effect of venereal disease).

34 **French velvet** The gentleman asserts that
Lucio's 'velvet' is decidedly threadbare.
There may be an allusion to the practice
of covering syphilitic scars with patches
of velvet (see Lavatch's jokes in *All's Well*
4.5.93–100), and there is an implied
contrast between the plain honest Eng-
lishman and the corrupt sophisticated
Frenchman.

feelingly powerfully, impressively

35–6 **with most painful feeling** Lucio deliberately misinterprets 'feelingly' as 'pain-

fully', implying that the gentleman has
sores in his mouth caused by disease,
which hurt him when he talks.

37–8 **begin thy health ... after thee** propose
a toast to you and so drink first from the
cup, but not drink from the same cup
after you because your mouth will have
contaminated it

39 **done myself wrong** done myself an injustice by laying myself open to mockery

42 **tainted or free** diseased or healthy. If he is
'tainted' he will have done himself wrong
in a different sense, 'injured himself'.

43–5 This speech is puzzling. Lucio has just
been taunting the First Gentleman for
venereal disease, and presumably would
not want to admit that he himself has
'purchased ... diseases' in a brothel.
Some editors re-assign the speech to the
First Gentleman, but it would then contradict his claim to be 'sound' at ll. 51–2.

43 **Madam Mitigation** Quoted in *OED*,
Madam 2d, as the first example of a
playful or ironic use. (*OED* has no example of *Madam* as 'prostitute' before 1719.)
Her allegorical name is 'Mitigation' because she helps to mitigate, or alleviate,
the pangs of desire. The mock title may be
a female equivalent of 'Monsieur Melancholy' (*As You Like It* 3.2.288) and

have purchased as many diseases under her roof as
come to—

SECOND GENTLEMAN To what, I pray?

LUCIO Judge.

SECOND GENTLEMAN To three thousand dolours a year.

FIRST GENTLEMAN Ay, and more.

LUCIO A French crown more.   50

FIRST GENTLEMAN Thou art always figuring diseases in me,
but thou art full of error; I am sound.

LUCIO Nay, not as one would say, healthy, but so sound
as things that are hollow. Thy bones are hollow;
impiety has made a feast of thee.

FIRST GENTLEMAN (*to Mistress Overdone*) How now, which
of your hips has the most profound sciatica?

MISTRESS OVERDONE Well, well. There's one yonder arrested and carried to prison was worth five thousand of
you all.   60

SECOND GENTLEMAN Who's that, I prithee?

MISTRESS OVERDONE Marry, sir, that's Claudio, Signor
Claudio.

61 prithee] This edition; pray'thee F

'Monsieur Remorse' (*1 Henry IV*
1.2.112).

45–7 **come to—... Judge** There may be a
play of words on *come to* ('amount to')
and *come to judge* ('make judgement on'),
as in such biblical phrases as 'he is come
to judge the earth', Psalm 98:9.

48 **dolours** pains (but with a pun on 'dollar',
in this context the German thaler, a large
silver coin). The same joke is found in
Tempest 2.1.19–20 and *Lear* 2.2.229.

50 **French crown** a gold coin minted in
France, but also used to mean 'baldness
caused by venereal disease'. Here again a
favourite joke of Shakespeare's: compare
Dream 1.2.88–91, *LLL* 3.1.138, and *All's
Well* 2.2.21.

51 **figuring** imagining

52 **sound** healthy

53–4 **so sound ... hollow** Playing on the
proverbial phrase, 'Empty vessels sound
most' (Tilley V36); compare 2.3.22–3
below, and *Lear* 1.1.153–4, 'Nor are
those empty-hearted whose low sounds |
Reverb no hollowness'.

54 **Thy bones are hollow** because they are

rotten with disease (compare 'hollow
bones' in *Timon* 4.3.152)

55 **impiety ... thee** your body has been eaten
away because of your sinful conduct

56–7 **How ... sciatica** Lever regards this as
the First Gentleman's reply to Lucio, but
'How now?' in Shakespeare usually indicates the opening of a fresh conversation
(compare Mistress Overdone's words to
Pompey at l. 83 below). The First Gentleman, perhaps feeling himself worsted in
the argument, at last deigns to notice
Mistress Overdone, but only in terms of a
jeer at her.

57 **most profound** deepest, most painful
sciatica possibly a euphemism for a symp-
tom of venereal disease, such as the
'bone-ache' mentioned in *Troilus* 2.3.18
and Additional Passage A, 6

61 **prithee** See 3.1.470 n.

62 The fact that she knows Claudio need not
necessarily indicate that he has been one
of her clients. She may know him as a
friend of Lucio, and she regards him as
'worth five thousand' of the men in front
of her.

FIRST GENTLEMAN Claudio to prison? 'Tis not so.

MISTRESS OVERDONE Nay, but I know 'tis so. I saw him
arrested, saw him carried away; and which is more,
within these three days his head to be chopped off.

LUCIO But after all this fooling, I would not have it so. Art .
thou sure of this?

MISTRESS OVERDONE I am too sure of it; and it is for getting   70
Madam Julietta with child.

LUCIO Believe me, this may be. He promised to meet me
two hours since, and he was ever precise in promise-
keeping.

SECOND GENTLEMAN Besides, you know, it draws something near to the speech we had to such a purpose.

FIRST GENTLEMAN But most of all, agreeing with the
proclamation.

LUCIO Away, let's go learn the truth of it.

Exeunt Lucio and two Gentlemen

MISTRESS OVERDONE Thus what with the war, what with   80
the sweat, what with the gallows, and what with
poverty, I am custom-shrunk.

Enter Pompey

How now, what's the news with you?

POMPEY Yonder man is carried to prison.

79.1 *Exeunt ... Gentlemen*] CAPELL; *Exit.* F   82.1 *Enter Pompey*] DYCE; *Enter Clowne.* F, *after*
l. 83 (F *uses 'Clowne' throughout the play*)

73 **precise** punctilious, scrupulous
75–6 Possibly implying that Lucio and the
two gentlemen had discussed Claudio
and his affairs earlier on.
80–2 Lever (Introduction, p. xxxii) sees this
speech as a series of topical allusions:
'Overdone's complaint links a number of
factors operative in the winter of
1603–4: the continuance of war with
Spain; the plague in London; the treason
trials and executions at Winchester in
connection with the plots of Raleigh and
others; the slackness of trade in the
deserted capital.' But she may simply be
listing the standard causes for a decline in
customers; it is surely perverse to look for
precise topicality in references to the
gallows and poverty, and the war may be
the one discussed in the opening lines of
this scene. 'Sweat' can refer to 'sweating-
sickness' (*OED sweat* 3b) but that is not

the same as bubonic plague, and the
word is more likely to allude to the
sweating-treatment (*OED* 4a) used for
venereal diseases (see the note on 'tub' at
3.1.323): the young men cannot visit
her establishment while they are
undergoing treatment.
80–1 The 'what with' construction can be
paralleled in *1 Henry IV* 5.1.49–50,
'What with our help, what with the
absent King, | What with the injuries of a
wanton time ...'
82 **custom-shrunk** short of customers (the
only example of the phrase in
Shakespeare and *OED*)
84 **Yonder man** This can hardly be anyone
other than Claudio (compare 'one yonder' at l. 58 above), but Mistress Overdone's failure to recognize this presents a
problem which is discussed in the Introduction, pp. 72–3. It is also odd that

MISTRESS OVERDONE Well, what has he done?

POMPEY A woman.

MISTRESS OVERDONE But what's his offence?

POMPEY Groping for trouts in a peculiar river.

MISTRESS OVERDONE What, is there a maid with child by
him?   90

POMPEY No, but there's a woman with maid by him. You
have not heard of the proclamation, have you?

MISTRESS OVERDONE What proclamation, man?

POMPEY All houses in the suburbs of Vienna must be
plucked down.

MISTRESS OVERDONE And what shall become of those in the
city?

POMPEY They shall stand for seed; they had gone down
too, but that a wise burgher put in for them.

MISTRESS OVERDONE But shall all our houses of resort in the   100
suburbs be pulled down?

Pompey should refer to him in this off-hand way, but later respectfully describe him as 'Signor Claudio' (l. 113).

85–6 **done ... A woman** playing on the sexual sense of *do*, 'copulate'

88 **Groping** catching fish by feeling for them in the water (sometimes referred to as 'tickling' trout). Eccles cites Chapman, *All Fools* 3.1.119, 'A man may grope and tickle 'em like a trout', and compare *Twelfth Night* 2.5.20–1.
peculiar privately owned. Tickling trout is a form of poaching, and the line as a whole would appear to mean 'seducing other men's wives', which does not accurately describe Claudio's offence. But Mistress Overdone's reply shows that she does not interpret it in this way, and Pompey may intend to be wittily paradoxical: 'he's accused of poaching fish in his own private river'. If so, however, we should expect 'his peculiar' rather than 'a peculiar'.

91 **woman with maid** Editors point out that *maid* (*OED* 7) can refer to the young of certain fish such as skate and shad, but the main point of the phrase may be rather different. Overdone's 'maid with child' (i.e. 'pregnant virgin') is a contradiction in terms, which Pompey corrects (the child carried by the pregnant woman will be a virgin). Note that 'maid' can be

applied to a male without sexual experience, as in *Twelfth Night* 5.1.259–61.

94 **houses** perhaps a discreet shortening of 'bawdy-houses', a phrase used, in singular or plural, six times elsewhere by Shakespeare
suburbs Most of the London brothels in the Elizabethan period were in the suburbs, outside the jurisdiction of the city authorities; *OED* quotes Nashe, *Christ's Tears over Jerusalem* (1593), 'London, what are thy suburbs but licenced stews?'

95 **plucked down** pulled down, demolished (see the Introduction, pp. 2–3)

98 **stand for seed** said of a plant left unharvested, so that it will provide seed for future crops (but with obvious obscene implications). This is the sole use of the phrase in Shakespeare, and the only quotation in *OED*, *stand v.* 17b dates from 1858.
had would have

99 **burgher** citizen (from the wealthy middle class)
put in *OED*, *put* 45d(b), quotes and glosses this as 'pleaded, interceded for', but it might also mean 'bid for, offered to buy'.

100 **houses of resort** The phrase 'houses of unlawful and disorderly resort' occurs in the Privy Council letter of 1596 mentioned in the Introduction, p. 3. Com-

POMPEY To the ground, mistress.

MISTRESS OVERDONE Why, here's a change indeed in the commonwealth! What shall become of me?

POMPEY Come, fear not you; good counsellors lack no clients. Though you change your place, you need not change your trade. I'll be your tapster still. Courage, there will be pity taken on you; you that have worn your eyes almost out in the service, you will be considered.   110

Enter Provost and Officers with Claudio and Julietta

MISTRESS OVERDONE What's to do here, Thomas tapster? Let's withdraw.

POMPEY Here comes Signor Claudio, led by the provost to prison, and there's Madam Juliet.

Exeunt Mistress Overdone and Pompey

CLAUDIO

Fellow, why dost thou show me thus to the world?
Bear me to prison, where I am committed.

110.1 *Enter . . . Julietta*] This edition; *for* F *see* 114.1 *n.*   114.1 *Exeunt . . . Pompey*] *Exeunt.* F (*at this point* F *inserts a new scene heading*, '*Scena Tertia.*', *omitted by* ROWE, *followed by* '*Enter Prouost, Iuliet, Officers, Lucio, & 2. Gent.*')

pare also the brothel-scene in *Pericles* Sc. 19.81–2, 'And do you know this house to be a place | Of such resort and will come into it?'

105–6 **good counsellors lack no clients** This sounds proverbial, but does not appear to be recorded in proverb-collections. In Drayton's *Matilda* (edition of 1594, C2ᵛ) a long passage on the allurements of female beauty, written in proverbial style, includes the lines 'The shrine of love doth seldom offerings want, | Nor with such counsel clients never scant'.

106 **change your place** live somewhere else

108–9 **worn your eyes** Lever sees this as 'a sly allusion to "Blind Cupid", traditionally the sign in front of brothels', but the only evidence to support this is Benedick's joke in *Much Ado* 1.1.234–7. It may be more to the point that partial blindness is one of the symptoms of advanced syphilis.

109 **service** perhaps used euphemistically in the chivalric sense (*OED* 2c 10), 'devotion or service to love', though a cruder sense is indicated in Lavatch's repeated use of the word in *All's Well* 4.5.24–31

109–10 **considered** *OED* glosses as sense 8,

'recompensed, remunerated', but it is surely more likely to be sense 7, 'treated with consideration, have allowances made for you'.

110.1 *Provost* an officer charged with the apprehension, custody, and punishment of offenders. The name does not apply to any English legal official of the time, and is not used by Shakespeare in any other play.

111 **Thomas tapster** apparently a generic or alliterative name for a tapster (equivalent to 'barman'); Eccles quotes 'You, Tom tapster, that tap your small cans of beer' from Greene's *A Quip for an Upstart Courtier* (1592), and *OED*, *tapster* 2, quotes 'Tom the tapster' from 1612. But it seems odd that Shakespeare did not use his memorable real name, Pompey Bum; if F is based on foul papers, perhaps he had not yet thought of it.

114.1 *Exeunt* Dover Wilson thinks it odd that they do not remain as spectators. But they are alarmed by the Provost's entrance, and make off as soon as they have identified the newcomers.

115 **show me thus to the world** The couple are being paraded through the streets as a kind of shame-punishment. But Claudio

97

PROVOST

I do it not in evil disposition,
But from Lord Angelo by special charge.

CLAUDIO

Thus can the demi-god, authority,
Make us pay down for our offence by weight.   120
The words of heaven: on whom it will, it will;
On whom it will not, so; yet still 'tis just.
    Enter Lucio and two Gentlemen

LUCIO

Why, how now, Claudio, whence comes this restraint?

CLAUDIO

From too much liberty, my Lucio, liberty.
As surfeit is the father of much fast,
So every scope by the immoderate use
Turns to restraint. Our natures do pursue,
Like rats that raven down their proper bane, *~Claudio's*
A thirsty evil, and when we drink, we die. *perception of love*
                                    marriage

120 weight.] WARBURTON; waight ∧ F   122.1 *Enter ... Gentlemen*] DYCE; *Lucio, & 2. Gent.* F
(*see* 114.1 *n.*)   124 liberty.] BALD; ~ ∧ F

resents it as an unjustified addition to his death-sentence, and asks to be taken directly to prison.

117 **in evil disposition** because of a malicious temperament

118 **by special charge** See the note on 'special' at 1.1.18; Angelo has made an order specifically relating to Claudio's case.

119 **demi-god** a being half human and half divine

120 **pay down ... by weight** This phraseology emphasizes the harshness of the punishment: to 'pay down' is to pay immediately or on the spot (*OED pay v.*¹ 5b), and 'by weight' means that the coins are not merely counted but weighed, to ensure that they are of full value.

121 **The words of heaven** an elliptical way of saying 'as in the Bible', with the next twelve words alluding to Romans 9: 15 and 18, 'For he saith to Moses, I will have mercy on him, to whom I will show mercy ... Therefore he hath mercy on whom he will, and whom he will, he hardeneth'. Claudio makes a daring, even blasphemous, comparison between Angelo's arbitrary punishment and God's election, for reasons known only to him, of the saved and the damned. In

both cases those selected for punishment must not dare to question it.

123 This line is discussed in the introduction, pp. 72–3.

124 **liberty** unrestrained action, licence; the flavour of the word is illustrated by Polonius's lines in *Hamlet* 2.1.22–4, 'such wanton, wild, and usual slips | As are companions noted and most known | To youth and liberty'. Tilley L225 gives 'Too much liberty spoils all' as proverbial.

125 **surfeit** gluttony or the sickness caused by it. Compare Tilley S1011, 'Every surfeit foreruns a fast'.

126–7 **every scope ... restraint** All the freedoms permitted to us turn into restrictions if we abuse them

128–9 **Like rats ... die** Compare Tilley | Dent R32.1, 'Like rats, men swallow sweet poison until they die', with a striking parallel from Joseph Hall's *Meditations and Vows* (1606), 1.95, 'Ambition is torment enough for an enemy, for it affords as much discontentment in enjoying as in want, making men like poisoned rats, which when they have tasted their bane cannot rest till they drink, and then can much less rest till their death'.

128 **raven** devour voraciously
    their proper bane (*a*) their own destruc-

LUCIO If I could speak so wisely under an arrest, I w
send for certain of my creditors. And yet, to say
truth, I had as lief have the foppery of freedom as th.
morality of imprisonment. What's thy offence, Claudio ?

CLAUDIO

What but to speak of would offend again.

LUCIO What, is't murder ?

CLAUDIO No.

LUCIO Lechery ?

CLAUDIO Call it so.

PROVOST Away, sir ; you must go.

CLAUDIO (*to the Provost*)

One word, good friend. Lucio, a word with you.   140

LUCIO A hundred, if they'll do you any good. Is lechery so
looked after ?

CLAUDIO

Thus stands it with me: upon a true contract
I got possession of Julietta's bed.
You know the lady ; she is fast my wife,
Save that we do the denunciation lack
Of outward order. This we came not to
Only for propagation of a dower

---

133 morality] DAVENANT ; mortality F

tion; (*b*) their own specific poison
(ratsbane, a compound of arsenic)

131 **creditors** who would then have Lucio
arrested for debt

132 **foppery** stupidity, folly (the sense
'behaviour typical of a fop or dandy'
does not appear until the end of the
17th c.)

133 **morality** wisdom. F reads 'mortality',
and Shakespeare never uses 'morality',
though he has 'moral', 'moraller' (a
unique usage in *Othello* 2.3.292, not
paralleled elsewhere) and 'moralize'.
Some editors retain the reading of F, but it
makes little sense in the context and does
not provide the required antithesis to
'foppery'.

140 **a word with you** See the Introduction,
p. 73.

142 **looked after** *OED, look* 12g, glosses 'look
after' in this context as 'keep watch
upon', but it could have various other

meanings such as 'search for', 'attend
to', and 'take care of'.

145 **fast** firmly, securely

146–7 **denunciation ... Of outward order**
declaration of the public ceremony (of
marriage). 'Outward' may perhaps also
imply that Claudio regards the matter as
one of mere formality or external appearance.

148 **propagation** *OED* quotes this as the
earliest example of sense 3, 'increase,
enlargement'. If so, presumably Julietta
would receive a larger dowry if she
married with the approval of her relatives. But it may simply mean 'generation, bringing into being' ; if she failed to
gain their approval she would not just
have a smaller dowry, she would lose it
altogether. The F spelling *propogation*,
though not found elsewhere in F, is not
necessarily a misprint ; the form *propogate*
occurs in Thomas Carew's masque, *Coe-
lum Britannicum* (1634), l. 791.

Remaining in the coffer of her friends
From whom we thought it meet to hide our love   150
Till time had made them for us. But it chances
The stealth of our most mutual entertainment
With character too gross is writ on Juliet.

LUCIO

With child, perhaps?

CLAUDIO   Unhappily, even so.
And the new deputy now for the Duke—
Whether it be the fault and glimpse of newness,
Or whether that the body public be
A horse whereon the governor doth ride,
Who, newly in the seat, that it may know
He can command, lets it straight feel the spur;   160
Whether the tyranny be in his place,
Or in his eminence that fills it up,
I stagger in—but this new governor
Awakes me all the enrollèd penalties
Which have, like unscoured armour, hung by the wall
So long that nineteen zodiacs have gone round,

149 **friends** in *OED*'s sense 3, 'relatives, family circle'

151 **made them for us** turned them into our allies

152 **mutual** *OED* glosses as sense 3, 'intimate', but the use of the word at 2.3.27 suggests that it has sense 1, 'reciprocal'. **entertainment** enjoyment of each other

153 **With character too gross** perhaps with a play of meaning: (*a*) written in large letters which are only too legible; (*b*) displayed in a blatant or indecent manner

156 **glimpse** momentary shining (implying that Angelo has been dazzled by his new position)

157 **body public** state or community as a whole. The phrase is not recorded in *OED*, though 'body politic' is fairly common; the only Shakespearian parallel is 'public body' in *Timon* 5.2.30.

161 **in his place** inherent in the office he holds

162 **his eminence** his personal sense of dignity and power

163 **stagger in** am uncertain about

164 **me** This may be intended to have an emphatic sense, 'in my case, for my benefit'. **enrollèd** entered in the rolls or records of the law

165 **unscoured** rusty because it has not been cleaned and used

166 **nineteen** The Duke at 1.3.21 refers to 'fourteen years' as the period of lax law-enforcement. The discrepancy may be explained in various ways. If F is based on foul papers, Shakespeare himself may not have bothered to reconcile the two numbers. There may at some stage have been a misreading of the figures 4 and 9, or xiv and xix, though it should be pointed out that both Crane and the writer of Hand D (probably Shakespeare) in *Sir Thomas More* use words for numbers, not figures. Claudio, who is a young man, may have been mistaken (he could be 19 himself and mean 'during my lifetime'). There is some plausibility in Norman Nathan's suggestion in *SQ* 20 (1969), 84, that 'nineteen zodiacs' refers to what *OED* calls the Metonic cycle or period, 'the cycle of 19 Julian years ... in which the moon returns (nearly) to the same apparent position with regard to the sun, so that the new and full moons occur at the same dates in the corresponding year of each cycle'. Each year was given a 'Golden Number' (see *OED golden a.* 6) corresponding to its place in the cycle, which helped to determine the date for

And none of them been worn; and for a name
Now puts the drowsy and neglected act
Freshly on me. 'Tis surely for a name.

LUCIO I warrant it is; and thy head stands so tickle on thy   170
shoulders that a milkmaid, if she be in love, may sigh it
off. Send after the Duke and appeal to him.

CLAUDIO

I have done so, but he's not to be found.
I prithee, Lucio, do me this kind service.
This day my sister should the cloister enter,
And there receive her approbation.
Acquaint her with the danger of my state,
Implore her, in my voice, that she make friends
To the strict deputy; bid herself assay him.
I have great hope in that, for in her youth   180
There is a prone and speechless dialect
Such as move men; beside, she hath prosperous art
When she will play with reason and discourse,
And well she can persuade.

LUCIO I pray she may, as well for the encouragement of
the like, which else would stand under grievous imposi-

186 the] F; thy OXFORD

Easter. The second prayer-book of
Edward VI (1552) contains 'An Almanac
for Nineteen Years' for the years
1552–70, with a Golden Number for
each year. If this interpretation is correct,
Claudio would mean something like 'for
many years, for ages'.

167 **worn** strictly relating back to the armour of l. 165 but obviously applying to
the neglected laws
for a name This is more likely to mean 'to
gain a reputation (for severity)' than
'because of a fault which is merely nomi-
nal'; Gildon in his 1700 version rewrites
it as 'to get himself a name'.
168 **puts** sets to work, imposes (though
possibly 'puts . . . on' follows from 'worn'
and continues the clothing imagery, i.e.
'makes me wear it')
170 **tickle** easily made to fall, insecure
171–2 **milkmaid . . . sigh it off** the gentle sigh
of an amorous girl would be enough to
dislodge it
176 **approbation** probation, novitiate
179 **herself** Isabella in person

179 **assay** attack with words. But it can also
mean 'make amorous advances to', and
in the next few lines it is hard to tell how
far Claudio, consciously or uncon-
sciously, wants Isabella to exploit her
sexuality in dealing with Angelo.
181 **prone** in *OED*'s sense 7, 'ready, eager'.
Lever's argument that it refers to 'the
abject posture of submission or help-
lessness' is surely unconvincing; this is
not what Claudio expects from his sister.
speechless dialect language that does not
express itself in the form of speech (perhaps what we should now call 'body-
language')
182 **move** arouse compassion in (but with
the implication 'arouse sexually'). The
word is probably in the subjunctive form,
equivalent to 'may move' (Abbott 367).
prosperous art a skill which makes her
successful in argument
186 **the like** love-making similar to Claudio's
stand under be exposed to, bear the
burden of
186–7 **imposition** punishment of the kind
imposed by Angelo

tion, as for the enjoying of thy life, who I would be sorry
should be thus foolishly lost at a game of tick-tack. I'll to
her.

CLAUDIO I thank you, good friend Lucio.   190

LUCIO Within two hours.

CLAUDIO Come, officer, away.   *Exeunt*

I.3   *Enter Duke and Friar Thomas*

DUKE

No, holy father, throw away that thought.
Believe not that the dribbling dart of love
Can pierce a complete bosom. Why I desire thee
To give me secret harbour hath a purpose
More grave and wrinkled than the aims and ends
Of burning youth.

FRIAR   May your grace speak of it?

DUKE

My holy sir, none better knows than you
How I have ever loved the life removed,
And held in idle price to haunt assemblies
Where youth and cost witless bravery keeps.   10
I have delivered to Lord Angelo,
A man of stricture and firm abstinence,
My absolute power and place here in Vienna;

1.3] *Scena Quarta.* F   10 witless] F; a witless WILSON

188 **tick-tack** described by *OED* as 'an old
form of backgammon, played on a board
with holes along the edge, in which pegs
were placed for scoring'; obviously used
by Lucio with an obscene implication.
Tilley/Dent gives 'To play tick-tack' as
proverbial (T281.1).

1.3.1 **that thought** that the Duke wishes to
be concealed in the monastery as part of a
love-intrigue

2 **dribbling** falling at random, ineffectual

3 **complete** without deficiency, perfectly
accomplished. The context hints at the
military use of the term to refer to armour
which totally protects the body, as in
Richard III 4.4.190, and *Hamlet* 1.4.33.

4 **harbour** shelter, lodging

5 **grave and wrinkled** mature, appropriate
to an older man; compare 'the grave
wrinkled senate', *Timon* 4.1.5

6 **burning** (with the heat of sexual desire)

8 **removed** retired, secluded

9 **held in idle price** considered (it) of very
slight value

10 **youth and cost** equivalent to 'youthful
extravagance'
witless bravery foolish ostentation, in the
form of expensive clothing (*OED bravery*
3, 3b)
keeps keeps up, maintains (with 'bravery' as object). Shakespeare frequently
inflects verbs in 's' when there are two
singular nouns as the subject (Abbott
336).

12 **stricture** *OED*, *sb.²*, defines as 'strictness',
with this use as the sole illustration. But
Lever may be right to gloss it as 'restric-
tion', relating it to Angelo's rigorous self-
control: he is totally unlike the kind of
young man described in ll. 9–10. The
word is very rare, and *OED* quotes no
other usage between 1400 and 1627.

And he supposes me travelled to Poland,
For so I have strewed it in the common ear
And so it is received. Now, pious sir,
You will demand of me why I do this.

FRIAR

Gladly, my lord.

DUKE

We have strict statutes and most biting laws,
The needful bits and curbs to headstrong weeds,   20
Which for this fourteen years we have let slip,
Even like an o'ergrown lion in a cave
That goes not out to prey. Now, as fond fathers,
Having bound up the threatening twigs of birch,
Only to stick it in their children's sight
For terror, not to use, in time the rod
Becomes more mocked than feared; so our decrees,
Dead to infliction, to themselves are dead,
And liberty plucks justice by the nose,
The baby beats the nurse, and quite athwart   30

27 Becomes more mocked] POPE; More mock'd F; More mock'd becomes OXFORD

15 **strewed** scattered, spread
16 **received** believed
19 **biting** with a range of metaphorical implications: (*a*) a restraint that cuts painfully into the flesh, like a horse's bridle; (*b*) the teeth of a hunting animal. Compare the punning use of 'biting statutes' in *Contention* (*2 Henry VI*), 4.7.15–16, and *Coriolanus* 1.1.82–3, 'piercing statutes ... to chain up and restrain the poor'.
20 **bits and curbs** The bit is the mouthpiece of a horse's bridle, and the curb is the chain or strap attached to the upper part of the bit.
   weeds See the longer note in Appendix A.
21 **this fourteen** See 1.2.166 n. For 'this' preceding a plural number compare 'this three mile', *Macbeth* 5.5.35.
   let slip This phrase seems to make appropriate sense if we relate it to the 'headstrong weeds' in the previous line and gloss it as 'allowed to escape through carelessness' (*OED let v.*¹ 28c).
22 **o'ergrown** fat and inactive. The term often refers to rank vegetation, and provides a slight link between weeds and animals.
23 **fond** foolish, doting

27 **Becomes** The shortness of the line suggests that a word has dropped out, and Pope's conjecture has been generally accepted. The word could also be inserted after *mocked* or *feared*.
28 **Dead ... dead** if not carried out are as good as dead
29 **liberty** See 1.2.124 n.
   plucks ... nose (as a gesture of contempt; compare 5.1.340–1 and Tilley N236)
30 **The baby beats the nurse** Broadside prints on the theme of 'The World Turned Upside Down' were popular throughout Western Europe from the 16th c. onward. These showed comic reversals, such as wives ruling husbands or animals controlling men, of what was accepted as the normal relationship. No English prints early enough for Shakespeare to have seen are known to survive, but Nashe testified to their existence in his *Preface* to Greene's *Menaphon* (1589), A4: 'It is no marvel if every alehouse vaunt the table of the world turned upside down, since the child beateth his father, and the ass whippeth his master'. The specific motif of the baby beating the nurse does not appear to occur in the existing prints; Steevens in

Goes all decorum.

FRIAR   It rested in your grace
To unloose this tied-up justice when you pleased;
And it in you more dreadful would have seemed
Than in Lord Angelo.

DUKE   I do fear, too dreadful.
Sith 'twas my fault to give the people scope,
'Twould be my tyranny to strike and gall them
For what I bid them do; for we bid this be done,
When evil deeds have their permissive pass
And not the punishment. Therefore, indeed, my father,
I have on Angelo imposed the office,   40
Who may in the ambush of my name strike home,
And yet my nature never in the fight
To do in slander. And to behold his sway
I will, as 'twere a brother of your order,
Visit both prince and people. Therefore, I prithee,
Supply me with the habit and instruct me
How I may formally in person bear

42 fight] F; sight POPE   43 To do in] F; To do it HANMER; T'allow in OXFORD

1793 claimed to have seen it in 'an ancient print', but this has not been subsequently identified. See Ian Donaldson, *The World Upside-Down* (Oxford, 1970), pp. 21–3, and David Kunzle, 'World Upside Down: the Iconography of a European Broadsheet Type', in *The Reversible World*, ed. Barbara Babcock (Ithaca, 1978), pp. 39–94.
    athwart in a perversely wrong direction

31 **decorum** either *OED* 1b, 'the dignity appropriate to one's social position', or 3, 'propriety of behaviour'

32 **unloose this tied-up justice** The friar continues the Duke's animal imagery: here the law is seen as a guard-dog which has been chained up.

33 **dreadful** awe-inspiring. The normal Shakespearian sense seems to be 'terrifying, horrifying', and there is a hint of this in the Duke's reply.

35 **Sith** Since

36 **my tyranny** tyrannical in me
    strike (of a horseman) beat with a whip
    gall make sore by chafing or rubbing (but also used figuratively to mean 'harass, oppress'). The term is often applied to a

horse which has a badly fitting collar or saddle, so that 'strike and gall' may be another of the play's repeated comparisons of government to horse-riding.

37–9 **we bid ... punishment** a semi-proverbial idea (Smith 172)

38 **permissive pass** authorization to proceed. This is the only use of 'permissive' in Shakespeare, and the earliest in this sense recorded in *OED*.

41–2 **name ... nature** title and authority as opposed to personal character; compare *Twelfth Night* 1.2.22–3, 'A noble duke, in nature | As in name'.

41 **home** directly at the target, effectively

43 **do in slander** ?act in a way that provokes slander. The phrase is obscure, and numerous emendations have been suggested.
    sway exercise of authority

45 **prince** ruler (i.e. Angelo)

46 **habit** friar's clothing

47 **formally** in the customary form or manner
    in person not the normal usage; perhaps *person* means 'body', and the Duke is thinking of the movements and gestures a friar would be expected to make
    bear conduct myself, behave.

Like a true friar. Mo reasons for this action
At our more leisure shall I render you;
Only this one: Lord Angelo is precise,   50
Stands at a guard with envy, scarce confesses
That his blood flows, or that his appetite
Is more to bread than stone. Hence shall we see
If power change purpose, what our seemers be. *Exeunt*

1.4   *Enter Isabella and Francisca, a Nun*

ISABELLA

And have you nuns no farther privileges?

NUN

Are not these large enough?

ISABELLA

Yes, truly. I speak not as desiring more,
But rather wishing a more strict restraint
Upon the sisterhood, the votarists of Saint Clare.

LUCIO (*within*)

Ho, peace be in this place!

ISABELLA (*to Francisca*)   Who's that which calls?

54 *Exeunt*] F2; *Exit* F
   1.4] *Scena Quinta.* F   5 sisterhood] F2; Sisterstood F   6 *within* (F has '*Lucio within.*' centred after l. 5)

48 **Mo** more (in number)
50 **Only this one** For the time being I will
   give you one only.
   precise correct, punctilious in behaviour.
   The term was applied to Puritans by
   those who regarded them as over-fastid-
   ious in their attitude to doctrine, but it is
   unlikely that this implication is present
   (the word is used of Claudio at 1.2.73).
51 **at a guard** on guard, in a defensive
   posture (said of swordplay or fencing)
   envy malice (implying that Angelo is
   much concerned about his reputation)
52 **blood** used in Elizabethan English to signify sexual appetite (*OED* 6) as well as the
   bodily fluid; the play exploits this ambiguity (e.g. 1.4.57–61 and 2.4.15 n.)
53 **to bread than stone** biblical vocabulary
   (Matthew 4: 3 and 7: 9) but used to
   convey Angelo's extraordinary lack of
   sensual appetites
54 **power change purpose** coming to power
   makes a man alter his behaviour (compare Tilley A402, 'Authority shows what
   a man is')

seemers those who make a pretence or
show. This is Shakespeare's only usage,
and the earliest example quoted in
OED.

1.4.1 **privileges** This seems to mean 'times
when you are not bound by the rules of
the order, and can behave in a relaxed
manner', though *OED* does not record
the word in precisely this sense.

5 **votarists** those bound by vows to a religious life
Saint Clare The order set up by St Clare
(1194–1253), a follower of St Francis of
Assissi, was rigorously enclosed and had
a strict rule (in theory if not always in
practice) of poverty, silence, and abstinence. Nunneries were established in
England in the late 13th c., but were
dissolved in 1539. How much
Shakespeare knew about the Clares or
Minoresses cannot be established, but it is
clear that Isabella would like an order
with a reputation for strictness to be
stricter still.

NUN

It is a man's voice. Gentle Isabella,
Turn you the key and know his business of him.
You may, I may not; you are yet unsworn.
When you have vowed you must not speak with men   10
But in the presence of the prioress;
Then if you speak you must not show your face,
Or if you show your face you must not speak.
     Lucio calls within
He calls again. I pray you answer him.

ISABELLA (*opening the door*)

Peace and prosperity! Who is't that calls?
     Enter Lucio

LUCIO

Hail, virgin, if you be—as those cheek-roses
Proclaim you are no less. Can you so stead me
As bring me to the sight of Isabella,
A novice of this place and the fair sister
To her unhappy brother Claudio?   20

ISABELLA

Why 'her unhappy brother', let me ask;
The rather for I now must make you know
I am that Isabella and his sister.

LUCIO

Gentle and fair, your brother kindly greets you.
Not to be weary with you, he's in prison.

13.1 *Lucio ... within*] OXFORD; *not in* F   15 *opening the door*] WILSON; *not in* F   15.1 *Enter
Lucio*] ROWE; *not in* F   21 Why 'her unhappy brother', let me ask;] This edition; Why her
vnhappy Brother? Let me aske, F

---

9 **are yet unsworn** have not yet taken your
   vows as a nun. Compare l. 19 below, and
   1.2.175–6, 2.2.21–2, and 5.1.73.
10–13 A Middle-English version of the rule
   (*Two Fifteenth-Century Franciscan Rules*,
   ed. W. W. Seton, EETS OS, no. 148,
   1914, p. 88) says that a sister may speak
   to a stranger only with the permission of
   the abbess and in the company of two
   other sisters, but it does not contain
   anything corresponding to ll. 12–13.
16 **if you be** Lucio cannot resist a cynical
   joke, but then realizes his tactlessness
   and does his best to recover from it.

cheek-roses sometimes glossed as 'rosy
cheeks', but it is more likely that Isabella
picks up Lucio's jest and blushes at it,
which he takes as a sign of modesty. This
is the sole example of the phrase in
Shakespeare and *OED*.
17 **stead** help
19 **novice** someone who is under probation
   for admission to a religious order, but has
   not yet taken vows (see l. 9 above)
20 **unhappy** unfortunate, ill-fated
22 **The rather for** the more readily because
25 **weary** tedious, prolix

ISABELLA

Woe me, for what?

LUCIO

For that which, if myself might be his judge,
He should receive his punishment in thanks:
He hath got his friend with child.

ISABELLA

Sir, make me not your story.

LUCIO   'Tis true.   30
I would not, though 'tis my familiar sin
With maids to seem the lapwing and to jest,
Tongue far from heart, play with all virgins so.
I hold you as a thing enskied and sainted,
By your renouncement an immortal spirit,
And to be talked with in sincerity
As with a saint.

ISABELLA

You do blaspheme the good in mocking me.

LUCIO

Do not believe it. Fewness and truth, 'tis thus:
Your brother and his lover have embraced.   40
As those that feed grow full, as blossoming time
That from the seedness the bare fallow brings
To teeming foison, even so her plenteous womb
Expresseth his full tilth and husbandry.

---

26 **Woe me** a contraction of 'Woe is (to) me'
(Abbott 230)

28 **in thanks** in the form of thanks (for
having performed a meritorious deed)

29 **friend** lover (a term used for both sexes)

30 **your story** the butt of one of your jokes

31 **familiar** usual, habitual

32 **lapwing** The lapwing or peewit was supposed to deceive predators of its young by
making the loudest noise when furthest
away from its nest, and the idea became
proverbial for deceit and hypocrisy (Tilley
L68). The lapwing as a symbol of a
treacherous lover can be found in Gow-
er's *Confessio Amantis* vii.6041–7.

34 **enskied** placed in the sky or heaven

35 **By your renouncement** because of your
renouncement of the world

38 **You do ... me** By mocking me with
excessive flattery you blaspheme against
those who are truly good. Isabella is

being modest, not arrogant.

39 **Fewness and truth** in few words and truly

41 **blossoming time** either (*a*) the time of year
at which blossoms are formed, or (*b*) time
which has the power to create blossoms
in plants. The two constructions in
ll. 41–3 beginning with 'as' are not
strictly symmetrical ('blossoming time' is
not followed by a verb) but the general
sense of the passage is clear enough.

42 **seedness** state of being sown with seed
fallow land ploughed and ready for sowing

43 **teeming foison** rich and plentiful crop or
harvest

44 **Expresseth** manifests, gives a visible
token of
tilth the act of ploughing (with a sexual
implication)
husbandry a play on words: (*a*) cultiva-
tion of the soil; (*b*) behaviour of a husband to his wife

ISABELLA

Someone with child by him? My cousin Juliet?

LUCIO

Is she your cousin?

ISABELLA

Adoptedly, as schoolmaids change their names
By vain though apt affection.

LUCIO   She it is.

ISABELLA

O let him marry her!

LUCIO   This is the point.

The Duke is very strangely gone from hence;   50
Bore many gentlemen, myself being one,
In hand, and hope of action; but we do learn,
By those that know the very nerves of state,
His givings-out were of an infinite distance
From his true-meant design. Upon his place
And with full line of his authority
Governs Lord Angelo, a man whose blood
Is very snow-broth, one who never feels
The wanton stings and motions of the sense,
But doth rebate and blunt his natural edge   60
With profits of the mind, study and fast.

---

54 givings-out] ROWE; giuing-out F

45 **cousin** The term had a range of meanings in Elizabethan English; here it is equivalent to 'intimate friend'. Lucio then asks if she is Isabella's cousin in the strict sense. The friendship must lie in the past if Isabella has no knowledge of Julietta's pregnancy.

47 **Adoptedly** as though by adoption (the sole example in Shakespeare and *OED*) **change** exchange (agree to call each other by affectionate names)

48 **vain though apt** childish or silly, but what you would expect from schoolgirls

51–2 **Bore ... In hand, and hope of action** Two distinct constructions are linked to the same verb: (*a*) *bore in hand*, 'deceived, deluded with false pretences' (*OED bear v*[1] 3e, Tilley H94); (*b*) *bore in hope of action*, 'kept soldiers waiting in the hope of active service'.

53 **very** an intensive used to emphasize the importance of the following word. The same usage occurs in l. 58.

nerves of state sinews controlling the operation of the state

54 **givings-out** announcements, statements of intent. F has the singular form, found also in *Hamlet* 1.5.179, and *Othello* 4.1.126, but the plural makes better sense; compare 'bringings-forth' at 3.1.405.

56 **line** limit (i.e. with an authority as extensive as the Duke's)

58 **snow-broth** melted snow; a slushy mixture of water and snow or ice

59 **stings and motions** goadings and provocations
sense sensuality, sexual desire (*OED* 4b)

60 **rebate** make dull or blunt
edge sharpness of his sexual urge; compare Hamlet to Ophelia, 3.2.237, 'It would cost you a groaning to take off mine edge'

61 **study and fast** probably verbs dependent on *doth* in the previous line rather than nouns in apposition to *profits*

He, to give fear to use and liberty,
Which have for long run by the hideous law
As mice by lions, hath picked out an act
Under whose heavy sense your brother's life
Falls into forfeit; he arrests him on it,
And follows close the rigour of the statute
To make him an example. All hope is gone,
Unless you have the grace by your fair prayer
To soften Angelo. And that's my pith of business   70
'Twixt you and your poor brother.

ISABELLA   Doth he so
Seek his life?

LUCIO   Has censured him already,
And as I hear the provost hath a warrant
For's execution.

ISABELLA
Alas, what poor ability's in me
To do him good?

LUCIO   Assay the power you have.

ISABELLA
My power, alas, I doubt.

LUCIO   Our doubts are traitors,
And makes us lose the good we oft might win
By fearing to attempt. Go to Lord Angelo
And let him learn to know, when maidens sue   80
Men give like gods; but when they weep and kneel
All their petitions are as freely theirs
As they themselves would owe them.

---

62 **use** custom or habit (of a disreputable kind)
   liberty See 1.2.124 n.
64 **mice by lions** Shakespeare may have had in mind a fable in which a group of mice play round and on top of a sleeping lion, which wakes and captures one of them but decides to spare it. Later the mouse helps to rescue the lion from a net in which it is trapped. In a version by the 15th-c. Scottish poet, Robert Henryson (*Fables*, printed in an anglicized form in London in 1577), the story is moralized in a highly political fashion: the sleeping lion is a king who neglects his duties, and the mice are the common people who will misbehave if they see that their rulers are negligent.

65 **heavy** harsh, oppressive
66 **Falls into forfeit** has to be given up, becomes liable to the death penalty
69 **grace** good fortune
70 **pith** essential part; *my pith of business* is equivalent to 'the pith of my business', and is a normal Shakespearian construction (see Abbott 423).
72 **Has** Shakespeare frequently omits nominative pronouns before such verbs as *has* or *is* (Abbott 400).
   censured passed judgement on
76 **Assay** put to the trial, test
80 **sue** plead
82–3 **as freely … owe them** granted in as complete a way as the girls themselves would wish to have them
83 **owe** own

ISABELLA

  I'll see what I can do.

LUCIO   But speedily!

ISABELLA

  I will about it straight,

  No longer staying but to give the mother

  Notice of my affair. I humbly thank you.

  Commend me to my brother; soon at night

  I'll send him certain word of my success.

LUCIO

  I take my leave of you.

ISABELLA   Good sir, adieu.   *Exeunt*   90

2.1   *Enter Angelo, Escalus, a Justice, and Servants*

ANGELO

  We must not make a scarecrow of the law,

  Setting it up to fear the birds of prey,

  And let it keep one shape till custom make it

  Their perch and not their terror.

ESCALUS   Ay, but yet

  Let us be keen, and rather cut a little

  Than fall and bruise to death. Alas, this gentleman

  Whom I would save had a most noble father.

  Let but your honour know—

  Whom I believe to be most strait in virtue—

  That in the working of your own affections,   10

  Had time cohered with place, or place with wishing,

2.1.0.1 *a Justice, and Servants*] *and seruants, Iustice.* F

86 **the mother** the mother-superior of a nunnery (the earliest use recorded in *OED* 3b)
88 **soon at night** early in the evening; a stock phrase used in *Romeo* 2.4.76, *Othello* 3.4.195, and elsewhere.
89 **my success** the outcome of my action (but not implying that it will necessarily be favourable)
2.1.1–4 Given as proverbial in Tilley/Dent S128.1, where close parallels are quoted from prose moralists of the period.
2 **fear** frighten away
3–4 **custom ... terror** they become so accustomed to the motionless scarecrow

that they perch on it instead of being frightened by it
5 **keen** having a sharp edge and thus able to cut precisely (said of a tool or appliance)
cut a little neatly cut out a small amount of corruption. The image may derive from surgery, or possibly from tree-pruning.
6 **fall** let fall (a heavy weight of punishment)
9 **strait** rigorous, scrupulous
10 **affections** sexual feelings
11 **Had ... wishing** had both the time and the place been convenient

Or that the resolute acting of your blood
Could have attained the effect of your own purpose,
Whether you had not sometime in your life
Erred in this point, which now you censure him,
And pulled the law upon you.

ANGELO

'Tis one thing to be tempted, Escalus,
Another thing to fall. I not deny
The jury passing on the prisoner's life
May in the sworn twelve have a thief or two   20
Guiltier than him they try. What's open made to
        justice,
That justice seizes. What knows the laws
That thieves do pass on thieves? 'Tis very pregnant,
The jewel that we find, we stoop and take't,
Because we see it; but what we do not see,
We tread upon and never think of it.
You may not so extenuate his offence
For I have had such faults, but rather tell me,
When I that censure him do so offend,
Let mine own judgement pattern out my death,   30
And nothing come in partial. Sir, he must die.
        Enter Provost

ESCALUS

Be it as your wisdom will.

ANGELO   Where is the Provost?

---

12 your] DAVENANT; our F   22 laws] F; law DAVENANT

12–13 **Or ... purpose** or if by decisively
  carrying out sexual activity you could
  have had your way with the woman in
  question. Escalus's language may seem
  awkward and circumspect, but he is
  naturally nervous at putting these ideas
  to Angelo.
12 **your** Some editors defend F's *our* as a
  temporary shift to general statement
  ('that which is common to all of us'), but
  the rest of the passage consistently uses
  you and *your*.
15 **which** for which
19 **passing** giving a verdict
21 **open** exposed, clearly visible
22 **What knows the laws** how can you
  expect the law to know

22 **knows** This could be a plural verb,
  though inflected in 's' (Abbott 333), or it
  may be that Shakespeare thought of *the
  laws* as a kind of collective noun which
  could be regarded as singular.
23 **thieves ... thieves** thieves in the jury are
  passing a verdict on thieves in the dock
  'Tis very pregnant it is a clear and
  convincing argument that
28 **For I have had** because I may have had
30 **pattern out** give an example for
31 **nothing come in partial** ambiguous, as
  nothing can be adverb or noun: (*a*) let my
  judgement in no way show itself to be
  partial; (*b*) let nothing which is partial to
  me intervene in the matter

PROVOST

Here, if it like your honour.

ANGELO   See that Claudio

Be execute by nine tomorrow morning.

Bring him his confessor, let him be prepared,

For that's the utmost of his pilgrimage.   *Exit Provost*

ESCALUS (*aside*)

Well, heaven forgive him, and forgive us all.

Some rise by sin, and some by virtue fall.

Some run from brakes of vice, and answer none,

And some condemnèd for a fault alone.   40

    Enter Elbow and Officers with Froth and Pompey

ELBOW Come, bring them away. If these be good people in
a commonweal, that do nothing but use their abuses in
common houses, I know no law. Bring them away.

ANGELO How now, sir, what's your name? And what's
the matter?

ELBOW If it please your honour, I am the poor Duke's
constable, and my name is Elbow. I do lean upon
justice, sir, and do bring in here before your good
honour two notorious benefactors.

ANGELO Benefactors? Well, what benefactors are they?   50
Are they not malefactors?

ELBOW If it please your honour, I know not well what they
are; but precise villains they are, that I am sure of, and
void of all profanation in the world that good Christians
ought to have.

34 execute] OXFORD; executed F   36 *Exit Provost*] ROWE; *not in* F   39 vice] ROWE; Ice F
40.1 *Enter . . . Pompey*] *Enter Elbow, Froth, Clowne, Officers.* F

34 **execute** F is very irregular metrically, and
the shorter form is common in the period
(see *OED execute pa. pple. Obs.*, and for
similar forms see Abbott 342).

35 **prepared** made spiritually ready for death

36 **pilgrimage** Life as a pilgrimage was a
proverbial idea (Tilley L249 and Whiting
P201), ultimately of biblical origin (Genesis 47: 9).

38 Printed in italic in F as a maxim or
sententia; compare F's use of inverted
commas at 2.4.186.

39–40 See the longer note in Appendix A.

41 **away** on, along

42 **use their abuses** carry out their corrupt
practices

43 **common houses** brothels (the only example given in *OED common house* 4b)

46–7 **the poor Duke's constable** possibly the
first of Elbow's 'misplacings' (see l. 85),
since it could suggest that the Duke
rather than the constable is poor. Compare 'the poor Duke's officers' in *Much
Ado* 3.5.19.

47 **lean upon** probably in *OED*'s sense 3,
'depend upon for support', but also a joke
on his own name

53 **precise** an error for *precious* in *OED*'s
sense 4a, 'arrant, egregious'; compare
'Precious villain!' in *Othello* 5.2.242

54 **void** devoid

ESCALUS This comes off well; here's a wise officer.

ANGELO (*to Elbow*) Go to. What quality are they of? Elbow
  is your name? Why dost thou not speak, Elbow?

POMPEY He cannot, sir, he's out at elbow.

ANGELO What are you, sir?   60

ELBOW He, sir? A tapster, sir, parcel bawd, one that serves
  a bad woman, whose house, sir, was, as they say,
  plucked down in the suburbs; and now she professes a
  hot-house, which I think is a very ill house too.

ESCALUS How know you that?

ELBOW My wife, sir, whom I detest before heaven and
  your honour—

ESCALUS How, thy wife?

ELBOW Ay, sir, whom I thank heaven is an honest
  woman—   70

ESCALUS Dost thou detest her therefore?

ELBOW I say, sir, I will detest myself also, as well as she,
  that this house, if it be not a bawd's house, it is pity of
  her life, for it is a naughty house.

ESCALUS How dost thou know that, constable?

ELBOW Marry, sir, by my wife, who if she had been a

---

59 POMPEY] F *has 'Clo.' or 'Clow.' throughout the play*

56 **comes off well** is a well-delivered speech
(compare Webster, *The Duchess of Malfi*
1.1.329–30, 'I think this speech between
you both was studied, | It came so roundly
off')

57 **Go to** a rebuke to Elbow
  quality rank or occupation

59 **out at elbow** a joke on the proverbial *out
at elbows*, said of worn clothing (Tilley
E102), and *out* meaning 'thrown out,
disconcerted' (he cannot speak when his
name is mentioned)

60 **What** who, of what profession

61 **parcel** partly

63 **plucked down** demolished; see
1.2.94–5, and Introduction, pp. 2–3.
There may be a hint of 'double time'
here; strictly speaking only a few hours
have elapsed since 1.2, but the account
that follows gives the impression that
Mistress Overdone's first house was
pulled down some while ago, and she has
set up another establishment in which
Froth has become a regular customer.

But the discrepancy is not noticed in the
theatre.
  professes claims to be running (but with a
hint of false pretences)

64 **hot-house** bathing-house which provided the luxury of hot baths; but such
places had a very dubious reputation in
the 16th c. and were often merely brothels (see Jonson, Epigram 7, and Dekker,
Westward Ho 1.1.8)

66 **detest** misused for *protest*, as in *Merry
Wives* 1.4.145

73–4 **it is pity of her life** it is a pity she
(Mistress Overdone) should live (a com-
mon construction; see Tilley/Dent
P368.1)

74 **naughty** wicked

76 **by my wife** We never learn what did
actually happen to Mrs Elbow, so perhaps
we should not enquire too closely; possibly an attempt was made to recruit her
as an amateur prostitute as Ursula tries to
recruit Mrs Overdo in Jonson's *Bartholomew Fair* 4.5.

woman cardinally given might have been accused in
fornication, adultery, and all uncleanliness there.

ESCALUS By the woman's means?

ELBOW Ay, sir, by Mistress Overdone's means; but as she   80
spit in his face, so she defied him.

POMPEY Sir, if it please your honour, this is not so.

ELBOW Prove it before these varlets here, thou honourable
man, prove it.

ESCALUS (*to Angelo*) Do you hear how he misplaces?

POMPEY Sir, she came in great with child, and longing,
saving your honour's reverence, for stewed prunes. Sir,
we had but two in the house, which at that very distant
time stood, as it were, in a fruit dish, a dish of some
three pence; your honours have seen such dishes, they   90
are not china dishes, but very good dishes—

ESCALUS Go to, go to, no matter for the dish, sir.

POMPEY No indeed, sir, not of a pin, you are therein in the
right; but to the point. As I say, this Mistress Elbow,
being, as I say, with child, and being great-bellied, and
longing, as I said, for prunes; and having but two in the
dish, as I said, Master Froth here, this very man, having
eaten the rest, as I said, and, as I say, paying for them

88 distant] F; instant F2

77 **cardinally** misused for *carnally*

78 **uncleanliness** moral impurity; see
2.4.54 n.

79 **By the woman's means** by instigation of
Mistress Overdone (but Elbow appears to
misunderstand it as 'by one of her agents
or customers')

81 **his** Froth's (for a similar vagueness on
Elbow's part see *this man* at l. 136 below)

83 **varlets** rogues, rascals

85 **misplaces** puts his words in the wrong
place

87 **saving your honour's reverence** a
proverbial phrase (Tilley R93) apologiz-
ing for a remark that might be considered
disrespectful

stewed prunes Elizabethan writers repeatedly associate stewed prunes with
brothels, as in *2 Henry IV* 2.4.142, and
Dekker's *2 Honest Whore* 4.3.36, and
OED asserts that *stewed* plays on *stew* as
meaning 'brothel'. The reasons for this
association are not fully clear: editors

have pointed out that William Clowes, in
A Profitable … Book of Observations
(1596), p. 161, recommends prunes as
part of a diet for those suffering from
venereal disease, but he mentions many
other foodstuffs as well, and Thomas
Cogan, in *The Haven of Health* (1584),
pp. 92–3, praises stewed prunes as a
laxative and says that they are popular
among Oxford students. Perhaps it was
simply a fact that Elizabethan brothels
tended to put a dish of prunes on the table
as a snack for customers, and the allusion
here would give a broad hint to the
audience that Mistress Overdone's house
was indeed a brothel.

88 **distant** The Second Folio of 1632 emends
to *instant*. This is probably what Pompey
means, but he does 'misplace' elsewhere
in the scene, notably at l. 148.

93 **not of a pin** a variant on the proverbial
not worth a pin (Tilley P334, Whiting
P213)

very honestly—for, as you know, Master Froth, I could
not give you three pence again—   100
FROTH No, indeed.
POMPEY Very well! You being then, if you be remembered,
cracking the stones of the foresaid prunes—
FROTH Ay, so I did indeed.
POMPEY Why, very well! I telling you then, if you be
remembered, that such a one and such a one were past
cure of the thing you wot of, unless they kept very good
diet, as I told you—
FROTH All this is true.
POMPEY Why, very well then—   110
ESCALUS Come, you are a tedious fool. To the purpose:
what was done to Elbow's wife that he hath cause to
complain of? Come me to what was done to her.
POMPEY Sir, your honour cannot come to that yet.
ESCALUS No, sir, nor I mean it not.
POMPEY Sir, but you shall come to it, by your honour's
leave. And I beseech you, look into Master Froth here,
sir, a man of fourscore pound a year, whose father died
at Hallowmas—was't not at Hallowmas, Master Froth?
FROTH All-hallond eve.   120
POMPEY Why, very well; I hope here be truths. He, sir,
sitting, as I say, in a lower chair, sir—'twas in the
Bunch of Grapes, where indeed you have a delight to sit,
have you not?

---

100 **give you three pence again** give you
    change for your coin
107 **wot** know (presumably that they suff-
    ered from venereal disease)
108 **diet** medical regime
113–14 **Come me ... that yet** Escalus means
    'bring me to the point in your story at
    which something happened to Elbow's
    wife', but Pompey quibblingly interprets
    it as 'let me experience the same thing
    that happened to her'.
118 **fourscore pound a year** With an
    unearned income of eighty pounds a year
    Froth was moderately wealthy by the
    standards of the time. Thomas Lodge
    asserted that half this amount, i.e. forty
    pounds a year, was enough to maintain a
    young man 'honestly and cleanly' (*An*

Alarum against Usurers, 1584, p. 5).
119 **Hallowmas** the feast of All Hallows or
    All Saints, 1 Nov.
120 **All-hallond eve** All-hallows' Eve, the
    evening of 31 Oct.
122 **lower chair** not satisfactorily explained;
    the only parallel so far discovered is the
    low chair mentioned in Barnabe Barnes's
    The Devil's Charter (1607), I2ᵛ. Perhaps it
    was the nearest Elizabethan equivalent to
    a couch or easy chair, on which the
    indolent Froth could relax himself.
122–3 **the Bunch of Grapes** Rooms in Eliza-
    bethan inns and taverns were often given
    names of this kind; compare the Half-
    moon and the Pomgarnet in *1 Henry IV*
    2.5.27, 36–7.

FROTH I have so, because it is an open room, and good for
    winter.
POMPEY Why, very well then; I hope here be truths.
ANGELO
    This will last out a night in Russia,
    When nights are longest there. I'll take my leave,
    And leave you to the hearing of the cause,   130
    Hoping you'll find good cause to whip them all.
ESCALUS
    I think no less. Good morrow to your lordship.

                                            Exit Angelo

    Now, sir, come on. What was done to Elbow's wife,
    once more?
POMPEY Once, sir? There was nothing done to her once.
ELBOW I beseech you, sir, ask him what this man did to
    my wife.
POMPEY I beseech your honour, ask me.
ESCALUS Well, sir, what did this gentleman to her?
POMPEY I beseech you, sir, look in this gentleman's face.   140
    Good Master Froth, look upon his honour; 'tis for a
    good purpose. Doth your honour mark his face?
ESCALUS Ay, sir, very well.
POMPEY Nay, I beseech you mark it well.
ESCALUS Well, I do so.
POMPEY Doth your honour see any harm in his face?
ESCALUS Why, no.
POMPEY I'll be supposed upon a book, his face is the worst
    thing about him. Good, then; if his face be the worst
    thing about him, how could Master Froth do the   150
    constable's wife any harm? I would know that of your
    honour.

132.1 *Exit Angelo*] THEOBALD; *Exit.* F (*at l.* 131)

125 **open** public
125–6 **good for winter** presumably because
    a fire was regularly lit in the room which
    Froth did not need to pay for
130–1 **cause … cause** in two senses: (*a*) the
    case being tried; (*b*) reason. It is not clear
    whether Angelo is consciously playing
    on words; the repetition of *leave* in
    ll. 129–30 has something of the same
    effect.

134 **once more** Escalus means 'to revert
    to our former topic', but Pompey assumes
    that his phrase is intended to qualify
    whatever was done to Mrs Elbow.
142 **mark** observe, watch
148 **supposed** an error for *deposed*; *OED*
    quotes the phrase *depose upon a book* from
    1566 under *depose* 5a(a), meaning 'give
    evidence upon oath'.

ESCALUS He's in the right, constable. What say you to it?

ELBOW First, an it like you, the house is a respected house;
next, this is a respected fellow, and his mistress is a
respected woman.

POMPEY By this hand, sir, his wife is a more respected
person than any of us all.

ELBOW Varlet, thou liest; thou liest, wicked varlet! The
time is yet to come that she was ever respected with   160
man, woman, or child.

POMPEY Sir, she was respected with him, before he married with her.

ESCALUS Which is the wiser here, Justice or Iniquity? Is this
true?

ELBOW O thou caitiff! O thou varlet! O thou wicked
Hannibal! I respected with her, before I was married to
her? If ever I was respected with her, or she with me, let
not your worship think me the poor Duke's officer.
Prove this, thou wicked Hannibal, or I'll have mine   170
action of battery on thee.

ESCALUS If he took you a box o' the ear you might have
your action of slander too.

ELBOW Marry, I thank your good worship for it. What is't
your worship's pleasure I shall do with this wicked
caitiff?

ESCALUS Truly, officer, because he hath some offences in
him that thou wouldst discover if thou couldst, let him
continue in his courses till thou know'st what they are.

ELBOW Marry, I thank your worship for it. (*To Pompey*)   180
Thou seest, thou wicked varlet now, what's come upon
thee. Thou art to continue now, thou varlet, thou art to
continue.

154 **respected** an error for *suspected*; compare the opposite error, *suspect* for *respect*,
in *Much Ado* 4.2.72–3

162–3 **she was respected ... her** Elbow is
here accused, like Claudio, of ante-nuptial fornication.

164 **Justice or Iniquity** These are commonly
assumed to be stock figures from morality
plays, but they may be no more than
personifications similar to Liberty and
Justice in 1.3.29. They are, of course,
ironical titles for Elbow and Pompey.

166 **caitiff** wretch, villain

167 **Hannibal** a mistake for *cannibal*; Jonson
had earlier made the same joke in *Every
Man in his Humour*, Quarto of 1601,
3.1.187–8, 'turn Hannibal and eat my
own fish and blood'. Pistol's *Cannibals* in
2 Henry IV 2.4.163 is no longer thought
to be an error.

171 **battery** assault (but a 'misplacing' for
slander, as Escalus humorously notes)

172 **took** gave

178 **discover** disclose, reveal

179 **courses** way of life

182 **continue** Elbow interprets this as a

ESCALUS (*to Froth*) Where were you born, friend?

FROTH Here in Vienna, sir.

ESCALUS Are you of fourscore pounds a year?

FROTH Yes, an't please you, sir.

ESCALUS So. (*To Pompey*) What trade are you of, sir?

POMPEY A tapster, a poor widow's tapster.

ESCALUS Your mistress' name?   190

POMPEY Mistress Overdone.

ESCALUS Hath she had any more than one husband?

POMPEY Nine, sir: Overdone by the last.

ESCALUS Nine! (*To Froth*) Come hither to me, Master
  Froth. Master Froth, I would not have you acquainted
  with tapsters; they will draw you, Master Froth, and
  you will hang them. Get you gone, and let me hear no
  more of you.

FROTH I thank your worship. For mine own part, I never
  come into any room in a taphouse but I am drawn in.   200

ESCALUS Well, no more of it, Master Froth; farewell.

                                             Exit Froth

  Come you hither to me, Master tapster. What's your
  name, Master tapster?

POMPEY Pompey.

ESCALUS What else?

POMPEY Bum, sir.

ESCALUS Troth, and your bum is the greatest thing about
  you, so that in the beastliest sense you are Pompey the
  Great. Pompey, you are partly a bawd, Pompey, howso-

201.1 *Exit Froth*] ROWE; *not in* F

restraint or punishment of Pompey,
though it is not clear precisely what he
thinks it means.

193 **Overdone** a play on words: (*a*) given the
name; (*b*) sexually exhausted. The word
can also mean 'carried to excess',
and thus refer to her fondness for
marriage.

196 **draw** used, as Dr Johnson noted, with
'a cluster of senses': (*a*) entice, draw
in; (*b*) draw out drink from the barrel;
(*c*) drain or empty (of money); (*d*) inflict
one of the punishments often associated
with hanging, either 'drag on a hurdle

to the place of execution' (*OED* 4), or
'disembowel' (*OED* 50)

197 **hang them** cause them to be hanged
(because they cannot resist tricking him)

200 **taphouse** house selling ale or beer in
small quantities
drawn in This could be read in a sense not
intended by Froth, 'ensnared, deluded'
(*OED draw v.* 82d).

207–8 **your bum ... about you** given as
proverbial in Tilley P73, and Whiting
P35, though only one parallel has been
noted, in John Heywood's *Dialogue ... of
... Proverbs* (1546)

208 **beastliest** crudest, most disgusting

ever you colour it in being a tapster, are you not? Come, 210
tell me true, it shall be the better for you.

POMPEY Truly, sir, I am a poor fellow that would live.

ESCALUS How would you live, Pompey? By being a bawd?
What do you think of the trade, Pompey? Is it a lawful
trade?

POMPEY If the law would allow it, sir.

ESCALUS But the law will not allow it, Pompey, nor it shall
not be allowed in Vienna.

POMPEY Does your worship mean to geld and splay all the
youth of the city? 220

ESCALUS No, Pompey.

POMPEY Truly, sir, in my poor opinion they will to't then.
If your worship will take order for the drabs and the
knaves, you need not to fear the bawds.

ESCALUS There is pretty orders beginning, I can tell you; it
is but heading and hanging.

POMPEY If you head and hang all that offend that way but
for ten year together, you'll be glad to give out a
commission for more heads. If this law hold in Vienna
ten year, I'll rent the fairest house in it after three pence 230
a bay; if you live to see this come to pass, say Pompey
told you so.

ESCALUS Thank you, good Pompey, and in requital of your
prophecy, hark you. I advise you let me not find you
before me again upon any complaint whatsoever; no,
not for dwelling where you do. If I do, Pompey, I shall
beat you to your tent and prove a shrewd Caesar to you;

210 **colour** cloak, disguise
212 **live** earn a living
219 **geld** castrate
   splay spay, remove the ovaries
220 **youth** young people
222 **to't** get to work (sexually)
223–4 **take order ... bawds** make arrangements for the prostitutes and their clients
   there will be no need to worry about the
   bawds (who will automatically be out of
   work)
225–6 **it is but heading and hanging** beheading and hanging will be the only
   punishments for sexual offences
229 **commission for more heads** official order authorizing procreation; *heads* may
   be a play of words, (*a*) units of popula-

tion; (*b*) maidenheads (which can now be
safely lost)
   hold remains valid
230–1 **after three pence a bay** at a ridiculously cheap rate; *OED* glosses *bay sb.*³ 2
   as 'the space lying under one gable, or
   included between two party-walls'
231–2 **say Pompey told you so** as Lever
   notes, a stock phrase of the time; compare 3.1.441 and Tilley S111
237 **beat you to your tent ... Caesar** Julius
   Caesar utterly defeated Pompey the Great
   at the battle of Pharsalia, in 48 BC. In
   Plutarch's *Life* of Pompey it is said that he
   retreated to his tent when he realized that
   the battle was lost. There may also be a
   play on *tent* meaning 'bandage' (*OED*

in plain dealing, Pompey, I shall have you whipped. So
for this time, Pompey, fare you well.

POMPEY I thank your worship for your good counsel—   240
(*aside*) but I shall follow it as the flesh and fortune shall
better determine.

Whip me? No, no, let carman whip his jade;

The valiant heart's not whipped out of his trade.   *Exit*

ESCALUS Come hither to me, Master Elbow; come hither,
Master constable. How long have you been in this place
of constable?

ELBOW Seven year and a half, sir.

ESCALUS I thought by the readiness in the office you had
continued in it some time. You say seven years to-   250
gether?

ELBOW And a half, sir.

ESCALUS Alas, it hath been great pains to you; they do you
wrong to put you so oft upon't. Are there not men in
your ward sufficient to serve it?

ELBOW Faith, sir, few of any wit in such matters. As they
are chosen, they are glad to choose me for them; I do it
for some piece of money, and go through with all.

ESCALUS Look you bring me in the names of some six or
seven, the most sufficient of your parish.   260

ELBOW To your worship's house, sir?

ESCALUS To my house. Fare you well.

Exeunt Elbow and Officers

What's o'clock, think you?

JUSTICE Eleven, sir.

ESCALUS I pray you home to dinner with me.

262.1 *Exeunt ... Officers*] ROWE; *not in* F

sb.³ 2): Pompey will be beaten so severely
that he will need to dress his wounds.

237 **shrewd** severe, harsh

241 **the flesh** probably in the biblical sense:
the weak and sinful part of human nature
(Romans 7–9)

243 **carman** driver of a cart or wagon
jade inferior horse in poor condition

249 **the readiness in the office** your skill and
promptness in performing your duties
(Escalus deliberately flatters Elbow outrageously as a prelude to dismissing him)

255 **sufficient** qualified in status and ability

256 **wit** intelligence. Constables were notorious for stupidity, though it must be said
that Shakespeare's comic constables do
not give a fair picture of reality (see Joan
R. Kent, *The English Village Constable
1580–1642*, Oxford, 1986). The
proverbial phrase, 'you might be a constable for your wit' (Tilley C616), is
intended to be an ironic joke.

258 **go through with all** carry out all the
duties of the post

264 **Eleven** i.e. eleven a.m., a normal time
for dinner in the 16th c.

JUSTICE I humbly thank you.
ESCALUS
　It grieves me for the death of Claudio,
　But there's no remedy.
JUSTICE
　Lord Angelo is severe.
ESCALUS   It is but needful.
　Mercy is not itself that oft looks so;   270
　Pardon is still the nurse of second woe.
　But yet—poor Claudio! There is no remedy.
　Come, sir.   *Exeunt*

2.2   *Enter Provost and a Servant*
SERVANT
　He's hearing of a cause; he will come straight.
　I'll tell him of you.
PROVOST   Pray you, do.   *Exit Servant*
　　　　　　　　　　　　　　　　　I'll know
　His pleasure, maybe he will relent. Alas,
　He hath but as offended in a dream!
　All sects, all ages smack of this vice, and he
　To die for't?
　　　　Enter Angelo
ANGELO   Now what's the matter, Provost?
PROVOST
　Is it your will Claudio shall die tomorrow?
ANGELO
　Did not I tell thee yea? Hadst thou not order?
　Why dost thou ask again?
PROVOST   Lest I might be too rash.

2.2.0.1 *Provost and a*] *Prouost*, F   2 *Exit Servant*] CAPELL; *not in* F

270–1 A group of overlapping proverbs
　makes the point that excessive mercy or
　pity has the effect of encouraging evil (see
　Tilley P50 and P366, and Smith 172 and
　229). For variants on the idea elsewhere
　in Shakespeare see *Lucrece* 1687, *Romeo*
　3.1.196, *Richard II* 5.3.81–2, and *Timon*
　3.6.3.
2.2.4 He Claudio
　but as ... in a dream merely as if in a
　dream (not reality)

5 **sects** classes or kinds of people
　ages either 'people of different ages,
　young and old', or 'periods of history'
　smack of have a flavour of, share in
8 **order** Coming after *tell thee* (a spoken
　command), this appears to imply a writ-
　ten order or warrant, and suggests that
　Angelo is a stickler for correct pro-
　cedures. Compare the same usage at l. 25
　below.

Under your good correction, I have seen   10
When, after execution, judgement hath
Repented o'er his doom.
ANGELO   Go to, let that be mine.
Do you your office, or give up your place,
And you shall well be spared.
PROVOST   I crave your honour's pardon.
What shall be done, sir, with the groaning Juliet?
She's very near her hour.
ANGELO   Dispose of her
To some more fitter place, and that with speed.
     Enter Servant
SERVANT
Here is the sister of the man condemned
Desires access to you.
ANGELO   Hath he a sister?
PROVOST
Ay, my good lord, a very virtuous maid,   20
And to be shortly of a sisterhood,
If not already.
ANGELO   Well, let her be admitted.   *Exit Servant*
See you the fornicatress be removed.
Let her have needful but not lavish means;
There shall be order for't.
     Enter Lucio and Isabella
PROVOST   Save your honour.
ANGELO
Stay a little while. (*To Isabella*) You're welcome; what's
     your will?

17.1 *Enter Servant*] CAPELL; *not in* F   22 *Exit Servant*] DAVENANT; *not in* F

10 **Under your good correction** correct me
    if I am wrong (a formula expressing
    deference to Angelo's authority and
    wisdom)
12 **Repented o'er his doom** regretted the
    sentence he had imposed (*judgement* in
    l. 11 is a personification)
    that responsibility for a decision which
    may prove to be wrong
14 **you ... spared** we shall manage perfectly
    well without you
15 **groaning** beginning to feel labour-pains
16 **hour** time to give birth

19 **Desires** who desires; see Abbott 244, and
    compare l. 34 below
23 **fornicatress** woman guilty of fornication
    (Shakespeare's only use of the word)
24 **means** means of living, subsistence
25 **Save** God save (see Introduction,
    pp. 68–9). The Provost's phrase indicates
    his acceptance of Angelo's orders and his
    intention to depart to carry them out.
26 **Stay ... while** Angelo detains the Pro-
    vost, either to act as a witness of the
    impending interview or to be a messenger
    if he should change his mind.

ISABELLA

   I am a woeful suitor to your honour,

   Please but your honour hear me.

ANGELO   Well, what's your suit?

ISABELLA

   There is a vice that most I do abhor,

   And most desire should meet the blow of justice;   30

   For which I would not plead, but that I must,

   For which I must not plead, but that I am

   At war 'twixt will and will not.

ANGELO   Well, the matter?

ISABELLA

   I have a brother is condemned to die.

   I do beseech you, let it be his fault,

   And not my brother.

PROVOST (*aside*)   Heaven give thee moving graces!

ANGELO

   Condemn the fault, and not the actor of it?

   Why, every fault's condemned ere it be done.

   Mine were the very cipher of a function,

   To fine the faults, whose fine stands in record,   40

   And let go by the actor.

ISABELLA   O just but severe law!

   I had a brother, then. Heaven keep your honour.

LUCIO (*aside to Isabella*)

   Give't not o'er so; to him again, entreat him,

   Kneel down before him, hang upon his gown.

   You are too cold; if you should need a pin,

31 **would not** would prefer not to
I must (because she is the condemned man's sister)

32 **must not** (because she would then be defending evil)

33 **will and will not** Compare Angelo's 'we would, and we would not', 4.4.32.
the matter get to the point

35 **let it be his fault** let it be his evil deed which is condemned to extinction

36 **moving** persuasive

37 **Condemn ... of it** Angelo generalizes from Isabella's particular case, alluding to the proverbial 'hate not the person but the vice' (Tilley, P238).

38 **condemned ... done** condemned by the law before it has even been carried out

39 **the very cipher of a function** an utterly empty or meaningless occupation

40 **To fine** to punish
whose fine ... record whose punishment has been set down in legal records. It is not fully clear how this qualifies *faults*; possibly it implies that since the penalties for wrongdoing, considered abstractly, have already been written down, it is pointless for Angelo simply to repeat them.

41 **let go by** allow to escape unpunished

43 **Give't not o'er so** do not give up so easily

44 **Kneel down** Editors do not make Isabella kneel here or in 2.4, though *how I prayed and kneeled*, 5.1.94, suggests that at some stage she does so. Compare 5.1.20 n.
hang upon cling to

You could not with more tame a tongue desire it.
To him, I say.
ISABELLA
  Must he needs die?
ANGELO   Maiden, no remedy.
ISABELLA
  Yes, I do think that you might pardon him,
  And neither heaven nor man grieve at the mercy.   50
ANGELO
  I will not do't.
ISABELLA   But can you if you would?
ANGELO
  Look what I will not, that I cannot do.
ISABELLA
  But might you do't, and do the world no wrong,
  If so your heart were touched with that remorse
  As mine is to him?
ANGELO   He's sentenced, 'tis too late.
LUCIO (*aside to Isabella*)
  You are too cold.
ISABELLA
  Too late? Why, no, I that do speak a word
  May call it back again. Well, believe this:
  No ceremony that to great ones longs,
  Not the king's crown, nor the deputed sword,   60
  The marshal's truncheon, nor the judge's robe,
  Become them with one half so good a grace

58 back] F2; *not in* F

52 **Look what** whatever (*OED look v.* 4b); Shakespeare uses the same construction in *Richard II* 1.1.87, and three times in the *Sonnets* (9.9, 37.13, and 77.9)
54 **remorse** pity, compassion
57–8 **I that … again** possibly alluding to (and contradicting) the proverb 'A word spoken cannot be called back' (Tilley W777)
58 **back** F2's insertion restores the metre of the line, and is also desirable on grounds of sense: *call* simply means 'summon', whereas *call back again* is a standard formation for 'cause someone to return who has just gone out', as in *Two Gentlemen* 1.2.51, and *Romeo* 4.3.17.

59–63 an expanded treatment of the proverbial theme (Tilley M898), 'It is in their mercy that kings come closest to gods'; compare *Titus* 1.1.117–19 and *Merchant* 4.1.181–94
59 **longs** is appropriate, belongs (but not a contraction of *belongs*; see *OED long v.*²)
60 **deputed** given by a ruler to a deputy as a sign of authority
61 **marshal** senior military officer
    truncheon symbol of authority; a modern equivalent would be the field marshal's baton
62 **grace** basically 'gracefulness, elegance', but with a hint of *grace* in its theological sense

As mercy does.
If he had been as you, and you as he,
You would have slipped like him, but he like you
Would not have been so stern.

ANGELO   Pray you be gone.

ISABELLA

I would to heaven I had your potency,
And you were Isabel; should it then be thus?
No, I would tell what 'twere to be a judge,
And what a prisoner.   70

LUCIO (*aside to Isabella*)

Ay, touch him, there's the vein.

ANGELO

Your brother is a forfeit of the law,
And you but waste your words.

ISABELLA   Alas, alas!

Why, all the souls that were were forfeit once,
And He that might the vantage best have took
Found out the remedy. How would you be
If He which is the top of judgement should
But judge you as you are? O, think on that,
And mercy then will breathe within your lips
Like man new made.

ANGELO   Be you content, fair maid.   80

It is the law, not I, condemn your brother;

---

64 **as you** in your position

65 **slipped** fallen into error, sinned; compare
5.1.475

67 **potency** power, ability to accomplish
something. Shakespeare's uses of this
word do not suggest that it had any
sexual implication for him.

68 **should** equivalent to modern 'would'
(Abbott 322)

69 **tell** make known, proclaim

71 **touch** perhaps in *OED*'s sense 19b, 'make
an apt or telling remark'
there's the vein that's the right way of
talking (*OED* vein sb. 12)

72 **forfeit of the law** See 1.4.66 n. and
compare 4.2.157–8.

74 **that were** that existed before the revelation of Christianity

75 **He** Christ
vantage opportunity (to punish mankind
because of original sin)
took taken

77 **top of judgement** supreme judge

80 **new made** In this explicitly theological
context the phrase refers to the Christian
concept that God's forgiveness of sin was
like a new or second creation: 'Now at
the same instant in which pardon shall be
granted, God likewise will once again
stretch forth that mighty hand of his,
whereby he made thee when thou wast
not, to make thee a new creature, to
create a new heart in thee, to renew a
right spirit in thee, and to stablish thee by
his free spirit' (W. Perkins, *A Direction for
the Government of the Tongue*, 1593,
pp. 2–3). For biblical sources see 2 Corinthians 5: 17, and Ephesians 4: 22–4.
The general sense of ll. 79–80 is that
someone who is fully conscious of God's
mercy to himself will be glad to show
mercy to his fellow-men.

81 **condemn** (attracted into the first person
because it immediately follows *I*)

Were he my kinsman, brother, or my son,
It should be thus with him. He must die tomorrow.

ISABELLA

Tomorrow? O, that's sudden—spare him, spare him!
He's not prepared for death. Even for our kitchens
We kill the fowl of season; shall we serve heaven
With less respect than we do minister
To our gross selves? Good, good my lord, bethink you:
Who is it that hath died for this offence?
There's many have committed it.

LUCIO (*aside to Isabella*)   Ay, well said.   90

ANGELO

The law hath not been dead, though it hath slept.
Those many had not dared to do that evil
If the first that did the edict infringe
Had answered for his deed. Now 'tis awake,
Takes note of what is done, and like a prophet
Looks in a glass that shows what future evils
Either now, or by remissness, new-conceived,
And so in progress to be hatched and born,

97 now] F; new POPE; raw OXFORD

82 **Were ... son** Evans notes that the family relationships are in an ascending order of closeness, from *kinsman*, to *brother*, to *son*. 'Though he were my brother' is proverbial (see 4.2.59 and Tilley/Dent B686.1). Dent surprisingly mentions only *Measure* as a Shakespearian illustration, but compare *Richard II* 1.1.116, 'Were he my brother, nay, my kingdom's heir' (and also 'Were he twenty times my son', 5.2.101), and *Henry V* 3.6.52, 'if, look you, he were my brother ...'

86 **of season** in season, in the best state for eating

86–7 **serve heaven│With less respect** (by 'serving up' souls to heaven before they are in a fit state to go there)

91 **The law ... slept** This may translate a legal maxim in Latin which can be found in the writings of Sir Edward Coke (see O. Hood Phillips, *Shakespeare and the Lawyers*, 1972, p. 43), but it should be noted that 'not dead but sleeping' is a stock formula: compare *Henry V* 3.6.118–19, 'though we seemed dead, we did but sleep', and Kyd's *The Spanish Tragedy* 3.15.23, 'Nor dies

Revenge although he sleep awhile'.

93 **If ... infringe** The line is unmetrical, and the compositor may have dropped out a word such as 'one' or 'man' after *first*, but any replacement must be a matter of guesswork.

96 **glass** globe or mirror in which the future reveals itself. Spenser discusses such devices at some length in *The Faerie Queene*, 3.2.18–21.

97 **now** ?now in existence, though not yet evident (for fuller discussion of this crux see Appendix A)
remissness negligence, laxity (in those who should suppress evil)
new-conceived recently formed in the criminal's mind (said of an idea or scheme for evil conduct). In the Fletcherian part of *Kinsmen*, 4.2.129, the phrase is applied more literally to women in the early stages of pregnancy.

98 **hatched** part of a Shakespearian image-cluster in which the gradual emergence of unpleasant events is compared to hatching an egg (see *Hamlet* 3.1.169–70, *Macbeth* 2.3.57–8, and, more elaborately, *2 Henry IV*

Are now to have no successive degrees,
But ere they live to end.

ISABELLA   Yet show some pity.   100

ANGELO

I show it most of all when I show justice,
For then I pity those I do not know,
Which a dismissed offence would after gall,
And do him right that, answering one foul wrong,
Lives not to act another. Be satisfied;
Your brother dies tomorrow; be content.

ISABELLA

So you must be the first that gives this sentence,
And he, that suffers. O, it is excellent
To have a giant's strength, but it is tyrannous
To use it like a giant.   110

LUCIO (*aside to Isabella*)

That's well said.

ISABELLA

Could great men thunder
As Jove himself does, Jove would never be quiet,

---

100 ere] HANMER; here F

3.1.75–87). In other contexts (see below, l. 100 n.) the egg is that of a poisonous animal, serpent or cockatrice, and the image-cluster as a whole may derive from Isaiah 59: 4–5, 'they conceive mischief, and bring forth iniquity. They hatch cockatrice eggs, and weave the spider's web; he that eateth of their eggs dieth, and that which is trod upon breaketh out into a serpent.'

99 **successive degrees** further stages of existence

100 **ere they live to end** are to be destroyed before they are born. Some editors defend and retain F's *here*, but *ere* is closer to a stock construction found in *Two Gentlemen* 2.4.30–1, 'you always end ere you begin', and *All's Well* 2.5.26, 'End ere I do begin'. It also hints at the proverb, 'Crush (or kill) the cockatrice/serpent in the egg' (Tilley C496), found in *Caesar* 2.1.32–4, 'And therefore think him as a serpent's egg, | Which, hatched, would as his kind grow mischievous, | And kill him in the shell'.

101–3 These lines echo such proverbs as 'To

punish evil-doers is a great work of mercy' (Tilley/Dent M899.1), and 'To spare the guilty is to injure the innocent' (Smith, 145).

103 **dismissed** sent away unpunished
gall pain, harass (because the pardoned criminal would repeat his offences against innocent people)

108 **And he, that suffers** and Claudio must be the first to undergo this punishment

108–10 Compare the proverb, 'To be able to do harm and not to do it is noble' (Tilley, H170).

109 **tyrannous** The Geneva Bible glosses 'giants' as 'tyrants' in its marginal annotation to Genesis 6: 4.

112–15 **Could … but thunder!** These lines are frequently compared to Ovid's *Tristia* 2.33–4, 'If Jupiter sent out his thunderbolts as often as men sin, he would soon use up his weapons and be defenceless'. But the point here is rather different: if men had the use of Jove's thunderbolts they would employ them for every offence, no matter how trivial (whereas Jove himself prefers to reserve his bolts for appropriate targets).

For every pelting petty officer
Would use his heaven for thunder, nothing but
     thunder!
Merciful heaven,
Thou rather with thy sharp and sulphurous bolt
Splits the unwedgeable and gnarlèd oak
Than the soft myrtle. But man, proud man,
Dressed in a little brief authority,   120
Most ignorant of what he's most assured,
His glassy essence, like an angry ape
Plays such fantastic tricks before high heaven
As makes the angels weep, who with our spleens
Would all themselves laugh mortal.

114 **pelting** paltry
    petty minor. Coming after *great men* in
l. 112, *pelting petty officer* is deliberately
sarcastic: 'even the lowest and most
contemptible of those in authority'.
115 **nothing but** normally in Shakespeare's
usage meaning 'exclusively' (no lesser
punishment would be used), rather than
'going on all the time', though this
implication may also be present.
117–19 **Thou ... myrtle** The oak was sacred
to Jupiter, and was thought particularly
liable to be struck by lightning. The
antithetical structure of the lines may
have been influenced by the proverb,
'Oaks may fall when reeds stand the
storm' (Tilley, O3).
118 **Splits** Shakespeare frequently ends the
second person singular form of verbs
ending in *-t* with *-ts* rather than *-test* for
the sake of euphony (Abbott 340).
    unwedgeable so strong that it cannot be
split open by having iron wedges driven
into it. This is the only instance of the
word recorded in *OED* before the 19th c.
    gnarlèd knotted. This spelling-form is not
otherwise recorded until the 19th c., but
OED gives *knar*, *knur*, and *knurl* as common 16th-c. words for a knot in a tree-
trunk, and the spelling interchange *gn/kn*
is fairly common (see for example *OED*
gnap/knap and *gnat/knat*). There is a
proverbial link between wedges and
knots; compare *Troilus* 1.3.310, 'Blunt
wedges rive hard knots', and Tilley,
P289.
119 **myrtle** perhaps chosen in this context
because it was a plant sacred to Venus
and an emblem of love

120 **brief** temporary
121 **assured** Since the passage is an attack
on human arrogance, the meaning is
probably 'certain, confident about', and
what is in apposition to *His glassy essence*:
man is ignorantly self-confident about his
innermost being.
122 **glassy** usually glossed as (*a*) brittle like
glass, and (*b*) as though seen or reflected
in a mirror. But (*b*) is not supported in
OED or elsewhere in Shakespeare (he
refers to objects reflected in a *glassy
stream*, as in *Hamlet* 4.7.139, but here it
means 'shiny and reflective like a mirror'). Perhaps the word is used in *OED*'s
sense 3a, 'transparent as glass'; man's
outward appearance, the clothing of authority referred to in l. 120, is contrasted
with his invisible essential nature. This
interpretation is given some support by
Othello 4.1.16, 'Her honour is an essence
that's not seen'.
    angry ape Apes were often thought to
mimic human behaviour, and in so doing
to make it ridiculous. Similarly man
becomes absurd when he pretends to be
God; *angry* refers back to Jove's anger in
ll. 112–13, but can also imply 'bad-
tempered, petulant'.
123 **tricks** capricious or foolish acts. The
word is often associated with apes, as in
Dekker's *Old Fortunatus* 2.2.25, 'like a
young ape, full of fantastic tricks'.
124 **with our spleens** if they had spleens
(regarded as the seat of laughter) like
human beings
125 **laugh mortal** 'laugh themselves either
to death, or into the condition of mortals;
ultimately the meanings are much the

LUCIO (*aside to Isabella*)

O, to him, to him, wench, he will relent.

He's coming, I perceive't.

PROVOST (*aside*)   Pray heaven she win him.

ISABELLA

We cannot weigh our brother with ourself.

Great men may jest with saints; 'tis wit in them,

But in the less, foul profanation.   130

LUCIO (*aside to Isabella*)

Thou'rt i' the right, girl, more o' that.

ISABELLA

That in the captain's but a choleric word,

Which in the soldier is flat blasphemy.

LUCIO (*aside to Isabella*)

Art advised o' that? More on't.

ANGELO

Why do you put these sayings upon me?

ISABELLA

Because authority, though it err like others,

Hath yet a kind of medicine in itself

That skins the vice o' the top. Go to your bosom,

---

same' (Lever). Compare Tilley/Dent L94.1, 'To die laughing (laugh oneself to death)'.

127 **coming** beginning to yield

128 **We ... ourself** This seems to mean 'we cannot compare our fellow human-beings to ourselves on a single scale of judgement (because those in authority can behave in ways that would not be tolerated in their inferiors)'. The point is then illustrated in ll. 129–30 and 132–3. Isabella however is not simply endorsing the idea, but using it to warn Angelo against the arrogance of power, and at l. 138 she openly asks him to compare himself with Claudio.
  our brother humanity in general, not specifically Claudio (see 2.4.186 n.)

129 **jest with saints** make jokes about holy people; compare Philip Stubbes, *Anatomy of Abuses*, Part II (1583), I8', 'You know the old proverb, *non bonum est ludere cum sanctis*, it is not good to meddle with these holy ones, for fear of thunderbolts to ensue', and Tilley B583

130 **the less** those lower down the social scale

132–3 **That ... blasphemy** An oath will be condoned when used by an officer, but will be a punishable offence in the mouth of an ordinary soldier.

132 **choleric** angry

133 **flat** absolute, downright

134 **advised** aware (Lucio is surprised at Isabella's worldly wisdom). *Are you advised of that* is a standard formula to express admiration at an unexpected remark; see *Merry Wives* 1.4.96, the collaborative *Sir John Oldcastle* (MSR, 1908), ll. 661–2, and Jonson, *Bartholomew Fair* 4.1.66

135 **put** impose, thrust. *OED put v.*[1] 23 shows that *put upon* can often refer to something felt as unwelcome or insulting; Angelo appears to resent the way Isabella is talking because he does not perceive its relevance to him.

138 **skins** covers over superficially. Compare *Hamlet* 3.4.138–40, 'It will but skin and film the ulcerous place | Whilst rank corruption, mining all within, | Infects unseen'.
  Go to your bosom a proverbial phrase (Tilley/Dent B546.1)

Knock there, and ask your heart what it doth know
That's like my brother's fault; if it confess   140
A natural guiltiness, such as is his,
Let it not sound a thought upon your tongue
Against my brother's life.

ANGELO (*aside*)   She speaks, and 'tis
Such sense that my sense breeds with it. (*To her*) Fare
    you well.

ISABELLA

Gentle my lord, turn back.

ANGELO

I will bethink me. Come again tomorrow.

ISABELLA

Hark how I'll bribe you; good my lord, turn back.

ANGELO

How? Bribe me?

ISABELLA

Ay, with such gifts that heaven shall share with you.

LUCIO (*aside to Isabella*)

You had marred all else.   150

ISABELLA

Not with fond sicles of the tested gold,
Or stones whose rate are either rich or poor
As fancy values them, but with true prayers

---

141 **natural guiltiness** inherent or innate
tendency to sin; compare *natural edge* at
1.4.60

144 **sense ... sense** a grim play on words: (*a*)
meaning, import; (*b*) sensuality (as at
1.4.59). It could be argued that the
ambiguity affects to some extent both
uses of the term: (*a*) 'her argument is
such that it provokes my own powers of
thought'; (*b*) 'her justification of sexual
desire as natural has stimulated my own
sexuality'. There is also a larger irony in
the speech as a whole; Angelo does
compare himself to Claudio, and finds
they have something in common, but his
deduction from this is totally at variance
with Isabella's.

    breeds used elsewhere in Shakespeare
simply to mean 'produces', but here the
sexual meanings are essential (there is
even a hint that by a kind of role-reversal
Isabella has impregnated Angelo's mind)

150 **You ... else** a compressed way of saying

'if you hadn't made it clear the bribe was
purely spiritual you would have ruined
everything'

151 **fond** trivial, valued only by fools
    sicles equivalent to 'shekels' (Hebrew
silver coins); this was the normal form of
the word in 16th-c. Bible translations
prior to the Geneva Bible of 1560
    tested (*a*) refined in the melting-pot (*OED
test sb.*[1] 1), free from impurity; (*b*) proved
genuine. This is the only use in
Shakespeare.

152 **stones** jewels
    rate value
    are in the plural because it refers back to
stones, as though the construction were
stones which are

153 **fancy** used here in its more pejorative
senses (*OED* 6–7), 'arbitrary notion, caprice'. The context expresses a proverbial
idea, 'The worth of a thing is as it is
esteemed' (Tilley W923).

That shall be up at heaven and enter there
Ere sunrise, prayers from preservèd souls,
From fasting maids whose minds are dedicate
To nothing temporal.

ANGELO

Well, come to me tomorrow.

LUCIO (*aside to Isabella*)

Go to, 'tis well; away.

ISABELLA

Heaven keep your honour safe.   160

ANGELO (*aside*)

Amen.
For I am that way going to temptation
Where prayers cross.

ISABELLA   At what hour tomorrow
Shall I attend your lordship?

ANGELO   At any time fore noon.

ISABELLA

Save your honour.   *Exeunt all but Angelo*

ANGELO   From thee, even from thy virtue!
What's this, what's this? Is this her fault or mine?
The tempter or the tempted who sins most, ha?
Not she, nor doth she tempt; but it is I

---

164 *Exeunt ... Angelo*] CAPELL; *not in* F; *Exeunt* F2

---

155 **preservèd** kept safe from harm or corruption (by entering an enclosed order of
nuns)

156-7 **dedicate | To   nothing   temporal**
wholly given up to religious concerns

160 **your honour** Isabella intends this simply as an honorific title, similar to 'your
worship' or 'your reverence', but it can
refer to Angelo's *honour* in its profoundest
sense, 'integrity, status as an honourable
person'. Angelo's comment shows that
he is fully aware of this implication; see
also l. 165 below.

163 **cross** thwart or contradict each other.
This could refer to a conflict between the
prayers of Isabella and the nuns on his
behalf and his own prayers to obtain
Isabella, or to an internal conflict in his
own mind between two kinds of desire,
for virtue and for sexual gratification. The
latter interpretation is perhaps more

likely, as it is taken up again at 2.4.1-7.

165 **Save ... From thee** The same play on
save ('God save' and 'protect') is found in
Marston's *The Malcontent* 2.3.3-4, where
Malevole cries out 'Save ye, Duke!' and
Duke Pietro replies 'From thee'.
even from thy virtue the phrase establishes the basic irony of Angelo's speech,
that his masculine honour needs to be
protected from something good, Isabella's feminine virtue.

167 **The tempter** in context clearly referring
to Isabella; but the line is also a generalization, and the devil is called 'the tempter' in Matthew 4: 3 and 1 Thessalonians
3: 5, an implication leading forward to
l. 183. For a moment Angelo tries to
escape his predicament by throwing the
blame on Isabella, but immediately realizes that he has no right to do so.

That lying by the violet in the sun
Do as the carrion does, not as the flower,   170
Corrupt with virtuous season. Can it be
That modesty may more betray our sense
Than woman's lightness? Having waste ground
          enough,
Shall we desire to raze the sanctuary
And pitch our evils there? O, fie, fie, fie!
What dost thou, or what art thou, Angelo?
Dost thou desire her foully for those things
That make her good? O let her brother live!
Thieves for their robbery have authority
When judges steal themselves. What, do I love her,   180

169–71 **lying ... season** an image used by contemporary moralists; John Carpenter asserts that some people derive no benefit from God's word 'as those carrions, that stink with the heat of the sun, which to the creatures is so comfortable' (*A Preparative to Contentation*, 1597, p. 108). For similar metaphors see Stubbes's *Anatomy of Abuses* (1583), G1ᵛ, quoted by Lever, and *Edward III* 2.1.438–9.

169 **violet** a flower associated with fragrancy, modesty, and chastity

170 **carrion** dead and putrefying flesh (but also applied, *OED* 3b, to the fleshly nature of man, the 'flesh' as at 2.1.241)

171 **virtuous season** the time of year that has power to promote growth. *Virtuous* means 'powerful, capable of producing great effects', but inevitably echoes Isabella's *virtue* at l. 165, suggesting that paradoxically Isabella is both the violet and the sun, simultaneously modest and sexually stimulating. Editors assert that *season* also means 'seasoning' (i.e. salt or spices added to improve the flavour of a dish, rather than 'preservative', as Lever glosses it), but the basic image is of the sun's heat producing growth or decay, and the culinary implication hardly seems relevant.

172 **betray our sense** Both key-words are ambiguous, so that two complementary interpretations are possible: (*a*) reveal the sensuality which we would prefer to keep hidden; (*b*) deceive our intellect.

173 **lightness** lewdness
waste uncultivated, unproductive; perhaps with a hint of the legal sense (*OED waste sb.* 2), 'a piece of land not in any

man's occupation, but lying common'. Angelo is thinking of common women, prostitutes, on whom men can dispose of their lustful impulses.

174 **raze** demolish, destroy completely
sanctuary holy place or building (the nun Isabella)

175 **pitch our evils** Both key-words are ambiguous: *pitch* can mean (*a*) 'throw down' or (*b*) 'place, set up' (normally used by Shakespeare of tents and the field of battle), and *evils* could mean (*a*) 'wicked thoughts and deeds' or (*b*) 'privies'. The phrase could thus mean (*a*) 'throw away, dispose of our sinful impulses' or (*b*) 'erect privies'. *OED evil sb.²* is sceptical of sense (*b*), 'privy', and quotes only one other example, from *All is True* (*Henry VIII*) 2.1.68, 'Nor build their evils on the graves of great men'. Malone and Lever, however, quote a further usage from the mid 17th c., and for the general idea we might compare 2 Kings 10: 27, 'And they destroyed the image of Baal, and threw down the house of Baal, and made a jakes of it unto this day', and Marston's *The Malcontent* 2.5.128–9, 'I ha' seen a sumptuous steeple turned to a stinking privy'. In the Revels edition of *The Malcontent* (1975), pp. 76–7), G. K. Hunter quotes a passage from John Weever's *Ancient Funeral Monuments* (1631, p. 373), deploring the way in which his contemporaries relieved themselves in churches and cathedrals.

fie in Shakespeare's day a powerful expression of disgust or revulsion, though its meaning weakened in later centuries

That I desire to hear her speak again,
And feast upon her eyes? What is't I dream on?
O cunning enemy, that to catch a saint
With saints dost bait thy hook! Most dangerous
Is that temptation that doth goad us on
To sin in loving virtue. Never could the strumpet
With all her double vigour, art and nature,
Once stir my temper, but this virtuous maid
Subdues me quite. Ever till now
When men were fond, I smiled and wondered how.   190

Exit

2.3   *Enter Duke, disguised as a Friar, and Provost*
DUKE

Hail to you, Provost—so I think you are.
PROVOST

I am the Provost. What's your will, good Friar?
DUKE

Bound by my charity, and my blessed order,
I come to visit the afflicted spirits
Here in the prison. Do me the common right
To let me see them, and to make me know
The nature of their crimes, that I may minister
To them accordingly.
PROVOST

I would do more than that, if more were needful.
     Enter Julietta
Look, here comes one, a gentlewoman of mine,   10

2.3.0.1 *disguised as a Friar*] DAVENANT; *not in* F

183 **enemy** the devil, as in Luke 10: 19 and
     Twelfth Night 2.2.28
183–4 **that to catch … hook** Lever refers to
     stories of saints tempted by the devil in
     the likeness of a beautiful and virtuous
     woman. But the rest of Angelo's speech
     shows that for him there is a horrible
     paradox: he is tempted to sin by a woman
     who is genuinely virtuous, not a devil in
     disguise, and it is precisely her virtue
     which excites him.
187 **art and nature** her skill as a courtesan
     combined with her inherent sexuality
188 **stir my temper** disturb my composure
190 **fond** infatuated, doting

2.3.1 **so I think you are** The Duke suddenly
     remembers that he is supposed to be a
     stranger, and pretends to be unsure of the
     Provost's identity.
3 **order** the religious order to which he
     belongs
4 **spirits** souls, persons. This may be a
     biblical echo of 1 Peter 3: 19, 'he also
     went and preached unto the spirits that
     were in prison'.
5 **common right** glossed by *OED, common a.*
     5c, as 'the right of every citizen', but the
     Duke is surely relying on the more spe-
     cialized right of a cleric to officiate inside a
     prison.

Who, falling in the flaws of her own youth,
Hath blistered her report. She is with child,
And he that got it, sentenced; a young man
More fit to do another such offence
Than die for this.

DUKE

When must he die?

PROVOST   As I do think, tomorrow.
(*To her*) I have provided for you; stay a while,
And you shall be conducted.

DUKE

Repent you, fair one, of the sin you carry?

JULIETTA

I do, and bear the shame most patiently.   20

DUKE

I'll teach you how you shall arraign your conscience
And try your penitence, if it be sound
Or hollowly put on.

JULIETTA   I'll gladly learn.

DUKE

Love you the man that wronged you?

JULIETTA

Yes, as I love the woman that wronged him.

DUKE

So then it seems your most offenceful act
Was mutually committed.

---

11 **flaws** The primary meaning is 'sudden blasts or gusts of wind' (*OED sb.²* 1), and *falling* suggests that she has been blown down by the wind. There is also a hint in *flaws* of 'faults, blemishes' (*OED sb.¹* 5b) and 'bursts of feeling or passion' (*OED sb.²* 2). Some editors have wanted to emend to *flames* because of *blistered* in the next line, but a Shakespearian link between infectious winds or fogs and blisters occurs in *Lear* 2.2.339–41 (Folio version) and *Tempest* 1.2.326–7, and see also *Coriolanus* 1.5.1–5.

12 **report** reputation

18 **conducted** escorted (to the place where she will lie in)

19 **carry** *OED*'s earliest quotation for sense 26c, 'are pregnant with', is from 1775, and Shakespeare does not use this sense elsewhere. The word may mean simply 'carry around with you or inside you' (*OED* 26, 26b), or it may have sense 28, 'exhibit, display' (her visible pregnancy is a sign of her sin).

20 **bear** endure

21 **arraign** Lever glosses as 'interrogate, examine' (*OED v.¹* 1), but *OED* gives no example of this later than 1447, so it is probably in sense 2, 'accuse, charge with a fault'.

22 **if** whether
   sound truthful, theologically correct

23 **hollowly** insincerely (used in the same way in *Tempest* 3.1.70). There may be a play on words here (see 1.2.53–4 n.).

26 **offenceful** full of offence, sinful (the sole example in Shakespeare and *OED* before 1970)

134

JULIETTA   Mutually.

DUKE

Then was your sin of heavier kind than his.

JULIETTA

I do confess it, and repent it, father.

DUKE

'Tis meet so, daughter, but lest you do repent   30
As that the sin hath brought you to this shame,
Which sorrow is always toward ourselves, not heaven,
Showing we would not spare heaven as we love it,
But as we stand in fear—

JULIETTA

I do repent me as it is an evil,
And take the shame with joy.

DUKE   There rest.
Your partner, as I hear, must die tomorrow,
And I am going with instruction to him.
Grace go with you; *Benedicite.*   *Exit*

JULIETTA

Must die tomorrow! O injurious law,   40

40 law] HANMER; Loue F

28 **Then ... his** It is not clear why the Duke
says this; Whetstone (*Heptameron*, 1582,
N2ᵛ) takes the opposite view: 'the man
was held to be the greatest offender and
therefore had the severest punishment'.
The relative weight of responsibility for
sexual sins between men and women was
much debated in the Renaissance; men
were supposed to have more powerful
intellects and were thus less excusable
than women in lapsing from morality,
but pregnancy made the woman's offence greater because it produced a public
sign of her sin (see Ian Maclean, *The
Renaissance Notion of Women*, Cambridge,
1980, pp. 15, 78).

30 **meet so** right that you should do so
lest in case (the Duke begins to wind his
way into an elaborate construction, but
never reaches a main clause because
Julietta interrupts him at l. 35)

31 **As that** in that, because

33–4 **we would not ... fear** we do not wish
to refrain from sin because we love God

but because we are afraid of His punishment

36 **There rest** Remain in that attitude

38 **instruction** moral teaching

39 *Benedicite* Bless you!

40 **law** Many editors defend F's *love*, on
the grounds that her love has led to
the pregnancy which is now saving
her life (*respites me a life* in l. 41 suggests that Julietta herself is due to be
executed, but has been granted a reprieve because of her pregnancy). But
the emendation to *law* gives a richer
meaning to *injurious*, not only 'harmful'
but 'unjust, the opposite of what it
should be' (perhaps with a hint of Latin
injurius, 'unjust'). In addition, though
love is the ultimate cause of the
couple's problems, it is law rather than
love which simultaneously condemns
Claudio to die immediately and spares
the woman who is emotionally dependent on him.

That respites me a life, whose very comfort
Is still a dying horror!

PROVOST   'Tis pity of him.   *Exeunt*

2.4   *Enter Angelo*

ANGELO

When I would pray and think, I think and pray
To several subjects. Heaven hath my empty words,
Whilst my invention, hearing not my tongue,
Anchors on Isabel: Heaven in my mouth,
As if I did but only chew his name,
And in my heart the strong and swelling evil
Of my conception. The state whereon I studied
Is like a good thing, being often read,
Grown seared and tedious; yea, my gravity,
Wherein—let no man hear me—I take pride,   10
Could I with boot change for an idle plume
Which the air beats for vain. O place, O form,
How often dost thou with thy case, thy habit,

2.4.4 Heaven] F; God NOSWORTHY   9 seared] HANMER; feard F

41 **very** See 1.4.53 n.
   comfort what gives life meaning to her, the man she loves
42 **dying horror** this seems to be ambiguous: Claudio himself is full of horror at the thought of his imminent death, and his plight creates a horror in Julietta which is bringing her to death
   'Tis pity of him He is much to be pitied
2.4.2 **several** separate and distinct
 3 **invention** mental powers, imagination
 4 **Anchors on** fastens on, is obsessed by
   Heaven possibly a substitution, by Crane or an earlier censor, for 'God' (see the Textual Introduction, pp. 68–9).
 5 **chew** quoted by *OED* as the earliest example of sense 3e, 'to keep saying or mumbling over'.
 7 **conception** creation, devising. Perhaps the stress should fall on *my*: Angelo admits that he alone is responsible for the evil. *Conception* and *swelling* may also hint at the evil as a kind of horrible pregnancy; compare Iago's language in *Othello* 1.3.395–6, 'It is engender'd. Hell and night | Must bring this monstrous birth to the world's light'.

   state state-affairs, matters of government; compare *Twelfth Night* 2.5.145–6, 'Let thy tongue tang arguments of state'.
 9 **seared** dried up, withered. F's *feared* might make sense ('regarded with unease'), but there is little support for this usage in *OED* or elsewhere in Shakespeare.
11 **boot** advantage
   idle useless, frivolous
   plume large feather, worn in the hat by fashionable young men
12 **for vain** *OED*, *vain a.* 5b, regards this as equivalent to 'in vain', but if *beats* could imply 'punish by beating' the phrase could also mean 'because of its vanity, foolishness'.
   place high rank
   form probably in *OED*'s sense 14, 'ritual, ceremony', though the earliest example given dates from 1612.
13 **thy case, thy habit** Both words mean 'clothing', but *case* may be the more general term (*OED sb.*² 2, 'outer-covering') and *habit* may refer to formal clothing worn to indicate rank or profession (*OED* 2).

Wrench awe from fools and tie the wiser souls
To thy false seeming! Blood, thou art blood.
Let's write 'good angel' on the devil's horn,
'Tis not the devil's crest.
    Enter Servant

                   How now? Who's there?
SERVANT One Isabel, a sister, desires access to you.
ANGELO
    Teach her the way.   *Exit Servant*
            O heavens,
Why does my blood thus muster to my heart,   20
Making both it unable for itself
And dispossessing all my other parts
Of necessary fitness?
So play the foolish throngs with one that swoons,
Come all to help him, and so stop the air
By which he should revive; and even so
The general, subject to a well-wished king,
Quit their own part, and in obsequious fondness
Crowd to his presence, where their untaught love

---

17 not] F; now OXFORD   *Enter Servant*] F (*at end of line*)   19 *Exit Servant*] CAPELL; *not in* F

14 **tie** In its context this may have *OED*'s sense 5c, 'bring into bondage, enthrall'; the fools are awe-struck, but even the wiser and more sceptical are forced to obey.

15 **seeming** deceptive appearance, hypocrisy (*OED vbl. sb.* 3). The term is used in the play with powerful resonances (compare l. 151 below and 3.1.306, and *seemers* at 1.3.54).
Blood, thou art blood Not merely a tautology; one meaning of *blood* is 'sexual appetite', as at 2.1.12, and Angelo now does confess 'That his blood flows' (1.3.52) and is not 'snow-broth' (1.4.58).

16–17 See the longer note in Appendix A.

19 **Teach** show

20 **muster** used of an army assembling for duty. In Elizabethan physiology it was assumed that the blood moved towards the heart in moments of crisis.

21 **unable for itself** incapable of carrying out its own functions

22 **dispossessing** depriving

27 **general, subject** F has no punctuation, and both words can be used as adjectives or nouns; for *the general* as 'the common people' cf. *Hamlet* 2.2.439, and for *the subject* as a ruler's subjects considered collectively cf. 3.1.398 and 5.1.15. The version given above would mean 'the ordinary people who are subjects'.
well-wished who has the good wishes of his people (a Shakespearian coinage not recorded elsewhere). For suggestions that this may be a topical allusion to King James I see the Introduction, p. 4.

28 **part** (*a*) office, duty in society; (*b*) theatrical role
obsequious fondness This could be glossed as 'dutiful affection', but both words had pejorative connotations (of servility and stupidity) at the time, and it is hard to tell whether these implications were intended to be present. If they are, Angelo presumably despises popularity.

29 **untaught** ignorant of correct behaviour

Must needs appear offence.
    Enter Isabella

                    How now, fair maid?   30

ISABELLA

I am come to know your pleasure.

ANGELO (*aside*)

That you might know it would much better please me
Than to demand what 'tis. (*To her*) Your brother
    cannot live.

ISABELLA

Even so. Heaven keep your honour.

ANGELO

Yet may he live a while, and it may be
As long as you or I; yet he must die.

ISABELLA

Under your sentence?

ANGELO

Yea.

ISABELLA

When, I beseech you? That in his reprieve,
Longer or shorter, he may be so fitted   40
That his soul sicken not.

ANGELO

Ha! Fie, these filthy vices! It were as good
To pardon him that hath from nature stolen
A man already made, as to remit
Their saucy sweetness that do coin heaven's image

30 *Enter Isabella*] F (*at end of line*)

32–3 **That ... 'tis** *Know* and *pleasure* in l. 31
have sexual connotations, unintended by
Isabella, which suggest that she is offer-
ing herself to him, and Angelo would like
this to be true, i.e. 'I would much rather
you gave me what I want without asking
me to spell out what it is'. Angelo himself
uses the same phrase as Isabella at
1.1.27.

37 **Under your sentence?** The stress is on
your; 'will it be you, rather than God,
who decides?'

39 **reprieve** time in prison awaiting execution

40 **fitted** spiritually prepared

41 **sicken** in the figurative sense, 'fall into
despair'

44 **remit** pardon

45 **Their saucy sweetness** the impudent las-
civiousness of those
    coin The collocation of *coin* and *stamps* in
l. 46 can be paralleled in other Shakespearian contexts which suggest that
Shakespeare equated the begetting of
illegitimate children with the counterfeit-
ing of coins; compare *Cymbeline* 2.5.2–6,
and the apocryphal *Edward III*
2.1.255–8. See also *Othello* 2.1.243–4,
'an eye can stamp and counterfeit advan-
tages'.
    heaven's image echoing Genesis 1: 26,
and perhaps intended to emphasize the
seriousness of the crime

In stamps that are forbid. 'Tis all as easy
Falsely to take away a life true-made,
As to put metal in restrainèd means
To make a false one.

ISABELLA

'Tis set down so in heaven, but not in earth. 50

ANGELO

Say you so? Then I shall pose you quickly.
Which had you rather, that the most just law
Now took your brother's life or, to redeem him,
Give up your body to such sweet uncleanness
As she that he hath stained?

ISABELLA   Sir, believe this,
I had rather give my body than my soul.

ANGELO

I talk not of your soul. Our compelled sins
Stand more for number than for account.

ISABELLA   How say you?

ANGELO

Nay, I'll not warrant that, for I can speak
Against the thing I say. Answer to this. 60
I, now the voice of the recorded law,
Pronounce a sentence on your brother's life;
Might there not be a charity in sin
To save this brother's life?

---

53 or] DAVENANT; and F

46 **stamps** blocks or dies; obviously also
figurative for a woman's womb
46–9 **'Tis all ... false one** These lines rather
seem to repeat the imagery of the previous four without substantially modifying
it.
47 **true-made** legitimately begotten
48 **restrainèd** forbidden
means methods, appliances. Steevens
suggested an emendation to 'mints' but
the abstract word can apply equally to a
mould used for making coins and the
womb.
50 **'Tis ... earth** i.e., 'God may regard murder and begetting a bastard as equally
weighty sins, but humans do not'.
51 **pose** set a problem difficult or impossible
to answer
54 **uncleanness** moral impurity, especially

sexual. The term is biblical (e.g. Romans
1 : 24 and 6 : 19) and was much used by
severer Elizabethan moralists.
57–8 **Our ... account** proverbial ('Compelled sins are no sins', Tilley S475)
57 **compelled** stress on the first syllable (Abbott 492)
58 **Stand ... account** ?will be numbered
among our sins but we shall not have to
pay for them at the last judgement
59 **warrant** guarantee, endorse. His previous assertion has alarmed Isabella and
pushed the argument in the wrong direction, so Angelo pretends that he was
merely putting forward a hypothesis
which he can reject if he wishes.
61 **recorded** set down in writing. As Lever
notes, Angelo stresses that he is merely
an agent of the law as it already exists.

ISABELLA   Please you to do't,
I'll take it as a peril to my soul
It is no sin at all, but charity.

ANGELO

Pleased you to do't, at peril of your soul,
Were equal poise of sin and charity.

ISABELLA

That I do beg his life, if it be sin
Heaven let me bear it; you granting of my suit,   70
If that be sin, I'll make it my morn prayer
To have it added to the faults of mine,
And nothing of your answer.

ANGELO   Nay, but hear me.
Your sense pursues not mine; either you are ignorant,
Or seem so craftily, and that's not good.

ISABELLA

Let me be ignorant, and in nothing good
But graciously to know I am no better.

ANGELO

Thus wisdom wishes to appear most bright
When it doth tax itself, as these black masks
Proclaim an enshield beauty ten times louder   80

75 craftily] DAVENANT; crafty F   76 me] F2; *not in* F

64 **Please you** if you decide

65–6 **I'll … charity** These lines are ambiguous, since *take it* can mean either 'assume as a fact' (with 'that' implied at the end of l. 65) or 'take on myself the spiritual burden'. Editors who prefer the latter replace F's comma after *soul* by a full stop. But at this point Isabella is merely trying to reassure Angelo that to forgive Claudio would not be a sin; she does not take upon herself any guilt involved in doing so until her next speech.

68 **poise** weight, balance

73 **nothing of your answer** not part of the sins you will have to answer for.

74 **Your sense pursues not mine** Angelo intends this to mean 'your argument does not follow logically from mine', hence 'you misunderstand me', but in view of 2.2.144 there is an inevitable undertone of 'your sensual desire is not responding to mine'.

75 **craftily** cunningly, in order to deceive. Some editors retain F's *crafty*, and adjec-

tives in Shakespeare are often used adverbially (Abbott 1); but *so crafty* is awkwardly ambiguous, the line in F is metrically clumsy, and the compositor (D) has omitted a word in the next line.

76 **Let … ignorant** Isabella willingly accepts the first of Angelo's alternatives; if she misunderstands him it is through lack of knowledge, not deceitfulness.

77 **graciously** through divine grace

79 **tax** rebuke

these used with a contemptuously generalizing effect ('the sort of thing you women wear')

masks Aristocratic women wore masks or mask-like devices to protect their complexions from the sun and keep them fashionably white; cf. 'her sun-expelling mask' in *Two Gentlemen* 4.4.150, and *Romeo* 1.1.227–8.

80 **enshield** apparently a shortened form of *enshielded*, 'concealed' (so *OED*; no other example quoted). See also Abbott 342.
ten times a stock phrase, common in the

Than beauty could displayed. But mark me:
To be receivèd plain, I'll speak more gross.
Your brother is to die.

ISABELLA

So.

ANGELO

And his offence is so, as it appears,
Accountant to the law upon that pain.

ISABELLA

True.

ANGELO

Admit no other way to save his life—
As I subscribe not that, nor any other—
But, in the loss of question, that you, his sister,   90
Finding yourself desired of such a person
Whose credit with the judge, or own great place,
Could fetch your brother from the manacles
Of the all-binding law, and that there were
No earthly mean to save him, but that either
You must lay down the treasures of your body
To this supposed, or else to let him suffer;
What would you do?

ISABELLA

As much for my poor brother as myself;
That is, were I under the terms of death,   100
The impression of keen whips I'd wear as rubies,

---

89 As] (As F   other-] OXFORD, *conj.* WATT; other, F   90 But,] OXFORD, *conj.* WATT; But F
question,] OXFORD, *conj.* WATT; question) F   94 all-binding] JOHNSON; all-building F

period, for 'many times, to a high degree'.
Cf. l. 129 below and 5.1.43 and 46.

82 **receivèd** understood (earliest quotation
in *OED* for sense 7)
gross openly, bluntly
85 **appears** is clearly evident
86 **Accountant** liable
upon that pain to receive that punishment (the death penalty)
88–90 **Admit ... sister** See longer note in
Appendix A.
89 **subscribe** assent to, endorse
93 **fetch** perhaps used in the same sense as
fetch off (*OED* 16), i.e. 'rescue, liberate'.
94 **all-binding** *binding* makes better sense

than F's *building* after *manacles*, and Lever
notes a similar error of *build* for *bind* in *The
Duchess of Malfi* 1.1.491 (Revels edn.),
now thought to be based on a Crane
transcript.
96 **treasures** For virginity as a kind of wealth
compare 'chaste treasure' in *Hamlet*
1.3.31, and Elaine in Malory, *Works* (ed.
Vinaver, Oxford Standard Authors,
p. 586), 'to fulfil this prophecy I have
given thee the greatest riches and the
fairest flower that ever I had, and that is
my maidenhood that I shall never have
again'.
97 **supposed** hypothetical person (Lever)
100 **terms of death** death sentence

And strip myself to death as to a bed
That longing have been sick for, ere I'd yield
My body up to shame.

handwritten margin note: language of sexuality in expressing death

ANGELO

Then must your brother die.

ISABELLA

And 'twere the cheaper way.
Better it were a brother died at once
Than that a sister by redeeming him
Should die for ever.

ANGELO

Were not you then as cruel as the sentence   110
That you have slandered so?

ISABELLA

Ignomy in ransom and free pardon
Are of two houses; lawful mercy
Is nothing kin to foul redemption.

ANGELO

You seemed of late to make the law a tyrant,
And rather proved the sliding of your brother
A merriment than a vice.

102–3 **strip ... sick for** 'To go to one's grave (death) like a bed' is given as proverbial in Tilley/Dent B192.1; the closest parallel is *Antony* 4.15.99–101, 'I will be | A bridegroom in my death, and run into't | As to a lover's bed'. Isabella is perhaps thinking of women saints who endured painful martyrdom rather than lose their virginity, e.g. St Margaret, 'Then the provost commanded her to be hanged in an instrument to torment the people, and to be cruelly first beaten with rods, and with iron combs to rend and draw her flesh to the bones, insomuch that the blood ran about out of her body, like as a stream runneth out of a fresh springing well', *The Golden Legend*, tr. Caxton (Temple Classics, 1900, 4.68).

103 **longing have** This may be a case of a singular subject with a plural verb (cf. 1.2.182), or *have* may be equivalent to 'I have' (Abbott 400–1).

106 **cheaper** entered in *OED* under *cheap adj.* 3, 'easily obtained'. The word is more likely to be in sense 2, 'less expensive, of better value'.

107 **at once** at one stroke, once for all

109 **die for ever** suffer eternal damnation

112 **Ignomy in ransom** freedom obtained by paying a shameful price. *Ignomy* is a shortened form of *ignominy*, common up to the end of the 18th c. and found also in the Folio texts of *1 Henry IV* 5.4.99, and *Troilus*, Additional Passage B, 2.
free (*a*) freely offered, without conditions; (*b*) free of charge

113 **of two houses** belonging to different families, totally unrelated

114 **nothing** in no way. Isabella makes the point twice, perhaps for emphasis (cf. 46–9 n. above).

115 **of late** in their first debate in 2.2

116 **sliding** moral lapse

117 **merriment** joke, light-hearted fooling. Elizabethan moralists repeatedly attacked those who condoned sexual offences as trivial. Angelo hardly gives a fair summary of Isabella's argument in 2.2, but he wants to steer her away from the exalted tone of her speeches at ll. 99–104 and 106–9, and tries to do so by accusing her of inconsistency in taking her own loss of chastity more seriously than her brother's.

ISABELLA

O pardon me, my lord, it oft falls out
To have what we would have, we speak not what we
     mean.
I something do excuse the thing I hate   120
For his advantage that I dearly love.

ANGELO

We are all frail.

ISABELLA   Else let my brother die,
If not a fedary but only he
Owe and succeed thy weakness.

ANGELO

Nay, women are frail too.

ISABELLA

Ay, as the glasses where they view themselves,
Which are as easy broke as they make forms.
Women?—Help heaven! Men their creation mar
In profiting by them. Nay, call us ten times frail,
For we are soft as our complexions are,   130
And credulous to false prints.

ANGELO   I think it well,

120 **something** somewhat

122 **We are all frail** biblical (cf. Ecclesiasticus
  8: 5, 'we are frail every one' in the
  Bishops' Bible version) and proverbial
  (Tilley F363)

  Else otherwise, if that is not so

123 **If ... he** if Claudio is the sole offender in
  this way, and has no accomplices in
  crime

  fedary a form of *feudary*, 'feudal tenant,
  retainer', but used by Shakespeare to
  mean 'confederate, accomplice', as in
  Cymbeline 3.2.21

124 **Owe** own

  suceed inherit

  thy weakness Isabella means 'the weakness you refer to', but Angelo assumes
  she means 'the exclusively male weakness', or even 'the weakness found in you
  as well as others' (though as yet she does
  not know this).

125 **women are frail** proverbial (Tilley/Dent
  W700.1)

126 **glasses** mirrors. Cf. Tilley W646, 'A
  woman and a glass are ever in danger'.

127 **are ... forms** can be destroyed as easily
  as they create images when people look
  in them

128–9 **Help heaven!** Heaven help them!
  **Men their creation mar | In profiting by
  them** i.e., 'Men, who were created superior to women, debase themselves by
  taking advantage of women's weakness'.
  Some editors gloss *their creation* as 'those
  who create them, i.e. women', but this
  gives a weaker reading in the context.

130 **complexions** Probably in *OED*'s sense
  2b, 'physical constitution or nature',
  rather than in the restricted sense applied
  to the face. Women were thought of as
  generically softer than men, and the term
  is repeatedly applied to Eve in Milton's
  Paradise Lost.

131 **credulous ... prints** Print has a variety
  of literal and figurative meanings, so that
  the phrase could be glossed in several
  overlapping ways: (*a*) easily made to take
  on false impressions or appearances; (*b*)
  ready to believe falsehoods; (*c*) easily
  moulded by the tools of the counterfeiter.
  Lines 129–31 may be a variation on the
  proverb 'soft wax will take any impression' (Tilley W136), often applied to
  women, as in *Dream* 1.1.49–51, *Twelfth
  Night* 2.2.29–30, and *Lucrece* 1240–6.
  I think it well (*a*) I consider your argu-

And from this testimony of your own sex—
Since I suppose we are made to be no stronger
Than faults may shake our frames—let me be bold;
I do arrest your words. Be that you are,
That is, a woman; if you be more, you're none.
If you be one, as you are well expressed
By all external warrants, show it now
By putting on the destined livery.

ISABELLA

I have no tongue but one; gentle my lord,   140
Let me entreat you speak the former language.

ANGELO

Plainly conceive I love you.

ISABELLA

My brother did love Juliet,
And you tell me that he shall die for it.

ANGELO

He shall not, Isabel, if you give me love.

ISABELLA

I know your virtue hath a licence in't,
Which seems a little fouler than it is
To pluck on others.

ANGELO   Believe me, on mine honour,
My words express my purpose.

144 for it] DAVENANT; for't F

ment well-constructed; (*b*) I thoroughly
agree with you

132 **of** possibly ambiguous: (*a*) relating to;
(*b*) coming from (a woman)

133 **suppose** posit, postulate

133–4 **we are made to be no stronger | Than
faults may shake our frames** i.e., 'God did
not create human beings to be so strong
that they cannot be shaken or disturbed
by the temptations of evil'

135 **arrest** take as security
that that which, what

136 **be more** try to do more than a woman is
naturally capable of. Cf. *Macbeth*,
1.7.46–7, 'I dare do all that may become
a man; | Who dares do more is none'.

137–8 **well expressed | By all external war-**

rants clearly shown to be (a woman) by
all the evidence of your outward appearance

139 **destined livery** uniform of frailty, which
women are destined to wear

140 **I have ... one** an implicit rebuke to
Angelo, as Shakespeare frequently uses
double tongue to mean 'deceitful speech,
lying' (e.g. *Much Ado* 5.1.166, *First Part
of the Contention* (*2 Henry VI*) 2.3.97)

141 **the former language** the simpler, more
intelligible language he had used earlier

142 **conceive** understand (that)

146 **licence** freedom allowed by his official
status

148 **pluck on others** draw other people into
exposing themselves

ISABELLA

Ha! Little honour, to be much believed,   150
And most pernicious purpose. Seeming, seeming!
I will proclaim thee, Angelo, look for't.
Sign me a present pardon for my brother,
Or with an outstretched throat I'll tell the world aloud
What man thou art.

ANGELO   Who will believe thee, Isabel?
My unsoiled name, the austereness of my life,
My vouch against you, and my place i' the state,
Will so your accusation overweigh
That you shall stifle in your own report
And smell of calumny. I have begun,   160
And now I give my sensual race the rein.
Fit thy consent to my sharp appetite;
Lay by all nicety and prolixious blushes
That banish what they sue for. Redeem thy brother
By yielding up thy body to my will,
Or else he must not only die the death,
But thy unkindness shall his death draw out
To lingering sufferance. Answer me tomorrow,
Or, by the affection that now guides me most,
I'll prove a tyrant to him. As for you,   170
Say what you can; my false o'erweighs your true. *Exit*

ISABELLA

To whom should I complain? Did I tell this,

150 **Little ... believed** Angelo is showing very little 'honour', but expects Isabella to believe deeply in his honourable intentions.

152 **proclaim** denounce publicly
look for't expect it

153 **present** immediate

154 **outstretched throat** ?mouth wide open so as to make the maximum sound

155 **What** what kind of

156 **unsoiled name** spotless reputation

157 **vouch** assertion, attestation of truth or fact (first quotation in *OED sb.* 2)

158 **overweigh** outweigh, crush

159 **report** (*a*) account of the event; (*b*) reputation. 'You will be smothered by your own story, and your reputation (as a slanderer) will stink.'

161 **give ... rein** *OED* glosses *race* as 'natural or inherited disposition' (*sb.*² 7), but this is a rare usage, and *give ... the rein* ('allow a horse to run uncontrolled') suggests that *race* could mean 'the act of riding rapidly on horseback' (*sb.*¹ 4a).

163 **nicety** coyness, affected modesty
prolixious protracted (but simply as a delaying tactic)

164 **banish what they sue for** either (*a*) reject what in fact they are eager for, or (*b*) are so alluring that they destroy any pity in the lover

166 **die the death** be put to death; a biblical phrase (e.g. several times in the Geneva version of Leviticus 20).

167 **unkindness** (*a*) harshness towards Angelo; (*b*) lack of sisterly feeling

168 **sufferance** suffering, torture

169 **the affection that now guides me most** the mood I am in at the moment

172 **Did I** If I were to (Abbott 361)

Who would believe me? O perilous mouths,
That bear in them one and the selfsame tongue
Either of condemnation or approof,
Bidding the law make curtsy to their will,
Hooking both right and wrong to the appetite,
To follow as it draws! I'll to my brother;
Though he hath fallen by prompture of the blood,
Yet hath he in him such a mind of honour   180
That had he twenty heads to tender down
On twenty bloody blocks, he'd yield them up
Before his sister should her body stoop
To such abhorred pollution.
Then Isabel, live chaste, and brother, die;
More than our brother is our chastity.
I'll tell him yet of Angelo's request,
And fit his mind to death, for his soul's rest.   *Exit*

3.1   *Enter Duke as a Friar, and Provost with Claudio*
DUKE

So then you hope of pardon from Lord Angelo?
CLAUDIO

The miserable have no other medicine
But only hope.
I've hope to live, and am prepared to die.
DUKE

Be absolute for death; either death or life

3.1.0.1 *as a Friar*] DAVENANT; *Enter Duke, Claudio, and Prouost.* F   4 I've] ROWE; I'haue F

174–5 **That … approof** Isabella seems to complain that Angelo talks in the same way (harsh and peremptory) when he is condemning sin in other people and approving it in himself.

176 **make curtsy** bow or bend the knee (as a token of obedience)

177 **Hooking** fastening, attaching

179 **prompture** prompting, instigation (earliest quotation in *OED*, and the only Shakespearian usage)

181 **tender down** lay down in payment

186 **More … chastity** Modern actresses find this line difficult to cope with (see the Introduction, pp. 38–9). It is the only line in the play to have double inverted commas, at the beginning of the line only, to indicate (as is common in Elizabe-

than printing) a maxim or sententia. These may have been supplied by Crane; they are frequent in the 1623 text of *The Duchess of Malfi*. It is clear, however, that Isabella herself is appealing to general principles to justify her own attitude: normally she refers to Claudio as 'my brother', and the only other place where she uses 'our brother', at 2.2.128, is also a generalization.

3.1.1 **of** for

2–3 **The miserable … hope** a variant on a proverb found in Erasmus and elsewhere, 'Hope preserves the afflicted' (see Smith 155 and Tilley H602)

2 **medicine** cure, remedy

5 **Be absolute for death** Accept with complete certainty that you must die

Shall thereby be the sweeter. Reason thus with life:
If I do lose thee, I do lose a thing
That none but fools would keep; a breath thou art
Servile to all the skyey influences
That dost this habitation where thou keep'st   10
Hourly afflict. Merely thou art death's fool,
For him thou labour'st by thy flight to shun,
And yet run'st toward him still. Thou art not noble,
For all the accommodations that thou bear'st
Are nursed by baseness. Thou'rt by no means valiant,
For thou dost fear the soft and tender fork
Of a poor worm. Thy best of rest is sleep,

6 **Reason ... life** Strictly speaking, the rest of the passage is a series of arguments offered by the Duke to Claudio, so that he can use them to counter the claims of *life*, personified as *thee* and *thou*. But we cannot avoid also reading the lines as direct address by the Duke, with *thou* as Claudio.

8 **keep** primarily in the sense 'continue to have' (opposite to *lose* in the previous line); but also having such implications as 'defend', 'watch over', 'maintain'
breath (*a*) a breathing, and hence living, being; (*b*) something unsubstantial and transitory, a trifle (*OED* 3d). See Tilley/Dent B641.1.

9 **Servile to** slavishly controlled by
skyey issuing from the sky; referring both to the weather and to emanations from heavenly bodies, thought at the time to have a powerful effect on human behaviour

10 **dost** usually taken as relating back to *influences*, which then become the subject of *afflict*. This makes good sense, and singular verbs with plural subjects are common in Elizabethan English; but no editor has produced a clear parallel for *dost* as a plural verb, so that it could refer back to *breath*, in which case it would be the breath or spirit which torments the body (compare Marvell's poem, 'A Dialogue between the Soul and Body').
habitation dwelling-place, used here figuratively for the body (compare Sonnet 95.10, and *2 Henry IV* 1.3.89)
keep'st reside, dwell

11 **Merely** utterly, completely
death's fool This has been related to illustrations of the Dance of Death in which the Fool is one of Death's victims, as in a broadsheet of 1569 entitled 'The Dance and Song of Death' (*STC* 6222). But it probably has a simpler meaning, 'tricked or made to appear foolish by death'; compare 'fortune's fool', *Romeo* 3.1.136, and 'time's fool', Sonnet 116.9, and *1 Henry IV* 5.4.80.

12–13 **For him ... still** You desperately struggle to run away from death, but in fact you are continually running towards it

14 **accommodations** The closest sense in *OED* is 6, 'conveniences, appliances' (earliest quotation from 1616), but the context of 'Unaccommodated man ... a poor, bare, forked animal' in *Lear* 3.4.100–1 suggests that Shakespeare is particularly thinking here of clothing and personal adornment. The word became fashionable in the early 17th c., and Jonson sneered at it as one of the 'perfumed terms of the time' in *Discoveries*, l. 2275.
bear'st carry about, wear

15 **Are nursed by baseness** have base or unworthy origins. Here again *Lear* 3.4.97–9 provides a gloss: 'Thou owest the worm no silk, the beast no hide, the sheep no wool, the cat no perfume'.

16 **fork** forked tongue of a poisonous snake (*OED* 1c, first recorded use)

17 **worm** snake (see previous note), not grave-worm, since the passage as a whole deals with the fear of death rather than with what happens after death; the man who thinks himself brave will be terrified of dying because of a snake-bite.
Thy best ... sleep sleep is the best and fullest way of resting yourself

And that thou oft provok'st, yet grossly fear'st
Thy death, which is no more. Thou art not thyself,
For thou exists on many a thousand grains   20
That issue out of dust. Happy thou art not,
For what thou hast not, still thou striv'st to get,
And what thou hast, forget'st. Thou art not certain,
For thy complexion shifts to strange effects
After the moon. If thou art rich, thou'rt poor,
For like an ass, whose back with ingots bows,
Thou bear'st thy heavy riches but a journey,
And death unloads thee. Friend hast thou none,
For thine own bowels which do call thee sire,
The mere effusion of thy proper loins,   30
Do curse the gout, serpigo, and the rheum
For ending thee no sooner. Thou hast nor youth, nor
    age,

29 thee sire] F4; thee, fire F   31 serpigo] ROWE; Sapego F

18 **provok'st** call upon, invite
    grossly (*a*) excessively; (*b*) stupidly
19 **no more** no more or worse than sleep; the
    same point is made in *Hamlet* 3.1.62–3
    (see the Arden edition by Harold Jenkins,
    3.1.61 n.). Lines 17–19 may be indebted
    to a passage in Cicero's *Tusculan Disputa-
    tions* 1.38, which uses the same argu-
    ments.
    not thyself The context suggests a mean-
    ing such as 'not self-sufficient' or 'not
    wholly of one substance'.
20 **exists on** continue to live by consuming a
    certain kind of diet (though *OED* does not
    record the phrasal verb, and the earliest
    example of sense 4, 'maintain an exis-
    tence', is from 1790). For the form of
    exists see the note on *splits* at 2.2.118.
    grains of wheat or similar food
21 **issue out of dust** grow out of the earth.
    Some commentators see an allusion to
    the dust from which Adam was created,
    Genesis 2 : 7, but *exists on* and *issue out of*
    point more strongly to the consumption
    of vegetable food.
23 **certain** (*a*) fixed in behaviour or opinions,
    consistent; (*b*) reliable, trustworthy
24 **complexion** disposition, temperament
    shifts alters
    to strange effects ?in very odd ways, with
    extraordinary results
25 **After** (*a*) in obedience to; (*b*) in imitation
    of. The moon was supposed to influence

human behaviour, and was also a symbol of changefulness (Tilley M1111).
26–8 **like ... thee** The closest parallel is in
    Caesar 4.1.21–7, 'He shall but bear them
    as the ass bears gold, | To groan and sweat
    under the business, | Either led or driven
    as we point the way; | And having
    brought our treasure where we will, |
    Then take we down his load, and turn
    him off, | Like to the empty ass, to shake
    his ears | And graze in commons'. Com-
    pare also the proverb, 'The ass though
    laden with gold still eats thistles' (Tilley
    A360).
26 **ingots** bars or slabs of gold and silver
29 **bowels** offspring, children (*OED sb.*[1] 5;
    Shakespeare's only use in this sense)
    call thee sire address you as father, regard
    you as their begetter
30 **mere** possibly in the sense 'pure, un-
    mixed' (*OED a.*[2] 1c); the child will be
    completely and genuinely his own, but it
    will none the less wish him dead
    effusion literally 'pouring out', hence
    'issue, product'
    loins the reproductive parts of the body
31 **serpigo** a general term for creeping or
    spreading skin diseases
    rheum any form of watery discharge,
    catarrh. In *Kinsmen* 5.6.8, *gout* and
    rheum are given as characteristic diseases
    of old age
32–8 **Thou hast ... pleasant** The general

But as it were an after-dinner's sleep
Dreaming on both, for all thy blessed youth
Becomes as agèd, and doth beg the alms
Of palsied eld; and when thou art old and rich,
Thou hast neither heat, affection, limb, nor beauty
To make thy riches pleasant. What's in this
That bears the name of life? Yet in this life
Lie hid mo thousand deaths; yet death we fear,   40
That makes these odds all even.

CLAUDIO   I humbly thank you.
To sue to live, I find I seek to die,
And seeking death, find life. Let it come on.

ISABELLA (*within*)
What ho! Peace here, grace, and good company.

---

38 in] POPE; yet in F   44 *within*] CAPELL; *not in* F

sense of these lines is: You never live fully
and contentedly in the present, because
youth lacks money to enjoy its pleasures
and age lacks the ability to extract pleasure from its money

33 **after-dinner** after the midday meal, in the
early afternoon (a period of drowsy stasis
which is neither morning nor evening)
34 **blessed** happy, fortunate (but obviously
used ironically)
35 **as agèd** sometimes regarded as corrupt
and emended, but the rest of the line
suggests that it may mean 'as though the
young man were an old beggar dependent on other people's charity'
36 **palsied eld** old people afflicted by palsy,
which produces paralysis or involuntary
tremors. Compare 'wrinkled eld', *Troilus*
2.2.103, and 'superstitious idle-headed
eld', *Merry Wives* 4.4.35.
37 **heat** ardour, energy
affection with a range of senses: emotion,
passion, love. To some extent the meanings of *heat* and *affection* overlap, and
both words can have strong sexual connotations.
limb full use of the various parts of the
body
beauty i.e., you are ugly and repulsive
through age
38 **What's in this** F's *yet* in this phrase is
superfluous and metrically clumsy, and
may be a compositorial anticipation of
the next line's *Yet in this*. It also seems
unlikely that Shakespeare would want to

use *yet* three times in three successive
lines.
39 **bears the name of life** is worthy of being
called 'life'
this life this so-called 'life', full of misery
40 **mo thousand** *mo* means 'more in number', and this turns *thousand* into a plural,
so that the phrase means 'thousands
more'. Compare 'many thousand' in
Winter's Tale 1.2.207, and *2 Henry IV*
2.3.66.
41 **makes these odds all even** Commentators
suggest that this could be a direct translation from various passages in Seneca's
writings, but seem to have ignored *OED*
odds sb. 1, which gives 'to make odds
even' as a stock phrase, with three examples from Scottish writings of the 16th c.,
and glosses it as 'to equalize or level
inequalities, to adjust or do away with
differences'. There is also a hint of the
proverbial idea of death as the leveller of
all things (Smith 54 and Tilley D143).
42–3 **To sue ... life** echoing the famous
paradox found four times in the New
Testament, as in Matthew 10: 39, 'He
that will save his life shall lose it, and he
that loseth his life for my sake shall save
it'
42 **To sue to live** in pleading for my life
43 **it** death
come on come towards me (used to refer
to the onset of a hostile army, as in *Caesar*
5.1.13)
44 **good company** may you enjoy good com-
panionship

PROVOST

Who's there? Come in, the wish deserves a welcome.

DUKE (*to Claudio*)

Dear sir, ere long I'll visit you again.

CLAUDIO

Most holy sir, I thank you.

        Enter Isabella

ISABELLA

My business is a word or two with Claudio.

PROVOST And very welcome. Look, signor, here's your sister.

DUKE (*aside to Provost*) Provost, a word with you.   50

PROVOST As many as you please.

DUKE Bring me to hear them speak, where I may be
    concealed.   *Exeunt Duke and Provost*

CLAUDIO

Now, sister, what's the comfort?

ISABELLA

Why,

As all comforts are, most good, most good indeed.

Lord Angelo, having affairs to heaven,

Intends you for his swift ambassador,

Where you shall be an everlasting lieger.

Therefore your best appointment make with speed;   60

Tomorrow you set on.

CLAUDIO   Is there no remedy?

ISABELLA

None, but such remedy as, to save a head,

To cleave a heart in twain.

47.1 *Enter Isabella*] DYCE; *after l.* 43 *in* F   52 me to hear them] MALONE; them to heare me F
53 *Exeunt . . . Provost*] DAVENANT; *not in* F; Exeunt F2

46 **sir** Mason's emendation to *son* is plausible; the Duke addresses Claudio as 'Son'
at l. 163 below, and Julietta as 'daughter' at 2.3.30.
52–3 **where I may be concealed** F has no
stage-direction. Lever (Introduction,
p. xxvi) argues that the Duke and Provost
should merely retire to the back of the
stage, but *concealed* suggests that he is not
visible, and it is better for Claudio and
Isabella to receive the undistracted attention of the audience, which will readily
assume that the Duke is somehow able to
hear what is going on.

57 **affairs to** business in
58 **Intends** intends to choose or appoint
(*OED* 19)
59 **lieger** resident or permanent ambassador
60 **appointment** preparation, both worldly
and spiritual
61 **set on** begin your journey
62–3 **such remedy . . . twain** the sort of
remedy that will save a head from execution by breaking someone else's heart
63 **cleave . . . in twain** split into two parts.
Winny argues that this is a form of death,
but *Hamlet* 3.4.147, 'O Hamlet, thou
hast cleft my heart in twain!', shows that

CLAUDIO

But is there any?

ISABELLA

Yes, brother, you may live.

There is a devilish mercy in the judge,

If you'll implore it, that will free your life,

But fetter you till death.

CLAUDIO   Perpetual durance?

ISABELLA

Ay, just, perpetual durance; a restraint,

Though all the world's vastidity you had,   70

To a determined scope.

CLAUDIO   But in what nature?

ISABELLA

In such a one as, you consenting to't,

Would bark your honour from that trunk you bear,

And leave you naked.

CLAUDIO   Let me know the point.

ISABELLA

O, I do fear thee, Claudio, and I quake

Lest thou a feverous life shouldst entertain,

And six or seven winters more respect

Than a perpetual honour. Dar'st thou die?

The sense of death is most in apprehension,

---

70 Though] ROWE; Through F

the phrase means 'break the heart, cause intense anguish'.

68 **Perpetual durance** life imprisonment
69 **just** exactly so
   restraint perhaps with a slight ambiguity: (*a*) imprisonment; (*b*) spiritual or moral confinement (because Claudio could never escape from shame and horror at the means used to save his life)
70 **Though all ... had** Even if you were free to travel to any part of the globe
   vastidity an irregular variant of *vastity*, 'vastness'; *OED* records no other example before 1812
71 **determined** limited, restricted
   in what nature of what sort (Claudio, who assumes that Isabella refers to a legal punishment, is puzzled by her cryptic remarks)

72 **you consenting** if you consent
73 **bark** strip away (as though stripping bark from a tree)
   trunk (*a*) body; (*b*) tree-trunk; and possibly (*c*) stem, family from which he is descended
74 **naked** exposed to hostile view, dishonoured
75 **quake** tremble for fear
76 **feverous** feverish, restless
   entertain the most probable sense seems to be *OED* 14c, 'cherish in the mind'
77 **respect** esteem, value
79 **sense** painful awareness
   apprehension anticipation. Compare Smith 57, 'The fear of death is worse than death itself', and Nashe, *The Unfortunate Traveller* (1594, M2), 'the fear of death's looks are more terrible than his stroke'.

And the poor beetle that we tread upon   80
In corporal sufferance finds a pang as great
As when a giant dies.
CLAUDIO   Why give you me this shame?
Think you I can a resolution fetch
From flowery tenderness? If I must die,
I will encounter darkness as a bride,
And hug it in mine arms.
ISABELLA
There spake my brother; there my father's grave
Did utter forth a voice. Yes, thou must die;
Thou art too noble to conserve a life
In base appliances. This outward-sainted deputy,   90
Whose settled visage and deliberate word
Nips youth i' the head, and follies doth enew

92 enew] KEIGHTLEY; emmew F

80-2 **the poor beetle ... dies** Isabella is
trying to comfort her brother, and must
intend to say that the death-sufferings of
a giant are no more or worse than those
of a small beetle, which dies suddenly
when trodden on. But *a pang as great*
inevitably invites a contrary reading:
death is equally horrible to all beings,
large or small. Perhaps Shakespeare intended this ambiguity to hint at the
implausibility of her argument.

82 **Why ... shame?** Why do you treat me in
this humiliating way?

83 **resolution** determination, steadiness of
mind

84 **flowery** wordy, full of flowers of speech
tenderness combining (*a*) compassion,
attempts at consolation, with (*b*) softness,
effeminacy (since the word was often
associated with women, as in *Coriolanus*
5.3.130)

85 **encounter** *OED v.* 6 glosses as 'go to
meet', but it can also mean 'confront in
battle' and 'engage with sexually' (compare l. 252 below). Compare ll. 85-6
with Isabella's own speech at 2.4.100-4,
and *Antony* 4.15.99-101, 'I will be|A
bridegroom in my death, and run into't
|As to a lover's bed'.

87 **my father's grave** This praise of Claudio
as worthy of his father (see 2.1.7) un-
obtrusively prepares for Isabella's violent
reversal of attitude at ll.144-6.

89 **conserve** preserve from destruction

90 **appliances** *OED* includes this under sense

1, 'compliance, subservience', but it is
more likely to mean 'medicines applied to
a disease', as in *Hamlet* 4.3.10, and
Pericles Sc. 12.84.
outward-sainted giving an outward appearance of holiness

91 **settled visage** fixed expression of the face
(indicating that he is not given to changing his mind)
deliberate word precise and careful way
of talking

92 **Nips...i' the head** This phrase appears to
refer to the way in which a bird of prey
seizes its victim by the back of the neck
and in effect paralyses it; hence the
figurative sense (*OED nip. v.*[1] 3b), 'to give
a decisive or final check to'. See also
Tilley/Dent H272.1.
follies *OED, folly sb.*[1] 3b, glosses as 'lewd
actions or desires'; compare the Old
Testament usage, 'she hath wrought
folly in Israel, by playing the whore in her
father's house' (Deuteronomy 22: 21),
echoed in *Othello* 5.2.141. As the word
follows *youth*, however, the sense of
'foolish behaviour' is also present.
enew F's *emmew* might be a form of
enmew or *immew*, 'mew up, keep in
confinement', but this is a very rare
word, with only one example in *OED*, and
the context shows that *enew*, 'drive into
the water', is much more appropriate.
This is a technical term of falconry: 'if ...
the fowl for fear of your hawk will spring
and fall again into the river ... and so lie

As falcon doth the fowl, is yet a devil;
His filth within being cast, he would appear
A pond as deep as hell.

CLAUDIO   The prenzie Angelo?

ISABELLA

O, 'tis the cunning livery of hell
The damnedst body to invest and cover
In prenzie guards! Dost thou think, Claudio,
If I would yield him my virginity
Thou mightst be freed?

CLAUDIO   O heavens, it cannot be.   100

ISABELLA

Yes, he would give't thee, from this rank offence,
So to offend him still. This night's the time
That I should do what I abhor to name,
Or else thou diest tomorrow.

CLAUDIO

Thou shalt not do't.

ISABELLA

O, were it but my life,

95, 98 prenzie] F; princely F2; precise KNIGHT   97 damnedst] F2; damnest F

still and dare not arise, ye shall say then
your hawk hath enewed the fowl into the
river', *The Book of Saint Albans* (1486,
D2).

94 **cast** *OED* gives 69 senses for *cast v.*; the
two most relevant are (*a*) 'cast up, vomit'
(*OED* 25), a usage sometimes occurring
in falconry when the bird needs to purge
itself, and (*b*) 'dig or clear out (a ditch or
the like), throwing the soil up on the
edges' (*OED* 29, quoting such illustrative
phrases as 'casting the ponds' and 'I will
not drain the fen, or stand casting the
pond'). Sense (*b*) is predominant: the
depth of Angelo's wickedness will not be
revealed until the obscuring mud or filth
is dredged out, and we perceive how
much there is of it. But the ambiguity
may have been present in Shakespeare's
mind, thus providing a transition from
falconry to cleaning out ponds.

95 **as deep as hell** a stock formula (Tilley/
Dent H397.1)
prenzie meaning obscure; see fuller discussion in Appendix A

96–8 **'tis ... guards** it is a cunning trick of

the devil to cover and disguise the
wickedest people in richly decorated garments so that they appear respectable

96 **livery** gift of clothing by a man of wealth
and position to his retainers and servants
(here by the devil to his followers). The
word may also have the implication
found elsewhere in Shakespeare of
'characteristic appearance': 'youth's
proud livery', Sonnet 2.3, and 'sorrow's
livery', *Lucrece* 1222.

97 **invest** clothe, adorn

98 **guards** contrasting facings or trimmings
on the front of a garment. As these were
often of rich fabrics like velvet, the word
occurs in contexts where the writer is
attacking extravagance and ostentation
Dost thou think could you believe it

101–2 **he would ... still** He would give you,
as a result of the vile deed I am to perform,
the power to continue committing offences against him as a magistrate. (Isabella may be assuming that Claudio could
get away with future misbehaviour because he could blackmail Angelo.)

101 **rank offence** Compare *Hamlet* 3.3.36, 'O,
my offence is rank! It smells to heaven'.

I'd throw it down for your deliverance
As frankly as a pin.

CLAUDIO   Thanks, dear Isabel.

ISABELLA

Be ready, Claudio, for your death tomorrow.

CLAUDIO

Yes. Has he affections in him   110
That thus can make him bite the law by the nose
When he would force it? Sure it is no sin,
Or of the deadly seven it is the least.

ISABELLA

Which is the least?

CLAUDIO

If it were damnable, he being so wise,
Why would he for the momentary trick
Be perdurably fined? O Isabel—

ISABELLA

What says my brother?

CLAUDIO

Death is a fearful thing.

ISABELLA

And shamèd life a hateful.   120

CLAUDIO

Ay, but to die, and go we know not where,

---

107 **deliverance** release from prison
108 **frankly** freely, unreservedly
110 **affections** See 2.1.10 n.
111 **bite ... by the nose** treat with contempt (*OED nose sb.* 9e). Compare 'snap (bite) off one's nose' (Tilley N241) and, in *Measure*, 'pluck by the nose', 1.3.29 and 5.1.340–1. An exact parallel is in Dekker's *Satiromastix* 5.2.199, 'to bite every motley-head vice by the nose'.
112 **force** *OED v.*[1] 9b glosses as 'enforce', but gives this as the only example. There seems to be an ironic undercurrent of other meanings, such as 'violate, ravish' and 'constrain by force'.
112–13 **Sure ... least** Proverbial; see 'Lechery is no sin' (Tilley/Dent L173.1), and the medieval quotations assembled under L167 in Whiting, such as *Piers Plowman*, B version, 3.58 (in a discussion of lechery), 'It is sin of the seven soonest released', and the anonymous play *Mankind* (*c.* 1475), l. 699, 'There are but six

deadly sins; lechery is none'. As might be expected, Elizabethan moralists bitterly attacked such notions, which were usually spoken by disreputable characters.
114 **Which is the least?** Perhaps intended to be contemptuous; by definition all the deadly sins led to damnation, and could not be graded in an order of seriousness.
115–17 **If it were ... fined** If it is a sin leading to damnation, why would Angelo, who is so wise, want to be damned for a brief pleasure?
116 **trick** with a range of meanings: (*a*) feat of dexterity (the sexual act); (*b*) trifle, caprice; (*c*) cheat, illusion
117 **perdurably fined** everlastingly punished
120 **shamèd life** Compare Smith 55, 'An honourable death is better than a shameful life', and Tilley H576. The sentiment was expressed by Seneca and Juvenal, and by numerous English writers from the Middle Ages onward (see Whiting D239).

To lie in cold obstruction, and to rot,
This sensible warm motion to become
A kneaded clod; and the delighted spirit
To bathe in fiery floods or to reside
In thrilling region of thick-ribbèd ice,
To be imprisoned in the viewless winds
And blown with restless violence round about
The pendent world, or to be worse than worst

122 **cold obstruction** *OED* glosses this as 'stoppage or cessation of the vital functions; the condition of the body in death'. *Obstruction* certainly refers to something impeding the movement of blood in *Twelfth Night* 3.4.19–20 ('This does make some obstruction in the blood, this cross-gartering'), but in the present context of *lie* and *rot* the phrase may refer to the constriction caused by pressure of earth on the buried corpse.

123 **sensible** primarily in *OED*'s sense 7, 'endowed with the faculty of sensation', but also with hints of senses 8, 'having acute powers of sensation; sensitive' and 1, 'perceptible by the senses'
warm motion a brilliant synecdoche for the living human body, warm-blooded and capable of movement

124 **kneaded** In view of *delighted* (see next note), Abbott, 375, seems right in suggesting that *kneaded* means 'kneadable' rather than 'which has been kneaded'; one of the many horrors of death is that the shapely human body turns into a formless clay-like substance which it is possible to manipulate at will.
delighted having the capacity to experience delight or give it to others. For the use of the suffix *-ed* in this sense see G. V. Smithers, *Shakespeare Survey 23* (Cambridge, 1970), p. 31. *OED* compares a quotation from 1600 given under *delightful*, 2, 'too chilling a doctrine for our delightful dispositions'. For *unshunned* as meaning 'unshunnable' see l. 326 below.

125–31 **To bathe ... horrible** This passage draws on a long and complex tradition, of mixed biblical, classical, and patristic origin, describing the pains of the afterworld. For a brief account of this tradition see J. E. Hankins, *Backgrounds of*

Shakespeare's Thought (Hamden, 1978), pp. 49–60.

125 **fiery floods** perhaps an allusion to the 'lake of fire, burning with brimstone' given as a place of punishment in Revelation 19: 20, or to the burning river Phlegethon, described in Virgil's *Aeneid* 6.550–1, and mentioned as a place of torture for 'damned ghost[s]' in Spenser's *Faerie Queene* 2.6.50.

126 **thrilling** piercing, causing shivering or shuddering (*OED thrilling ppl. a.* 1b)
thick-ribbèd piled or compressed into ridges; apparently a Shakespearian coinage, though the phrase 'ribs of ice' can be found in Jonson's *Catiline* 1.1.214, and in l. 30 of a poem, 'The Expostulation' ('To make the doubt clear that no woman's true ...'), printed as Donne's in 1633 and as Jonson's in 1640

127–9 **To be imprisoned ... world** Compare 'Blow me about in winds', *Othello* 5.2.286. The concept may derive ultimately from a passage in Cicero's *Dream of Scipio*, a work which survived only as quoted by Macrobius, 'For the souls of those who have given themselves up to the pleasures of the body, and have become as it were the slaves of the body, and who at the instigation of desires subservient to pleasure have broken the laws of gods and men, when they have left their bodies fly around the earth itself, and do not return to this place except after many ages of torment' (trans. D. S. Brewer in his edition of Chaucer's *The Parlement of Foulys*, 1972, p. 137). Cicero influenced ll. 78–84 of Chaucer's poem, and possibly Dante's description of the carnal sinners continually blown about by a stormy wind, *Inferno* 5.28–45.

127 **viewless** invisible

129 **pendent** hanging or floating unsupported in space

Of those that lawless and incertain thought   130
Imagine howling—'tis too horrible.
The weariest and most loathèd worldly life
That age, ache, penury, and imprisonment
Can lay on nature is a paradise
To what we fear of death.

ISABELLA   Alas, alas!

CLAUDIO

Sweet sister, let me live.
What sin you do to save a brother's life,
Nature dispenses with the deed so far
That it becomes a virtue.

ISABELLA   O you beast!
O faithless coward, O dishonest wretch!   140
Wilt thou be made a man out of my vice?
Is't not a kind of incest to take life
From thine own sister's shame? What should I think?
Heaven shield my mother played my father fair,

---

133 penury] F2; periury F

130–1 **those ... howling** Mary Lascelles
(*Shakespeare's Measure for Measure*,
1953, p. 166) has argued that the
thought is *lawless* because those howling
are undergoing the pains of purgatory,
and Protestantism explicitly repudiated
the doctrine of purgatory. But
Shakespeare uses *howling* to refer to the
cries of the damned in *Romeo* 3.3.47–8
('O friar, the damnèd use that word in
hell.|Howling attends it') and *Hamlet*
5.1.237. The parallels quoted above suggest that Claudio is consistently referring
to the pains of damned souls, and *worse
than worst* implies that ll. 130–1 form a
climax to this list of punishments and
refer to the most horrible agonies of hell.
Lawless may mean 'uncontrolled, freely
speculating' rather than 'illegal': the
frenzied imaginations of those about to
die lead them to think that they can hear
the screams of the damned souls who are
being actively tortured by devils.

130 **incertain** uncertain, wavering

133 **ache** used collectively in its strongest
and widest sense: all the various kinds of
pain suffered by the body

134 **nature** here meaning 'the vital or physical powers of man' (*OED* 6), whereas at
l. 138 below it means 'natural feeling or

affection' (9e) or possibly the personified
figure of nature (11b), acting as a kind of
judge

135 **To** compared to

138 **dispenses with** excuses, pardons

139 **beast** clearly enough a term of abuse,
but it should perhaps be noted that in
Shakespeare *beast* is often contrasted
with *man*, implying behaviour lacking
the rational control that distinguishes
men from beasts ('a beast that wants
discourse of reason', *Hamlet* 1.2.150)

140 **faithless** treacherous
dishonest (*a*) dishonourable, shameful;
(*b*) lewd

141 **made a man** The primary meaning
seems to be 'given good fortune or prosperity' (*OED man sb.*[1] 7); compare *All is
True* (*Henry VIII*) 5.4.64, 'Thou hast
made me now a man'. But in this context
made can mean 'procreated' (as in
Richard II 1.2.22–4, 'That bed, that
womb,|That mettle, that self mould that
fashioned thee,|Made him a man'), so
there is a hint that Angelo would give
Claudio life by begetting him on his sister.

144 **shield** This can mean both 'forbid' and
'protect' (as at 5.1.119), but the former
gives a much more powerful and gram-
matically consistent reading: 'Heaven

For such a warpèd slip of wilderness
Ne'er issued from his blood. Take my defiance,
Die, perish! Might but my bending down
Reprieve thee from thy fate, it should proceed.
I'll pray a thousand prayers for thy death,
No word to save thee.   150

CLAUDIO

Nay, hear me, Isabel—

ISABELLA   O fie, fie, fie!
Thy sin's not accidental, but a trade.
Mercy to thee would prove itself a bawd,
'Tis best that thou diest quickly.

CLAUDIO

O hear me, Isabella—
        Enter Duke as a Friar

DUKE Vouchsafe a word, young sister, but one word.

ISABELLA What is your will?

DUKE Might you dispense with your leisure, I would by
and by have some speech with you. The satisfaction I
would require is likewise your own benefit.   160

155.1 *Enter ... Friar*] F2 (*Duke steps in*); *not in* F

forbid that my mother was faithful to my
father when you were conceived, because you cannot possibly be his true
issue'. In the intensity of her revulsion
Isabella would like to be able to regard
her brother as a bastard.

144 **fair** according to the rules, without
cheating; but a sexual implication is
clearly present (compare the context of
play false in *Errors* 2.2.145, where it
clearly means 'commit adultery')

145 **warpèd slip of wilderness** The phrase
consistently works on two levels, the
horticultural and moral: *warped* can be
applied to a plant growing in a contorted
way, or to a morally distorted person
('thy warped soul', Dekker, *Satiromastix*
4.3.225); *slip* is a shoot or cutting from a
plant, or a scion or descendant ('Brave
slip, sprung from the great Andronicus',
Titus 5.1.9); *wilderness* can refer to a
plant growing wild, or to wildness of
character, licentiousness (*OED* 5b, only
quotation given).

146 **Take my defiance** *OED* glosses the
phrase as a declaration of aversion or

contempt (*defiance* 5, only quotation), but
it could have its stronger military sense of
a declaration of war ('Then take my
king's defiance from my mouth', *K. John*
1.1.21); Isabella no longer regards him
as her brother and proclaims her open
enmity to him.

152 **accidental** happening by chance, occasional
trade 'habitual practice' or possibly even
'profession, livelihood', which would
give a powerful irony: 'you're trying to
make a living by illicit sin'

153 **prove itself** turn out to be (in that it
would allow him to continue sinning).
Under *bawd sb.*[1], sense b, *OED* quotes a
parallel from 1607: 'The mercy of God ...
is made ... a bawd to all manner of
ungodliness'; compare also *Richard II*
5.3.65, 'So shall my virtue be his vice's
bawd'.

156 **Vouchsafe** grant
158 **dispense with** forgo, do without
158–9 **by and by** The phrase could mean
'immediately' or 'before long, soon';
probably the latter is intended.

159–60 **The satisfaction ... benefit** You

157

ISABELLA I have no superfluous leisure, my stay must be
    stolen out of other affairs; but I will attend you a while.
DUKE (*taking Claudio aside*) Son, I have overheard what
    hath passed between you and your sister. Angelo had
    never the purpose to corrupt her; only he hath made an
    assay of her virtue, to practise his judgement with the
    disposition of natures. She, having the truth of honour
    in her, hath made him that gracious denial which he is
    most glad to receive. I am confessor to Angelo, and I
    know this to be true; therefore prepare yourself to   170
    death. Do not satisfy your resolution with hopes that are
    fallible: tomorrow you must die. Go to your knees, and
    make ready.
CLAUDIO Let me ask my sister pardon. I am so out of love
    with life that I will sue to be rid of it.
DUKE Hold you there. Farewell. (*Exit Claudio*) Provost, a
    word with you.
        Enter Provost
PROVOST What's your will, father?
DUKE That now you are come, you will be gone. Leave me

163 *taking ... aside*] OXFORD; *not in* F   171 satisfy] F; falsify HANMER   176 *Exit Claudio*]
CAPELL; *not in* F; *Exit* F2 (*after l.* 175)   177.1 *Enter Provost*] DYCE; *not in* F

would be doing a favour to yourself as
well as me by granting my request

162 **attend** This could mean 'listen to', but is
    more likely in the context to mean 'wait
    for'.
165 **only he hath** he has merely
166 **assay** trial, test. In Whetstone's *Heptam-
    eron* (1582, N3ᵛ), Cassandra, the equiva-
    lent of Isabella, imagines when Promos
    first tries to seduce her that he 'used this
    speech but to try her behaviour'.
166–7 **practise ... natures** ?exercise his skill
    as a judge of human nature
167 **truth** in *OED*'s sense 4, 'honesty, integ-
    rity'; cf. l. 209 below
168 **gracious** (*a*) righteous, full of grace; (*b*)
    happy, fortunate
169 **I am confessor to Angelo** clearly a lie
    (and at 4.3.126 he pretends that another
    friar, unnamed, is Angelo's confessor.
    But his previous remarks about Angelo
    are also untrue; the Duke puts things in
    this way partly in an attempt to restore
    harmonious relations between brother
    and sister (because Claudio will no longer

believe that Isabella is refusing to save his
life) and partly because he feels, with
some justification, that it would be unwise at this stage to give Claudio the
impression that a solution has been
found to his problems.

171 **satisfy your resolution** ?maintain your
    firmness of mind, comfort yourself
174 **Let ... pardon** F makes no provision of
    any kind for Claudio to do this, but the
    director can let him do so (see Introduc-
    tion, p. 30). In Peter Brook's Stratford
    production of 1950 the Duke shook his
    head in refusal, and in Adrian Noble's
    Stratford production of 1983 Claudio
    tried to approach his sister but was pulled
    away by prison guards.
176 **Hold you there** remain in that state of
    mind
179 **now ... gone** Critics dislike this little
    touch (Lever calls it 'deliberately fatu-
    ous'). But it may be self-consciously delib-
    erate, part of the mannered and antitheti-
    cal prose-style of this section of the scene.
    As a stage-manœuvre it is not absurd: the
    Duke has not yet decided to take the

a while with the maid. My mind promises with my habit   180
no loss shall touch her by my company.

PROVOST In good time.   *Exit*

DUKE The hand that hath made you fair hath made you
good. The goodness that is cheap in beauty makes
beauty brief in goodness, but grace, being the soul of
your complexion, shall keep the body of it ever fair.
The assault that Angelo hath made to you, fortune hath
conveyed to my understanding; and but that frailty
hath examples for his falling, I should wonder at
Angelo. How will you do to content this substitute, and 190
to save your brother?

ISABELLA I am now going to resolve him. I had rather my
brother die by the law than my son should be un-
lawfully born. But O, how much is the good Duke
deceived in Angelo! If ever he return, and I can speak
to him, I will open my lips in vain, or discover his
government.

DUKE That shall not be much amiss. Yet, as the matter
now stands, he will avoid your accusation: he made

Provost into his confidence, and does not
want him to overhear the arrangement
with Isabella.

180 **My mind ... habit** both my inward
intention and outward appearance as a
friar give assurance that

181 **touch** injure, harm

182 **In good time** a stock phrase expressing
approbation or agreement; roughly
equivalent to 'certainly' or 'very well'.
According to *OED* (*time sb.* 6c, section d)
the phrase commonly has a note of irony
or incredulity, but that can hardly be
present here.

183–4 **The hand ... good** a contradiction of
the proverb, 'Beauty and chastity seldom
meet' (Tilley B163), as in *As You Like It*
1.2.36–7, 'those that she [Fortune]
makes fair she scarce makes honest'

184–5 **The goodness ... goodness** The exact
nature of the antithesis is not fully clear.
Goodness may mean both 'moral virtue'
and 'high quality, excellence', and *cheap*
in Shakespeare commonly means 'held
cheap, despised'. If so, the meaning
would be in effect 'if a beautiful woman
despises virtue her beauty will prove to be

of poor quality and not long-lasting'.

185 **grace** moral excellence implanted by
God
soul essential, fundamental quality
('brevity is the soul of wit', *Hamlet*
2.2.91)

186 **complexion** possibly with a wider sense
than in l. 24 above: 'the distinctive com-
bination of qualities granted you at your
creation'

187 **assault** disreputable attack on a woman's chastity, as in *Cymbeline* 1.4.59,
1.6.151, and 3.2.8

188–9 **frailty ... falling** in the records of
frailty we can find other examples of
Angelo's kind of behaviour. There is no
need to make this a specific allusion to the
fall of the angels, or of Adam.

190 **substitute** someone exercising deputed
authority; not necessarily contemptuous
in tone (in *Richard II* 1.2.37–8, the king is
described as 'God's substitute, | His deputy
appointed in his sight')

192 **resolve** answer

196 **discover** reveal, expose

197 **government** 'personal moral conduct'
(*OED* 2b) as well as 'political rule' (1a)

199 **avoid** make void, refute (a legal term)

trial of you only. Therefore fasten your ear on my   200
advisings; to the love I have in doing good a remedy
presents itself. I do make myself believe that you may
most uprighteously do a poor wronged lady a merited
benefit, redeem your brother from the angry law, do no
stain to your own gracious person, and much please the
absent Duke, if peradventure he shall ever return to
have hearing of this business.

ISABELLA Let me hear you speak farther. I have spirit to do
anything that appears not foul in the truth of my spirit.

DUKE Virtue is bold, and goodness never fearful. Have you   210
not heard speak of Mariana, the sister of Frederick, the
great soldier, who miscarried at sea?

ISABELLA I have heard of the lady, and good words went
with her name.

DUKE She should this Angelo have married; was affianced
to her oath, and the nuptial appointed. Between which
time of the contract and limit of the solemnity, her
brother Frederick was wrecked at sea, having in that
perished vessel the dowry of his sister. But mark how
heavily this befell to the poor gentlewoman. There she   220
lost a noble and renowned brother, in his love toward
her ever most kind and natural; with him, the portion
and sinew of her fortune, her marriage dowry; with

201 advisings; ... good ∧] POPE; aduisings, ... good; F   216 oath] F; by oath F2

202 **do make myself believe** have persuaded
myself, am convinced
203 **uprighteously** apparently a Shakespearian coinage not found elsewhere, a
mixture of 'uprightly' and 'righteously'
208–9 **spirit ... spirit** courage ... soul
210 **Virtue is bold** a variant on the proverb
'Innocence is bold' (Tilley I82), as in *First
Part of the Contention* (*2 Henry VI*)
4.4.58–9
212 **miscarried** died by accident
215 **She** used as equivalent to 'her' (a common construction; see *OED she* 4a, and
Abbott 211, and compare 5.1.528). The
nominative form is used because
Shakespeare wants it to act as subject to
the next phrase in the sentence.
215–16 **affianced to her oath** Eccles regards
this as nonsense, and accepts F2's emendation of *oath* to *by oath* (with Angelo as
subject). But *affianced* may mean

'pledged' (*OED affiance v.* 1), or the phrase
may be a justifiable licence: 'she was
betrothed to her promise, which she still
regards as valid, not to Angelo who
abandoned her'. The construction may
be similar to 'bestowed her on her own
lamentation' (i.e. married her to her
sorrow) at ll. 229–30.
216 **nuptial appointed** wedding arranged
217 **limit** appointed time (the earliest example quoted in *OED* 2f, but found also in
Richard III 3.3.7, and *Richard II* 1.3.145)
220 **heavily** grievously, painfully
222 **natural** full of brotherly affection
portion This commonly means 'dowry,
marriage portion', but as *dowry* is used in
the next line it probably means 'her share
of the family estate' (*OED* 2).
223 **sinew** main strength, most powerful
factor

both, her combinate husband, this well-seeming Angelo.

ISABELLA Can this be so? Did Angelo so leave her?

DUKE Left her in her tears, and dried not one of them with his comfort; swallowed his vows whole, pretending in her discoveries of dishonour; in few, bestowed her on her own lamentation, which she yet wears for   230
his sake, and he, a marble to her tears, is washed with them but relents not.

ISABELLA What a merit were it in death to take this poor maid from the world! What corruption in this life, that it will let this man live! But how out of this can she avail?

DUKE It is a rupture that you may easily heal, and the cure of it not only saves your brother, but keeps you from dishonour in doing it.

ISABELLA Show me how, good father.   240

DUKE This forenamed maid hath yet in her the continuance of her first affection. His unjust unkindness, that in all reason should have quenched her love, hath, like an impediment in the current, made it more violent and unruly. Go you to Angelo, answer his requiring with a plausible obedience, agree with his demands to the

---

224 **combinate** a rare and puzzling word; in the only other Elizabethan usage recorded in *OED* it is clearly equivalent to 'combined'. *OED* rather cautiously agrees with Johnson in glossing it here as 'betrothed, promised, settled by contract', though in a different context it might have suggested that Angelo had actually married Mariana.
well-seeming with a speciously good appearance; also used in *Romeo* 1.1.176

228 **swallowed** retracted (compare the modern usage 'to swallow one's words')
whole without any attempt to chew them, without hesitation

228–9 **pretending ... dishonour** falsely alleging that she had been found out in sexual misconduct. Clearly a hypocritical excuse for Angelo to break off his contract, though the real reason was financial. See 5.1.218–23.

229 **in few** in few words, in short

229–30 **bestowed ... lamentation** married her to her grief

230 **wears** possibly with a double meaning:

(*a*) is dressed in (as though she were wearing mourning); (*b*) carries about in her heart (compare *Hamlet* 3.2.70–1, 'I will wear him | In my heart's core, ay, in my heart of heart')

231 **a marble** hard, unresponsive

233 **What ... in death** how praiseworthy death would be

234 **What ... life** how corrupt life is

236 **avail** benefit herself

242 **unjust** faithless, dishonest

243–5 **like an impediment ... unruly** Compare *Two Gentlemen* 2.7.25–6, 'The current that with gentle murmur glides, | Thou know'st, being stopped, impatiently doth rage'; a form of the proverb, 'The stream stopped swells the higher' (Tilley S929).

245 **requiring** request, demand

246 **plausible** affable, ingratiating (*OED* 2b); the word at the time did not necessarily imply 'specious, deceptive', but the context seems to suggest it

246–7 **to the point** to the smallest detail

point. Only refer yourself to this advantage: first, that
your stay with him may not be long; that the place may
have all shadow and silence in it; and the time answer
to convenience. This being granted in course, and now   250
follows all: we shall advise this wronged maid to stead
up your appointment, go in your place. If the encounter
acknowledge itself hereafter, it may compel him to her
recompense; and here, by this is your brother saved,
your honour untainted, the poor Mariana advantaged,
and the corrupt deputy scaled. The maid will I frame
and make fit for his attempt; if you think well to carry
this as you may, the doubleness of the benefit defends
the deceit from reproof. What think you of it?

ISABELLA The image of it gives me content already, and I   260
trust it will grow to a most prosperous perfection.

DUKE It lies much in your holding up. Haste you speedily
to Angelo; if for this night he entreat you to his bed,
give him promise of satisfaction. I will presently to Saint

248–9 place ... time] LEVER; time ... place F

247 **refer** commit, entrust (perhaps in this
    context meaning 'throw yourself on his
    mercy, ask him to grant you these fa-
    vourable circumstances')
248–9 **place ... time** This transposition of F,
    suggested by Ridley, improves the sense:
    shadow and silence are more appropriate
    to a place, and Isabella could more rea-
    sonably demand that the time should be
    convenient to her than the place. A
    similar shift occurred at l. 52 above,
    though the two passages were set by
    different compositors.
249–50 **answer to convenience** suit Isabel-
    la's convenience
250 **in course** in due course
251–2 **stead up** fulfil, go instead of someone
    else (*OED v.* 3, only example quoted)
252 **encounter** See l. 85 n. above.
253 **acknowledge itself** reveal itself, become
    publicly known (perhaps by Mariana
    becoming pregnant)
253–4 **to her recompense** to make repara-
    tion or compensation to her
255 **advantaged** benefited
256 **scaled** weighed as in scales; com-
    pare *Coriolanus* 2.3.249, 'Scaling his
    present bearing with his past'. There
    may be an allusion to Daniel 5: 27,
    'thou art weighed in the balance and

art found too light'.
    frame direct, put in the right frame of
    mind
257 **fit** prepared, ready
    attempt attack on her honour (*OED* 3b)
    think well consider it a good idea
257–8 **carry this as you may** manage this
    affair as skilfully as you can
258 **doubleness** to the two women, Isabella
    and Mariana. The word is ambiguous
    ('twofold quality' and 'duplicity, deceit-
    fulness') and a hint of the latter meaning
    is perhaps also present ('a beneficial
    trickery').
260 **image** idea, description by the Duke
261 **perfection** completion, fulfilment
262 **It lies ... up** the success of the trick
    largely depends on your skill in perform-
    ing it
    Haste you speedily a tautology, but one
    which is common in Shakespeare: 'all
    the speedy haste you may', *Richard III*
    3.1.60; 'all swift haste', *Troilus* 1.1.116;
    'all swift speed', *Richard II* 5.1.54. See
    also 4.1.7 and 4.2.110 n.
264 **satisfaction** gratification, the granting
    of his wishes
    presently immediately
264–5 **Saint Luke's** 'Saint Luke's church' is
    mentioned in *Shrew* 4.5.15.

Luke's; there at the moated grange resides this dejected
Mariana. At that place call upon me, and dispatch with
Angelo, that it may be quickly.

ISABELLA I thank you for this comfort. Fare you well, good
father.   *Exit*

Enter Elbow and Officers with Pompey

ELBOW Nay, if there be no remedy for it, but that you will   270
needs buy and sell men and women like beasts, we shall
have all the world drink brown and white bastard.

DUKE O heavens, what stuff is here?

POMPEY 'Twas never merry world since of two usuries the
merriest was put down, and the worser allowed by order
of law a furred gown to keep him warm—and furred

269.1 *Enter ... Pompey*] *Enter Elbow, Clowne, Officers.* F   276 law ∧] CAPELL; Law; F

265 **moated grange** 'an outlying farm-house
with barns, etc. belonging to a religious
establishment' (*OED grange* 2b); *moated*
could mean (*a*) surrounded by a moat, or
(*b*) equipped with a fish-pond (*OED moat
sb.*¹ 2). The quotations given in *OED* and
Eccles indicate that a grange was typi-
cally thought of as a lonely and isolated
place: Mariana is nursing her grief in
seclusion. If she has no money, it is
possible that she has been given lodging
at the grange as a charity by a religious
institution; she leaves it to get married,
so that her destiny is somewhat like
Isabella's.

dejected (*a*) cast down by fortune; (*b*)
low-spirited, melancholy

266 **dispatch** make arrangements rapidly

269.1 **Enter ...** Most later editors follow
Pope in indicating a fresh scene at this
point, on the assumption that the action
has now moved from the inside to the
outside of the prison. But the setting
could be at some place inside the prison
where an interview could take place, and
also where fresh prisoners could be
brought in. (It has not been in Claudio's
cell, because he goes out at l. 176.) It is
true that Lucio casually wanders in at
l. 307, but he does so again at 4.3.146,
another prison scene. The Duke remains
on stage to provide linkage, and all recent
productions have played Act 3 in one
continuous sweep without causing any
problems to the audience.

272 **brown and white bastard** a sweet Spanish wine, but with an obvious play of

meaning: (*a*) red and white wine; (*b*)
dark and fair-skinned illegitimate children

273 **stuff** nonsense, rubbish

274 **'Twas never merry world since** the
world ceased to be a cheerful place as
soon as (a stock phrase; see *OED merry
adj.* 1b, and Tilley/Dent W878.1)
two usuries (*a*) prostitution (compare
?Tourneur, *The Revenger's Tragedy*
4.4.102–3, 'To prostitute my breast to
the duke's son, | And put myself to com-
mon usury'); (*b*) money-lending

275 **merriest** most enjoyable
put down suppressed, abolished

275–6 **allowed ... warm** F has a semicolon
after *law* which most editors have removed. Lever retains it on the grounds
that 'no legal regulation ever mentioned
such a gown for usurers'. But Pompey is
not a legal historian, and his point is
made symbolically: the bawds and
whores are punished, but the usurer is
legally condoned, so that he becomes rich
and wears expensive clothing.
order of law A statute of 1570 restricted
permissible interest on loans to 10 per
cent; some moralists were distressed by
this because they felt that usury should
be banned completely. There may also be
an allusion to the abolition in 1603 of the
sumptuary laws controlling types of
clothing worn by different classes of
society, with the result that anyone who
could afford to do so could wear ostenta-
tiously rich clothing.

with fox on lambskins too, to signify that craft, being
richer than innocency, stands for the facing.

ELBOW Come your way, sir. Bless you, good father friar.

DUKE And you, good brother father. What offence hath   280
this man made you, sir?

ELBOW Marry, sir, he hath offended the law; and, sir, we
take him to be a thief too, sir, for we have found upon
him, sir, a strange picklock, which we have sent to the
deputy.

DUKE

Fie, sirrah, a bawd, a wicked bawd!
The evil that thou causest to be done,
That is thy means to live. Do thou but think
What 'tis to cram a maw, or clothe a back
From such a filthy vice; say to thyself,   290
From their abominable and beastly touches
I drink, I eat, array myself, and live.
Canst thou believe thy living is a life,
So stinkingly depending? Go mend, go mend.

277 on] RANN; and F   292 eat, array] THEOBALD; eate away F

277 **fox** fox-fur (but obviously invoking the
unscrupulous cunning traditionally associated with the animal). There is a
reference to 'fox-furred usurers' in a little
pamphlet of 1604, *The Meeting of Gallants
at an Ordinary*, C4 (*STC* 17781) and
similar phrases occur elsewhere.
craft craftiness, deceit

278 **richer** (*a*) wealthier; (*b*) a costlier fabric
stands for the facing *facing* is trimming on
the outside of a garment, and *stands for*
presumably means 'represents, acts as'. If
so, the phrase could imply that the usurer
presents a crafty face to the world. But
there may be a joke here which is now
lost; compare Herrick's epigram 'Upon
Crab': 'Crab faces gowns with sundry
furs; 'tis known, | He keeps the fox-fur for
to face his own'.

279 **Come your way** come on

279–80 **father friar … brother father** *friar*
means 'brother', so the Duke is returning
Elbow's absurd form of address to him.

282 **he hath offended the law** Elbow is
pompous and literal-minded: 'he has
offended the law, not me'.

284 **picklock** Elbow naïvely assumes that
Pompey is a thief or burglar, but as he is a

bawd the locks he picks are those on
chastity belts intended to prevent women
from being unfaithful (so editors assert;
lock meaning 'chastity belt' occurs in
Jonson's *Volpone* 2.5.57, and Middleton's
A Chaste Maid in Cheapside 4.4.4–5, but
no parallel has yet been found for *picklock*
in this specific sense).

286 **sirrah** a contemptuous form of address

289 **maw** stomach, belly

291 **abominable** offensive, loathsome. The
word is spelt *abhominable* in F; according
to *OED* this is the normal spelling
throughout the First Folio, and reflects
what was mistakenly thought to be the
etymology of the word, *ab homine*, 'away
from man, inhuman'.
touches sexual contacts; see 5.1.141 n.
and compare *Othello* 4.2.87, 'foul unlawful touch'

292 **array** dress, clothe. The emendation is
supported by l. 289 above, and compare
Jonson, Epigram 12, 'On Lieutenant
Shift', ll. 5–6: 'By that one spell he lives,
eats, drinks, arrays | Himself'.

293 **thy living is a life** your livelihood is an
admirable way of life

294 **depending** (*a*) relying for maintenance

POMPEY Indeed it does stink in some sort, sir, but yet, sir, I
would prove—

DUKE

Nay, if the devil have given thee proofs for sin,
Thou wilt prove his. Take him to prison, officer.
Correction and instruction must both work
Ere this rude beast will profit.   300

ELBOW He must before the deputy, sir, he has given him
warning. The deputy cannot abide a whoremaster; if he
be a whoremonger and comes before him, he were as
good go a mile on his errand.

DUKE

That we were all, as some would seem to be,
Free from our faults, as faults from seeming free!

ELBOW His neck will come to your waist—a cord, sir.

          Enter Lucio

POMPEY I spy comfort, I cry bail! Here's a gentleman, and
a friend of mine.

LUCIO How now, noble Pompey? What, at the wheels of   310

306 Free from] F2 ; From F   307.1 *Enter Lucio*] ALEXANDER ; *after l.* 306 *in* F

on such a sordid occupation; (*b*) dependent, servile

294 **mend** reform yourself, behave better

296–8 **prove ... prove** prove by argument
... turn out to be (a prey to the devil). The
Duke picks up Pompey's word and gives it
a different meaning.

297 **proofs for sin** There may be a connection with the kind of idea found in
Donne's *The Progress of the Soul*, l. 118,
'Arguing is heretic's game': a wish to
argue in defence of evil is in itself a proof
of corruption.

299 **Correction** punishment, probably in the
form of corporal punishment, a whipping
work operate, take effect

300 **rude** uncivilized, barbarous

302–3 **whoremaster ... whoremonger** Elbow appears to be making a distinction,
but according to *OED* both words mean
'one who has dealings with whores,
fornicator'.

303–4 **he were ... errand** a proverbial
phrase ('I will go twenty miles on your
errand first', Tilley M927), but its exact
implications are not fully clear, and editors gloss it in various ways. Perhaps it
means 'it would be better for him to be

doing something else (because if he
comes up before Angelo he will be
severely punished)'.

305–6 **That ... seeming free** a difficult couplet. As it follows Elbow's simple-minded
comparison of the whoremaster Pompey
and the rigidly virtuous Angelo, Dover
Wilson is probably right in arguing that
the Duke contrasts Angelo's hypocrisy in
virtue with Pompey's honesty in sin:
'would that all men were as free from sin
as Angelo seems, or as Pompey is free
from hypocrisy'.

306 **Free from** F2's emendation does not
radically alter the sense, but it does
improve the rhythm, which ought to be
regular in a rhyming couplet of this type.
from seeming free an inversion: free from
'seeming' or hypocrisy

307 **come to** arrive at the condition of (in
having a cord or rope round it)
cord (*a*) girdle worn by the Duke round
his friar's robes; (*b*) hangman's rope

308 **cry** entreat, call for

310–11 **at the wheels of Caesar** in disgrace,
being led as a prisoner behind Caesar's
chariot in a triumphal procession. Compare 2.1.236–7.

Caesar? Art thou led in triumph? What, is there none of
Pygmalion's images newly-made woman to be had now
for putting the hand in the pocket and extracting
clutched? What reply, ha? What sayst thou to this
tune, matter, and method? Is't not drowned i' the last
rain, ha? What sayst thou, trot? Is the world as it was,
man? Which is the way? Is it sad, and few words? Or
how? The trick of it?

DUKE Still thus and thus; still worse!

LUCIO How doth my dear morsel, thy mistress? Procures   320
she still, ha?

POMPEY Troth, sir, she hath eaten up all her beef, and she
is herself in the tub.

313 extracting] F; extracting it ROWE

312 **Pygmalion's   images   newly-made
woman** beautiful young women whose
looks are so unspoiled that they appear to
have come into existence only recently
(and would thus be very successful as
prostitutes). The story of Pygmalion's
statue transformed into a live woman by
Venus is told in Ovid's *Metamorphoses*,
Book 10.

312–14 **to be had ... clutched** perhaps an
elaborate way of saying 'to be had for
money': 'to be obtained by putting your
hand in your pocket and taking it out
clutching money'

313 **extracting** Many editors have followed
Rowe in inserting *it* after *extracting*; this
clarifies the sense, but there are various
circumstances in which Shakespeare
does not use *it* where we should expect it
in modern English (Abbott 404) and this
may well be one of them.

315 **tune, matter, and method** Some earlier
editors asserted that at *tune* Lucio should
chink a purseful of money. But the last
four lines of Lucio's speech seem to be
basically an extravagant and repetitive
way of saying 'What have you got to say
for yourself?', and these three terms can
all have a rhetorical significance: *tune* is
the style or 'tone' of a discourse, *matter* its
subject-matter, and *method* its order or
disposition. Lucio's sentence would thus
mean 'What do you reply to my way of
putting it?'

315–16 **Is't not ... rain** This sounds a
colloquial saying, but no exact parallel
has yet been discovered. Probably the *it* of
Is't refers to Pompey's answer, and

drowned i' the last rain may mean 'lost,
destroyed, as farm animals are drowned
when heavy rain causes floods'. The
ward in Middleton's *Women Beware
Women* 3.3.154–5 refers to a 'ballad ...
of the lamentable drowning of fat sheep
and oxen'.

316 **trot** elsewhere applied to an ugly old
woman, a hag, as in *Shrew* 1.2.78–9, 'an
old trot with ne'er a tooth in her head'
Is the world as it was perhaps another
way of saying 'How goes the world with
thee?', *Richard III* 3.2.92, but obviously a
piece of brutal mockery

317 **Which is the way?** How are you going
to answer me?
sad, and few words sadly and briefly
(because you are unhappy)

318 **trick** way, manner

319 **thus and thus** equivalent to 'in minute
detail'; see *OED thus adv.* 1e and Tilley/
Dent TT13. The Duke's speech might be
glossed as 'he keeps on spinning out his
words, getting steadily more spiteful'.

320 **morsel** titbit, here applied to a woman,
as in *Antony* 1.5.30–1, 'I was | A morsel
for a monarch'

322 **eaten up all her beef** (*a*) eaten up her
supplies of salted beef; (*b*) used up or
worn out another kind of flesh, the
prostitutes in her establishment

323 **tub** (*a*) the barrel in which beef is stored;
(*b*) the 'powdering-tub' of *Henry V*
2.1.73, used for treating venereal disease
with the fumes of cinnabar or mercuric
sulphide. The engraved title-page of *Cornelianum Dolium*, a Latin comedy by
'T. R.' published in 1638, shows a man

LUCIO Why, 'tis good; it is the right of it; it must be so.
Ever your fresh whore and your powdered bawd, an
unshunned consequence; it must be so. Art going to
prison, Pompey?

POMPEY Yes, faith, sir.

LUCIO Why, 'tis not amiss, Pompey. Farewell. Go say I
sent thee thither. For debt, Pompey, or how?   330

ELBOW For being a bawd, for being a bawd.

LUCIO Well, then, imprison him. If imprisonment be the
due of a bawd, why, 'tis his right. Bawd is he doubtless,
and of antiquity too, bawd-born. Farewell, good Pompey. Commend me to the prison, Pompey. You will turn
good husband now, Pompey, you will keep the house.

POMPEY I hope, sir, your good worship will be my bail.

LUCIO No indeed will I not, Pompey, it is not the wear. I
will pray, Pompey, to increase your bondage; if you
take it not patiently, why, your mettle is the more.   340
Adieu, trusty Pompey. Bless you, friar.

DUKE And you.

LUCIO Does Bridget paint still, Pompey, ha?

ELBOW (*to Pompey*) Come your ways, sir, come.

POMPEY (*to Lucio*) You will not bail me then, sir?

339–40 bondage; ... patiently,] THEOBALD; bondage ∧ ... patiently: F

standing in a large wooden tub to
undergo this treatment (see the Introduction p. 10).

325 **Ever ... bawd** the healthy young prostitute always turns into the diseased elderly bawd
powdered with a play on words: (*a*)
preserved with salt (contrasted with
fresh, as with fresh or salted meat); (*b*)
undergoing treatment for venereal
disease; (*c*) wearing cosmetics

326 **unshunned** unshunnable, unavoidable
(for the grammatical form compare
kneaded and *delighted*, l. 124 n. above)

329–30 **say I sent thee thither** This could
imply that Lucio informed on Pompey to
get a reward (see ll. 455–6 below), or it
may refer to Lucio's refusal to supply
Pompey with bail.

330 **For debt** a spiteful touch; Lucio knows
perfectly well why Pompey is going to
prison

334 **of antiquity** for many years
bawd-born probably 'son of a bawd', and
hence born into his profession (only use
in Shakespeare; not recorded in *OED*)

336 **good husband** *OED*, *husband* 5, gives
this as a stock phrase: 'one who manages
his affairs with skill and thrift; a saving,
frugal, or provident man'.
keep the house stay indoors (*OED house
sb.*[1] 17d); ostensibly a compliment ('you
will live quietly and economically') but
obviously an insult in the light of Pompey's imprisonment

338 **wear** current fashion

339 **bondage** in the most literal sense,
chains used to keep him a prisoner

340 **your mettle is the more** playing on the
common Elizabethan *mettle/metal* ambiguity: (*a*) you will show your courage
more clearly; (*b*) you will receive more
metal (in the form of shackles)

343 **paint** wear cosmetics

LUCIO Then, Pompey, nor now. What news abroad, friar,
   what news?
ELBOW Come your ways, sir, come.
LUCIO Go to kennel, Pompey, go.
                           Exeunt Elbow and Officers with Pompey
   What news, friar, of the Duke?   350
DUKE I know none; can you tell me of any?
LUCIO Some say he is with the Emperor of Russia; other
   some, he is in Rome; but where is he, think you?
DUKE I know not where, but wheresoever, I wish him
   well.
LUCIO It was a mad fantastical trick of him to steal from
   the state, and usurp the beggary he was never born to.
   Lord Angelo dukes it well in his absence, he puts
   transgression to't.
DUKE He does well in't.   360
LUCIO A little more lenity to lechery would do no harm in
   him. Something too crabbed that way, friar.
DUKE It is too general a vice, and severity must cure it.
LUCIO Yes, in good sooth, the vice is of a great kindred, it
   is well allied; but it is impossible to extirp it quite, friar,
   till eating and drinking be put down. They say this
   Angelo was not made by man and woman after this
   downright way of creation; is it true, think you?
DUKE How should he be made, then?
LUCIO Some report, a sea-maid spawned him. Some, that 370

349.1 *Exeunt ... Pompey*] ROWE; *not in* F; *Exeunt* F2

346 **Then ... nor now** a kind of play on *then*
      as (*a*) therefore, consequently, and (*b*) in
      the past
      What news abroad a stock phrase; com-
      pare l. 477 below, *Richard Duke of York* (3
      Henry VI) 2.1.95, and *Richard III* 1.1.135
      abroad current in the outside world
352–3 **other some** some others
356 **fantastical** fanciful, irrational
      steal from steal away from
357 **usurp the beggary** not an indication
      that Lucio sees through the Duke's dis-
      guise (if this was so, his exposure of the
      Duke at 5.1.352–6 would fall completely
      flat); he despises the Duke for leaving
      Vienna incognito, in a way quite un-
      worthy of his high birth
358 **dukes it** plays the part of the Duke
358–9 **puts transgression to't** harasses evil-
      doers, makes life difficult for them
361 **lenity** mildness
362 **crabbed** harsh, severe
364 **of a great kindred** belonging to a large
      family, having many relatives
365 **is well allied** has powerful allies and
      relations
      extirp extirpate, root out
367 **after** according to
368 **downright** straightforward, normal
370 **sea-maid** mermaid
      spawned used contemptuously for 'gave
      birth to'

he was begot between two stockfishes. But it is certain
that when he makes water his urine is congealed ice,
that I know to be true. And he is a motion generative,
that's infallible.

DUKE You are pleasant, sir, and speak apace.

LUCIO Why, what a ruthless thing is this in him, for the
rebellion of a codpiece to take away the life of a man!
Would the Duke that is absent have done this? Ere he
would have hanged a man for the getting a hundred
bastards, he would have paid for the nursing a   380
thousand. He had some feeling of the sport; he knew the
service, and that instructed him to mercy.

DUKE I never heard the absent Duke much detected for
women, he was not inclined that way.

LUCIO O sir, you are deceived.

DUKE 'Tis not possible.

LUCIO Who, not the Duke? Yes, your beggar of fifty; and
his use was to put a ducat in her clack-dish. The Duke
had crotchets in him. He would be drunk too, that let
me inform you.   390

DUKE You do him wrong, surely.

LUCIO Sir, I was an inward of his. A shy fellow was the
Duke, and I believe I know the cause of his withdrawing.

373 generative] F; ungenerative THEOBALD

371 **stockfishes** a name for cod and other
    fishes cured by splitting open and drying
    hard in the air without salt (*OED*); here
    the type of something cold and sexless
372 **congealed ice** The phrase seems tautolo-
    gous, but is perhaps part of Lucio's extra-
    vagance: 'it comes out as hard ice-pellets'.
373 **motion generative** sexless puppet as far
    as generation is concerned. Some editors
    emend *generative* to *ungenerative*, by
    analogy with *ungenitured* at l. 431 below.
374 **infallible** certain
375 **pleasant** facetious
    speak apace chatter idly
377 **codpiece** a bagged appendage to the
    front of the close-fitting hose or breeches
    worn by men from the 15th to the
    17th c.: often conspicuous and orna-
    mented (*OED*). Here equivalent to the
    male genitals.
381 **feeling of** feeling for, response to

382 **service** See 1.2.109 n.
383–4 **detected for women** accused of le-
    chery
387 **beggar of fifty** beggarwoman 50 years
    old
388 **use** habit, custom
    ducat gold coin issued by several coun-
    tries, of varying value
    clack-dish an alternative form of *clap-
    dish*, a wooden dish with a lid carried and
    clacked by beggars as an appeal for
    contributions. A sexual innuendo has
    been suggested, and Lever comments
    that 'the Duke's secret charities are made
    by Lucio into occasions for slander'.
389 **crotchets** whimsical fancies
392 **inward** intimate friend
    shy cautious, reserved. Compare 5.1.55,
    where it is applied to Angelo (these are
    Shakespeare's only uses of the word).
393–4 **withdrawing** departure

DUKE What, I prithee, might be the cause?

LUCIO No, pardon. 'Tis a secret must be locked within the
    teeth and the lips. But this I can let you understand: the
    greater file of the subject held the Duke to be wise.

DUKE Wise? Why, no question but he was.

LUCIO A very superficial, ignorant, unweighing fellow.   400

DUKE Either this is envy in you, folly, or mistaking. The
    very stream of his life, and the business he hath helmed,
    must upon a warranted need give him a better procla-
    mation. Let him be but testimonied in his own
    bringings-forth, and he shall appear to the envious a
    scholar, a statesman, and a soldier. Therefore you speak
    unskilfully, or if your knowledge be more, it is much
    darkened in your malice.

LUCIO Sir, I know him and I love him.

DUKE Love talks with better knowledge, and knowledge   410
    with dearer love.

LUCIO Come, sir, I know what I know.

DUKE I can hardly believe that, since you know not what
    you speak. But if ever the Duke return, as our prayers are
    he may, let me desire you to make your answer before
    him. If it be honest you have spoke, you have courage to
    maintain it. I am bound to call upon you, and I pray you
    your name.

411 dearer] HANMER; deare F

396 **must** that must

398 **greater file of the subject** the greater
    part or majority of the Duke's subjects

400 **unweighing** unthinking, lacking in
    judgement

401 **envy** malice

402 **stream** course, direction
    helmed steered, guided

403 **upon a warranted need** if there should
    be a genuine need for the Duke to defend
    his reputation (implying that he does not
    regard the present occasion as a serious
    challenge)

403-4 **proclamation** public statement con-
    cerning him, assessment

404 **testimonied in** judged by the evidence of

405 **bringings-forth** recorded in *OED* under
    bringing vbl. sb., but not glossed; only
    example quoted. *Bring forth* can mean
    'give birth to children' and 'create poetry'
    (as in the Sonnets, 38.11, 72.13, and

103.1), so the phrase appears to mean
'creations, achievements'.

405-6 **a scholar, a statesman, and a soldier**
    The Duke regards himself as conforming
    to a Renaissance ideal in being simulta-
    neously a man of learning and a man of
    action. Compare *Merchant* 1.2.110, and
    Hamlet 1.5.145 and 3.1.154.

407 **unskilfully** ignorantly

408 **darkened in** blackened, made evil, by

410-11 **Love ... love** If you truly loved him
    you would know him better, and if you
    really knew him you would love him
    more

412 **I know what I know** I know what I'm
    talking about (a proverbial phrase, Tilley
    K173)

416 **honest** sincere, truthful

417 **call upon you** summon you to testify to
    the truth of what you have said

LUCIO Sir, my name is Lucio, well known to the Duke.

DUKE He shall know you better, sir, if I may live to report   420
you.

LUCIO I fear you not.

DUKE O, you hope the Duke will return no more, or you
imagine me too unhurtful an opposite—but indeed I can
do you little harm. You'll forswear this again?

LUCIO I'll be hanged first; thou art deceived in me, friar.
But no more of this. Canst thou tell if Claudio die
tomorrow or no?

DUKE Why should he die, sir?

LUCIO Why? For filling a bottle with a tundish. I would the   430
duke we talk of were returned again; this ungenitured
agent will unpeople the province with continency.
Sparrows must not build in his house-eaves, because
they are lecherous. The Duke yet would have dark deeds
darkly answered; he would never bring them to light.
Would he were returned! Marry, this Claudio is condemned for untrussing. Farewell, good friar, I prithee
pray for me. The Duke—I say to thee again—would eat
mutton on Fridays. He's now past it, yet—and I say to
thee—he would mouth with a beggar though she smelt   440
brown bread and garlic. Say that I said so. Farewell.
                                                        Exit

439 now] F; not HANMER

424 **unhurtful** weak, powerless
 opposite opponent
424–5 **but indeed ... harm** The Duke suddenly remembers that he is supposed to
be a friar.
425 **forswear** repudiate, swear that you
have not said it
 again on another occasion
430 **tundish** funnel (but with an obvious
double meaning)
431 **ungenitured** lacking genitals (only example in *OED*)
432 **agent** deputy, substitute
 unpeople depopulate
433–4 **Sparrows ... lecherous** Sparrows
were proverbially lecherous (Tilley
S715).
434–5 **dark deeds darkly answered** sexual
acts, performed in darkness, accounted
for in private, not subjected to public
trial. For *dark deeds* compare 'deed of

darkness', *Pericles* Sc. 19.37, and 'act of
darkness', *Lear*, 3.4.81.
437 **untrussing** untying the lower garments; also used to mean 'relieving oneself, passing water', so Lucio may mean
'undressing' or 'relieving himself'
438–9 **eat mutton on Fridays** break the
ecclesiastical laws that forbade the eating
of meat on Friday; but with a pun on
mutton as 'prostitute' (*OED* 4)
439 **now** Hanmer and other editors
emended to *not*, but this ruins Lucio's
final crashing insult: the Duke is now
impotent, so full sexuality is a thing of the
past, but he would still *mouth* (kiss in a
repulsive way) a filthy old beggarwoman.
441 **brown bread** coarse bread made from
rye or rye and wheat; according to Lever
it rapidly turned musty and affected the
breath. Eccles quotes an exact parallel
from Thomas Powell's *Art of Thriving*

DUKE

No might nor greatness in mortality
Can censure scape; back-wounding calumny
The whitest virtue strikes. What king so strong
Can tie the gall up in the slanderous tongue?
But who comes here?

> *Enter Escalus, Provost, and Officers with Mistress
> Overdone*

ESCALUS Go, away with her to prison.

MISTRESS OVERDONE Good my lord, be good to me; your
honour is accounted a merciful man. Good my lord!

ESCALUS Double and treble admonition, and still forfeit in   450
the same kind? This would make mercy swear and play
the tyrant.

PROVOST A bawd of eleven years' continuance, may it
please your honour.

MISTRESS OVERDONE My lord, this is one Lucio's information against me. Mistress Kate Keepdown was with child
by him in the Duke's time, he promised her marriage.
His child is a year and a quarter old come Philip and

446.1–2 *and ... Overdone*] THEOBALD; *and Bawd* F

(1635, p. 93), 'if the clown is predominant, he will smell all brown bread and
garlic'.

442–3 **No might ... scape** neither political
power, nor nobility of character, among
human beings can escape hostile criticism

443 **back-wounding** ?given to wounding or
stabbing in the back; perhaps equivalent
to *back-biting*, 'slandering behind one's
back'

443–4 **calumny ... virtue** a proverbial idea
(Tilley E175), but Shakespeare likes to
link these particular words: compare
Hamlet 1.3.38, 'Virtue itself scapes not
calumnious strokes', and *Winter's Tale*
2.1.75–6, 'calumny will sear | Virtue it-
self'

444 **so strong** is so strong that he

445 **tie the gall up** a kind of transference: 'tie
up the tongue so that it cannot express its
gall or bitterness'

450–1 **forfeit in the same kind** liable to
punishment for the same offence (that
she has repeatedly been warned not to
commit)

451–2 **play the tyrant** usually interpreted as

'indulge in noisy rant like the tyrants in
medieval and early Elizabethan drama',
but it might simply mean 'inflict savage
punishment'

453 **continuance** perhaps with the sense of
'persistence' (*OED* 3a); the Provost
wants to stress that she has stubbornly
plied her trade over a long period

455–6 **information** a legal term (*OED* 5): a
complaint or charge against a person
lodged with a court or magistrate. The
complainant would often receive a share
of any fine imposed, and the term suggests
that Lucio is an informer who gets money
by betraying his associates to the law.

456 **Keepdown** possibly a joking name to
indicate her profession: 'one who keeps
on lying down'

457 **in the Duke's time** Mistress Overdone's
speech implies that the Duke has been
absent for more than a year, not merely a
couple of days.

458–9 **come Philip and Jacob** next 1 May,
the day of St Philip and St James. It was
also May Day, a time of rituals and
festivities which frequently led to sexual
licence; presumably the child was conceived on this occasion.

Jacob. I have kept it myself, and see how he goes about
to abuse me.   460
ESCALUS That fellow is a fellow of much licence; let him be
called before us. Away with her to prison—go to, no
more words.   *Exeunt Officers with Mistress Overdone*
Provost, my brother Angelo will not be altered, Claudio
must die tomorrow. Let him be furnished with divines,
and have all charitable preparation. If my brother
wrought by my pity, it should not be so with him.
PROVOST So please you, this friar hath been with him, and
advised him for the entertainment of death.
ESCALUS Goode'en, good father.   470
DUKE Bliss and goodness on you.
ESCALUS Of whence are you?
DUKE

Not of this country, though my chance is now
To use it for my time. I am a brother
Of gracious order, late come from the See
In special business from his Holiness.
ESCALUS What news abroad i' the world?
DUKE None, but that there is so great a fever on goodness
that the dissolution of it must cure it. Novelty is only in

---

463 *Exeunt ... Overdone*] ROWE; *not in* F   470 Goode'en] This edition; Good'euen F
475 See] THEOBALD; Sea F

459–60 **goes about to abuse** tries to slander
461 **licence** unrestrained behaviour, licen-
    tiousness
464 **brother** fellow-officer (compare *brother-
    justice* at l. 507 below)
467 **wrought by my pity** administered jus-
    tice with the same degree of pity that I feel
469 **entertainment** acceptance, willingness
    to undergo
470 **Goode'en** F's unusual spelling-form,
    which recurs at 4.3.147 but not else-
    where in the Folio, appears to derive from
    Crane. In his transcripts of Middleton's *A
    Game at Chess* Crane sometimes expanded
    contractions but retained the apostrophe
    (e.g. writing *you'are* for Middleton's
    you're). It is therefore probable that the
    copy of *Measure* he was working from had
    a contracted form at this point. (Compare
    prithee at 1.2.61.)
474 **for my time** ?for the time being
475 **See** Holy See, Rome. F's spelling *Sea* is

also used for the other three occurrences
of the word in the Folio, and is common
in the period (*OED see sb.*[1] 2c).
477 **news abroad** In Marston's *The Malcon-
    tent*, 1.3.17–22, Pietro asks Malevole
    'what's the common news abroad?' and
    Malevole replies with a series of cynical
    generalizations.
478–9 **there is ... cure it** Presumably both
    uses of *it* refer back to *goodness*: 'goodness
    is so ill that it can get rid of its sickness
    only by dying'.
479 **Novelty** used contemptuously: 'new-
    ness for its own sake, the latest thing'.
    Nashe makes the same complaint, 'in all
    things men haste unto novelties, and run
    to see new things, so that whatsoever is
    not usual, of the multitude is admired',
    The Anatomy of Absurdity, 1589, E1ᵛ.
479–80 **only in request** the only thing in
    demand

request, and it is as dangerous to be aged in any kind of   480
course as it is virtuous to be inconstant in any
undertaking. There is scarce truth enough alive to make
societies secure, but security enough to make fellow-
ships accursed. Much upon this riddle runs the wisdom
of the world. This news is old enough, yet it is every
day's news. I pray you, sir, of what disposition was the
Duke?

ESCALUS One that above all other strifes contended especially to know himself.

DUKE What pleasure was he given to?   490

ESCALUS Rather rejoicing to see another merry than merry
at anything which professed to make him rejoice. A
gentleman of all temperance. But leave we him to his
events, with a prayer they may prove prosperous, and
let me desire to know how you find Claudio prepared. I
am made to understand that you have lent him visitation.

DUKE He professes to have received no sinister measure
from his judge, but most willingly humbles himself to
the determination of justice. Yet had he framed to   500

480 it] F3; as it F   481 inconstant] HUDSON; constant F

480–2 **it is ... undertaking** it is as dangerous
to your reputation to persist in a particular kind of behaviour as it is considered
virtuous to be shifting and unreliable in
any action you undertake. The antithesis
is not very powerful, in that both halves
of the sentence say much the same thing,
but attempts to defend F readings (*as it is*
as and *constant*) are strained and implausible.

480 **aged** in a metaphorical sense not recorded in *OED*: persistent, constant

482–4 **There is scarce ... accursed** Most
commentators argue for a financial implication in the second half of the sentence, with *security* meaning 'financial
pledge guaranteeing a loan' and *fellowship* meaning, in Lever's gloss, 'corpora-
tion formed for trading ventures'. But the
play on *secure* and *security* may be
slightly different, with *secure* meaning
'safe, reliable' and *security* meaning 'foolish optimism, ignorant belief that all is
well' (*OED* 3 and *Macbeth* 3.5.32): 'there
is hardly enough trustworthiness or reli-
ability around to make it safe to associate

with other people, but there is enough
foolish confidence to make such associa-
tions accursed (because the rogues will
take advantage of this naïvety)'.

484 **upon this riddle** according to this paradox

488 **strifes** objectives to be striven for, efforts

489 **know himself** The maxim 'know thyself' originated in Greek thought, was
taken up by Roman moralists, and was
repeated innumerable times in the Middle
Ages and Renaissance (see Smith 167,
Whiting K100, and Tilley K175). Christianity welcomed the phrase because it
inculcated the duty of severe and strenu-
ous self-examination.

492 **professed** intended

493–4 **his events** the outcome of his activities

496–7 **lent him visitation** made him a visit
(*visitation* is Shakespeare's normal word
for 'visit', which he never uses as a noun)

498 **professes** declares, affirms
sinister measure unjust punishment

500 **determination** verdict
framed devised, invented

himself, by the instruction of his frailty, many deceiving promises of life, which I by my good leisure have discredited to him, and now is he resolved to die.

ESCALUS You have paid the heavens your function, and the prisoner the very debt of your calling. I have laboured for the poor gentleman to the extremest shore of my modesty, but my brother-justice have I found so severe that he hath forced me to tell him he is indeed justice.

DUKE If his own life answer the straitness of his proceed-   510
ing, it shall become him well; wherein if he chance to fail, he hath sentenced himself.

ESCALUS I am going to visit the prisoner. Fare you well.

DUKE Peace be with you.   *Exeunt Escalus and Provost*
He who the sword of heaven will bear
Should be as holy as severe;
Pattern in himself to know,
Grace to stand, and virtue, go;

514 *Exeunt ... Provost*] CAPELL; *not in* F; *Exit* F2

502 **by my good leisure** a stock phrase (*OED leisure* 5c) implying that the Duke went about it deliberately and patiently

504–5 **You have ... calling** a somewhat laborious way of saying 'you have completely fulfilled your responsibilities as a priest both to God and to the prisoner'

506–7 **to the extremest shore of my modesty** *shore* is used figuratively for 'limit': 'as far as I could possibly go without becoming impudent to my superior'

508–9 **indeed justice** justice itself, the personified figure of Justice. Compare *2 Henry IV* 5.2.101, 'You are right Justice, and you weigh this well' (this is the reading of both Q and F, though many modern editors add a comma after *right*).

510 **answer the straitness** correspond to the strictness

515–36 **He who ... contracting** For a general discussion of this passage see Appendix A. Its literary and dramatic function is considered in the Introduction, p. 52.

515 **the sword of heaven** The sword is an emblem, not of warfare, but of legal authority to punish wrongdoers; compare 'the deputed sword', 2.2.60, Whetstone's *An Heptameron of Civil Discourses* (1582, O2ʳ), 'the sword of justice, appointed to chasten the lewd', and *2 Henry*

IV 5.2.86–7, 102, and 112–16. There may be an allusion to Romans 13 : 4 (in a passage urging respect for the 'powers that be'): 'if thou do evil, fear, for he beareth not the sword for nought; for he is the minister of God to take vengeance on him that doeth evil'. The fact that the sword is of divine origin suggests that the Duke has no theoretical objection to capital punishment.

516 **as holy as severe** presumably 'holy in equal proportion to his severity', implying that he can be as severe as he wishes provided that he has the right degree of holiness. To some extent this is a generalized form of the Duke's earlier speech at ll. 510–12.

517 **Pattern ... know** he should be able to find a pattern or model of virtuous behaviour by looking into himself

518 **Grace ... go** *stand* and *go* are used as a stock pair of verbs in Elizabethan English, with *stand* meaning 'remain steadily upright, support oneself erect' and *go* meaning 'move about on one's legs'. In Part 2 of Thomas Lupton's *Siuqila* (1581, V4) the story is told of a girl who spends all night tied to a tree: 'I unbound her, who was so frozen with the cold that then she could neither go nor stand', and under

> More nor less to others paying
> Than by self-offences weighing.   520
> Shame to him whose cruel striking
> Kills for faults of his own liking;
> Twice treble shame on Angelo,
> To weed my vice and let his grow!
> O what may man within him hide,
> Though angel on the outward side!
> How may likeness made in crimes,
> Making practice on the times
>
>   .   .   .   .   .
>
> To draw with idle spiders' strings
> Most ponderous and substantial things!   530
> Craft against vice I must apply:
> With Angelo tonight shall lie
> His old betrothèd, but despisèd;
> So disguise shall by the disguisèd

528 Making] F; Make my OXFORD   528–9] *hiatus indicated by* LEVER; *not in* F

stand v. 9, *OED* quotes from 1592, 'the
old man ... by cold taken at that being in
the hole was never after able to go or
stand'. The line thus means 'he must
have divine grace to keep him morally
upright, and virtue to provoke him into
action'. For a similar paraphrase see
Abbott 504.

519–20 **More ... weighing** paying out, or
inflicting, neither more nor less punishment to others than is determined by
weighing up the amount of evil in himself
(a negative way of putting the idea
expressed in l. 516)

524 **my vice** Several editors gloss this as 'the
vice of other people' but there is an
antithesis between *my* and *his*, and the
phrase is surely more powerful as a
reference to the Duke (the vice he allowed
to exist through failing to enforce the law
properly). Lines 521–2 lead up to
ll. 523–4: 'it is shameful when someone
inflicts the death-penalty for vices he is
sympathetic to, but it is several times
more shameful for Angelo to weed out
the vice for which I was responsible and
at the same time to let his own vice
flourish'.

526 **angel on the outward side** Compare
'outward-sainted deputy', l. 90 above;
there is an obvious play on Angelo's

name. Lines 521–6 indicate that what
the Duke most objects to in Angelo is his
hypocrisy, not his severity.

527–30 **How may ... things** For discussion
of these lines see Appendix A.

528 **practice** deceit, trickery

529 **strings** threads of a spider's web. Charlton Hinman is mistaken in his assertion
that a variant uncorrected form, *stings*,
can be found in the Elizabethan Club copy
of F in Yale University Library (Introduction to the Norton Facsimile of *The First
Folio of Shakespeare*, London, 1968,
p. xxi). In fact the Yale copy has a crease
in the page which has swallowed up a
number of letters; see my note in *SQ* 39
(1988), 360.

531 **apply** with a hint of its medical sense;
'put on (as though to a wound), use as a
remedy'

534–5 **So disguise ... exacting** The general
sense of the couplet is fairly clear, but as
the Duke, Mariana, and Angelo either are
or will be in some sort of disguise it is not
certain how far the audience is intended
to make personal identifications. Probably *disguise* is best taken as an abstrac-
tion: 'disguise (as a form of trickery) will,
by means of a disguised person
(Mariana), repay with deception Angelo's treacherous and disloyal exaction
from Isabella'. The verbal balance (*dis-*

Pay with falsehood false exacting,
And perform an old contracting.   *Exit*

4.1   *Enter Mariana and a Boy singing*
BOY (*sings*)

    Take, O take those lips away,
      That so sweetly were forsworn,
    And those eyes, the break of day,
      Lights that do mislead the morn;
    But my kisses bring again, bring again,
    Seals of love, though sealed in vain, sealed in vain.
    Enter Duke as a Friar

MARIANA

Break off thy song, and haste thee quick away.
Here comes a man of comfort, whose advice
Hath often stilled my brawling discontent.   *Exit Boy*
I cry you mercy, sir, and well could wish   10
You had not found me here so musical.
Let me excuse me, and believe me so,
My mirth it much displeased, but pleased my woe.

DUKE

'Tis good; though music oft hath such a charm

4.1.1 BOY (*sings*)] WILSON; Song. F   3 day,] ROWE; day ∧ F   6 though] OXFORD; but F
6.1 *as a Friar*] ROWE; *not in* F   9 *Exit Boy*] CAPELL; *not in* F

guise ... disguised, falsehood false) is
another aspect of the play's concern with
measure for measure.

536 **perform** fulfil, bring to completion
4.1 For the textual problems associated with
this scene see Introduction, pp. 69–71.
The song is discussed in Appendix A.
 2 **so sweetly were forsworn** swore false
vows of fidelity in such a sweet and
beguiling way
 4 **Lights** a subdued pun, because *lights* can
mean 'eyes' (*OED* 4) as well as 'lamps'
 5 **again** back again
 6 **Seals of love** a stock Shakespearian metaphor for kisses; compare Sonnet
142.5–7, *Shrew* 3.2.123, and *Two
Gentlemen* 2.2.7
though All other 17th-c. texts of this
poem, printed or manuscript, read
though, and F's *but* seems to be an
accidental repetition, by scribe or compo-

sitor, from the preceding line. See Introduction, p. 71.
 7 **haste thee quick** See 3.1.262 n.
 9 **often** This implies a long acquaintance,
which would contradict the impression
given in 1.3 that the Duke has only very
recently started to disguise himself as a
friar (and see also l. 52 n. below and
5.1.530). An explanation is suggested in
the Introduction, pp. 43–4.
brawling clamorous, noisy
10 **cry you mercy** beg your pardon (a stock
phrase)
12 **excuse me** excuse myself
believe me so believe that what I say of
myself is true
13 **My mirth ... woe** The music did not
incite me to frivolity, but helped to soothe
my melancholy
14 **charm** power of the type associated with
magic or witchcraft

To make bad good, and good provoke to harm.
I pray you tell me, hath anybody enquired for me here
today? Much upon this time have I promised here to meet.

MARIANA You have not been enquired after; I have sat
here all day.

Enter Isabella

DUKE I do constantly believe you; the time is come even   20
now. I shall crave your forbearance a little, maybe I will
call upon you anon for some advantage to yourself.

MARIANA I am always bound to you.   *Exit*

DUKE

Very well met, and welcome.
What is the news from this good deputy?

ISABELLA

He hath a garden circummured with brick,
Whose western side is with a vineyard backed,
And to that vineyard is a planchèd gate
That makes his opening with this bigger key;
This other doth command a little door,   30
Which from the vineyard to the garden leads.
There have I made my promise,
Upon the heavy middle of the night,
To call upon him.

DUKE

But shall you on your knowledge find this way?

ISABELLA

I have ta'en a due and wary note upon't.
With whispering and most guilty diligence,

---

24 welcome] WARBURTON; well come F

15 **make ... harm** Shakespeare normally
celebrates the beneficial effects of music;
in this case the Duke may feel that
Mariana is using music in order to luxuri-
ate in grief.

17 **Much upon** near to, round about
meet keep an appointment (*OED* 8c)

20 **constantly** firmly, confidently

21 **forbearance** absence, departure (a sense
not recorded in *OED*)

24 **welcome** Crane normally writes this as
one word, but occasionally, as in his
transcript of Middleton's *The Witch* (MSR,
1950), l. 853, he leaves a small gap
between the two syllables which does not

appear to have any grammatical significance.

26 **garden** See the note on *garden-house* at
5.1.211.
circummured walled round (earliest quotation in *OED*)

27 **is ... backed** has a vineyard adjoining it

28 **planchèd** made of planks or boards (earliest quotation in *OED*)

33 **heavy** with a range of senses: (*a*) gloomy;
(*b*) slow-moving; (*c*) inducing sleep

35 **on your knowledge** ?with the knowledge
you have at present

36 **due** (*a*) fitting, suitable; (*b*) adequate
wary cautious

In action all of precept, he did show me
The way twice o'er.

DUKE   Are there no other tokens
Between you 'greed concerning her observance?   40

ISABELLA

No, none but only a repair i' the dark;
And that I have possessed him my most stay
Can be but brief, for I have made him know
I have a servant comes with me along,
That stays upon me, whose persuasion is
I come about my brother.

DUKE   'Tis well borne up.
I have not yet made known to Mariana
A word of this. What ho, within, come forth!
          Enter Mariana
I pray you be acquainted with this maid;
She comes to do you good.

ISABELLA   I do desire the like.   50

DUKE (*to Mariana*)

Do you persuade yourself that I respect you?

MARIANA

Good friar, I know you do, and so have found it.

DUKE

Take then this your companion by the hand,
Who hath a story ready for your ear.
I shall attend your leisure, but make haste,
The vaporous night approaches.

48.1 *Enter Mariana*] ROWE; *after l. 47 in* F   52 SO] LEVER; *not in* F

38 **all of precept** wholly consisting of verbal
instructions (Angelo did not show her the
way by actually taking her there)
39 **tokens** perhaps in *OED*'s sense 7a, 'pre-
arranged sign or password'
40 **her observance** the formalities she must
observe
41 **repair** visit
42 **possessed** informed
   most utmost, longest
45 **stays upon** waits for
   persuasion belief
46 **'Tis well borne up** the intrigue against
Angelo has been skilfully kept going
47-8 **I have ... this** Clearly the Duke has not
carried out his promise at 3.1.256-7 (see

Introduction, p. 44, n. 1).
50 **I do ... like** I wish to do the same, i.e.
good to Mariana (Isabella is not completely certain she will be able to)
51 **Do you ... you** Are you convinced that I
have a high regard for you?
52 **have found it** have had experience of it in
the past (another indication of a long
acquaintance between Mariana and the
Duke)
55 **attend your leisure** wait until you are at
leisure, have finished the business (a
stock formula)
56 **vaporous** damp (and hence injurious to
health)

MARIANA (*to Isabella*)

  Will't please you walk aside?

                        Exeunt Mariana and Isabella

DUKE

  O place and greatness, millions of false eyes

  Are stuck upon thee; volumes of report

  Run with their false and most contrarious quests   60

  Upon thy doings; thousand escapes of wit

  Make thee the father of their idle dream,

  And rack thee in their fancies.

     Enter Mariana and Isabella

                    Welcome, how agreed?

ISABELLA

  She'll take the enterprise upon her, father,

  If you advise it.

DUKE   It is not my consent,

  But my entreaty too.

ISABELLA   Little have you to say

  When you depart from him but, soft and low,

  'Remember now my brother'.

MARIANA   Fear me not.

DUKE

  Nor, gentle daughter, fear you not at all.

57.1 *Exeunt ... Isabella*] ROWE; *Exit.* F   60 their] HANMER; these F   quests] F2; Quest F
63 *Enter ... Isabella*] F (*at end of line*)

58–63 **O place ... fancies** The Duke should
meditate while the two women confer,
but this speech has seemed to most
editors neither long enough nor appropriate (see Introduction, p. 68). Similar
ideas are expressed by the Duke at
3.1.442–6. The general sense of the
passage is that those who have power
and authority are scrutinized by millions
of hostile onlookers, and are pursued by
spiteful gossip and made the butt of
irresponsible jokes.

58 **false** treacherous (*not* 'artificial')

59 **stuck upon** in the sense of 'watching
obsessively', like modern 'glued to',
rather than implying that place and
greatness have artificial eyes dotted over
their clothes like sequins, as some editors
suggest. For this sense of *stuck* compare
Complaint, l. 81, and *Timon* 4.3.264.
volumes very large amounts (*OED* 7b,
earliest example from 1647)

59 **report** rumour, gossip

60–1 **Run ... Upon** run towards, in order to
attack (*OED run* 5); compare *Venus*,
l. 1112, 'He ran upon the boar with his
sharp spear'

60 **contrarious** (*a*) inconsistent; (*b*) hostile;
(*c*) wilful, perverse
quests in sense 6b of *OED quest sb.*¹, 'a
peculiar barking uttered by dogs when in
sight of game'. This would make *Run*
imply the pursuit of its prey by a pack of
hounds.

61 **escapes** sudden outbursts, sallies (earliest
quotation in *OED sb.*¹ 5)

62 **Make ... dream** attribute to you, father
on you, their own irresponsible fancies

63 **rack** distort, misinterpret

65–6 **It is ... too** I not only agree to it, but
beg you to do it

68 **Fear me not** don't worry about my ability
to do what is needed

69 **fear you not at all** The Duke turns her

He is your husband on a pre-contract; 70
To bring you thus together 'tis no sin,
Sith that the justice of your title to him
Doth flourish the deceit. Come, let us go;
Our corn's to reap, for yet our tilth's to sow. *Exeunt*

4.2 *Enter Provost and Pompey*

PROVOST Come hither, sirrah. Can you cut off a man's head?

POMPEY If the man be a bachelor, sir, I can; but if he be a married man, he's his wife's head, and I can never cut off a woman's head.

PROVOST Come, sir, leave me your snatches, and yield me a direct answer. Tomorrow morning are to die Claudio and Barnardine. Here is in our prison a common executioner, who in his office lacks a helper. If you will take it on you to assist him, it shall redeem you from 10 your gyves; if not, you shall have your full time of imprisonment, and your deliverance with an unpitied whipping, for you have been a notorious bawd.

POMPEY Sir, I have been an unlawful bawd time out of mind, but yet I will be content to be a lawful hangman. I would be glad to receive some instruction from my fellow-partner.

74 tilth's] THEOBALD; Tithes F

phrase back on her with a slightly different meaning: 'don't you worry at all about the rightness of your action'.

70 **pre-contract** a contract of marriage made in the past (see Introduction, pp. 6–8)
73 **flourish** *OED* quotes under the figurative sense of *v* 6, 'embellish, decorate'; the specific force here seems to be 'give an attractive appearance to what would otherwise seem repulsive'.
74 **to reap ... to sow** still to be reaped ... to be sown (Abbott 359); 'we still have more to do before we can reap the rewards of our efforts'
tilth Editors who retain F's *tithe* gloss it as 'crop, harvest', but there is no support for this in *OED* or elsewhere in Shakespeare, and *tilth*, 'arable land, ploughed field'

(*OED* 4), gives a much better sense: the ground has been prepared, and now is the time to sow the seed.
4.2.4 **his wife's head** a play of words on the literal sense of *head* and the figurative ('lord, master'), as found in Ephesians 5 : 23, 'for the husband is the wife's head', and 1 Corinthians 11 : 3
6 **snatches** quibbles, jokes
8 **common** public
11 **gyves** shackles or fetters for the leg
12 **deliverance** release from prison
unpitied which no one will pity (though the sense 'pitiless, merciless' may also be present)
14–15 **time out of mind** for longer than I can remember (a stock phrase; see *OED mind sb.*¹ 2f, and Tilley/Dent T332.2)

PROVOST What ho, Abhorson! Where's Abhorson there?
    Enter Abhorson

ABHORSON Do you call, sir?

PROVOST Sirrah, here's a fellow will help you tomorrow in   20
your execution. If you think it meet, compound with
him by the year, and let him abide here with you; if not,
use him for the present and dismiss him. He cannot
plead his estimation with you, he hath been a bawd.

ABHORSON A bawd, sir? Fie upon him, he will discredit our
mystery.

PROVOST Go to, sir, you weigh equally, a feather will turn
the scale.   *Exit*

POMPEY Pray, sir, by your good favour—for surely, sir, a
good favour you have, but that you have a hanging   30
look—do you call, sir, your occupation a mystery?

ABHORSON Ay, sir, a mystery.

POMPEY Painting, sir, I have heard say, is a mystery; and
your whores, sir, being members of my occupation,
using painting, do prove my occupation a mystery. But
what mystery there should be in hanging, if I should be
hanged, I cannot imagine.

ABHORSON Sir, it is a mystery.

POMPEY Proof.

ABHORSON Every true man's apparel fits your thief—   40

4.2.40–1 thief-/POMPEY If] F(*Clo.*); thief, Clown: If THEOBALD; thief. If CAPELL

18 **Abhorson** a portmanteau word combining *abhor* and *whoreson* ('son of a whore, wretch'); for the repulsion with which the common executioner and common hangman were regarded see *As You Like It* 3.5.3–7 and *Pericles* Sc. 19.199–202

21–2 **compound … by the year** agree on an annual wage

24 **plead his estimation** argue that he is too respectable to carry out such work

26 **mystery** craft, profession (*OED mystery*[2] 2). This is etymologically distinct from *mystery*[1] 8, a 'secret' or skilled practice in a trade, known only to the initiated, but the two usages were often confused and Abhorson may have both in mind. Pompey however finds it difficult to regard those who hang other people as belonging to a highly skilled profession.

27–8 **a feather … scale** A similar metaphor

occurs in *2 Henry IV* 2.4.255–6, 'the Prince himself is such another—the weight of a hair will turn the scales between their avoirdupois'.

29 **by your good favour** a stock phrase ('by your leave, if you don't mind my saying so'), but Pompey goes on to play on *good favour* as meaning 'handsome face'

30–1 **hanging look** (*a*) grim appearance (because his profession is to hang other people); (*b*) the look of someone who is destined for the gallows

33 **Painting** the occupation of an artist (but in l. 35 meaning 'the application of cosmetics')

40 **true** honest (the *true man* and the *thief* are regularly contrasted; see *LLL* 4.3.185 and *1 Henry IV* 2.3.1)
    fits (*a*) is of the right size for; (*b*) is appropriate for, will be welcome to

POMPEY If it be too little for your thief, your true man
thinks it big enough. If it be too big for your thief, your
thief thinks it little enough. So every true man's apparel
fits your thief.

    Enter Provost

PROVOST Are you agreed?

POMPEY Sir, I will serve him, for I do find your hangman is
a more penitent trade than your bawd; he doth oftener
ask forgiveness.

PROVOST You, sirrah, provide your block and your axe
tomorrow, four o'clock.   50

ABHORSON Come on, bawd, I will instruct thee in my
trade. Follow.

POMPEY I do desire to learn, sir, and I hope, if you have
occasion to use me for your own turn, you shall find me
yare. For truly, sir, for your kindness I owe you a good
turn.

PROVOST

Call hither Barnardine and Claudio.

                    Exeunt Abhorson and Pompey

The one has my pity, not a jot the other,

Being a murderer, though he were my brother.

    Enter Claudio

Look, here's the warrant, Claudio, for thy death.   60

'Tis now dead midnight, and by eight tomorrow

Thou must be made immortal. Where's Barnardine?

---

55 yare] THEOBALD; y'are F   57.1 *Exeunt ... Pompey*] CAPELL; *Exit* F (*at l.* 56)

41–4 **If it ... thief** The Folio attribution of
this speech is discussed in Appendix A.
41–2 **little ... big** As Lever remarks, there is
a play on these words in relation to (*a*)
size and (*b*) value. It is hard to see how
proving that *every true man's apparel fits
your thief* also proves that the executioner's trade is a mystery, and attempts by
modern commentators to provide a connection are unconvincing. Possibly
Abhorson intended l. 40 to lead on to an
extended argument, but was silenced by
Pompey's intervention.
46 **I do find** This must mean 'in my experience I find it to be true'; Pompey has not
just discovered it from his conversation
with Abhorson.
48 **ask forgiveness** The executioner nor-

mally asked the condemned person to
forgive him.
54 **for your own turn** when you come to be
executed
55 **yare** quoted in *OED yare* 1, 'ready, prepared'. When applied to a hangman in
Antony 3.13.132, it means 'brisk, nim-
ble', and this implication could be present
also.
55–6 **good turn** (*a*) act of kindness; (*b*) skilful
execution (from the verb *turn off* meaning
'execute', *OED turn v.* 74d). There is in
addition an allusion to the proverbial 'one
good turn deserves another' (Tilley T616).
59 **though he were my brother** See 2.2.82 n.
62 **made immortal** turned into an immortal
spirit through the death of his mortal
body

CLAUDIO

As fast locked up in sleep as guiltless labour
When it lies starkly in the travailer's bones.
He will not wake.

PROVOST   Who can do good on him?
Well, go, prepare yourself. (*Knocking within*) But hark,
      what noise?
Heaven give your spirits comfort!   *Exit Claudio*
      (*Knocking within*)   By and by!
I hope it is some pardon or reprieve
For the most gentle Claudio.
      Enter Duke as a Friar

                              Welcome, father.

DUKE

The best and wholesom'st spirits of the night   70
Envelop you, good Provost! Who called here of late?

PROVOST None since the curfew rung.

DUKE Not Isabel?

PROVOST No.

DUKE They will then ere't be long.

PROVOST What comfort is for Claudio?

DUKE There's some in hope.

PROVOST It is a bitter deputy.

DUKE

Not so, not so; his life is paralleled
Even with the stroke and line of his great justice.   80

64 travailer's] F (Trauellers)   66 *Knocking within*] ROWE; *not in* F   67 *Exit Claudio*] CAPELL;
not in F   *Knocking within*] WILSON; *not in* F   69 *Enter Duke*] F (*at end of line*)   *as a Friar*] ROWE;
not in F

64 **starkly** stiffly
    travailer This spelling indicates the cor-
    rect sense ('labourer', not 'voyager') to a
    modern reader; it should however be
    stressed in the same way as modern
    traveller. The two spellings overlapped in
    the 16th c. Lines 63–4 allude to Ecclesi-
    astes 5: 11 (Geneva version; 5: 12 in
    AV), 'the sleep of him that travaileth is
    sweet'.
65 **do good on** benefit, improve
72–8 Most editors try to rearrange these
    lines as verse, but it is impossible to do so
    systematically, and they are better left as
    a series of brief prose sentences.
72 **curfew** In London the curfew-bell rang at

nine o'clock at night as a signal that the
regulations governing nocturnal behaviour had come into force.
78 **bitter** severe, cruel
80 **Even** exactly, precisely
    stroke and line This phrase has a rich
    complexity of meaning. The primary
    sense is geometrical: *stroke* as 'linear
    mark' (*OED* 17) is virtually a doublet for
    line, and Angelo's private life and his
    behaviour as a judge are compared to a
    pair of parallel lines. The phrase can also
    refer to the marks and lines made on
    paper by Angelo in writing out his legal
    judgements. In addition, *stroke* can mean
    the infliction of punishment, including

He doth with holy abstinence subdue
That in himself which he spurs on his power
To qualify in others. Were he mealed with that
Which he corrects, then were he tyrannous,
But this being so, he's just. (*Knocking within*) Now are
    they come.   *Exit Provost*
This is a gentle Provost; seldom-when
The steelèd gaoler is the friend of men.
    Enter Provost. Knocking within
How now? What noise? That spirit's possessed with
    haste
That wounds the unshifting postern with these strokes.

PROVOST

There he must stay until the officer   90
Arise to let him in; he is called up.

DUKE

Have you no countermand for Claudio yet,
But he must die tomorrow?

PROVOST   None, sir, none.

DUKE

As near the dawning, Provost, as it is,
You shall hear more ere morning.

PROVOST   Happily
You something know, yet I believe there comes

---

85 *Knocking within*] ROWE; *not in* F   *Exit Provost*] THEOBALD; *not in* F   87.1 *Enter Provost*] THEOBALD (*after l.* 88); *not in* F   *Knocking within*] COLLIER; *not in* F   89 unshifting] CAPELL; unsisting F; unlisting WHITE

capital punishment (*OED stroke sb.*[1] 3a does not record *the stroke of justice* until 1665, but compare *the blow of justice* at 2.2.30), and *line* can mean 'course, direction, conduct' (*OED*, 26, 27). Dover Wilson ingeniously suggests that *stroke* is the blow of the executioner's axe, and *line* the hangman's cord, but *OED* does not support the latter interpretation.

83 **qualify** control, regulate (perhaps with a hint of 'mitigate, moderate', as at 1.1.66)
   mealed stained, spotted
85 **this** the virtuous conduct described above
85–91 F has no stage-directions here. The present arrangement sends off the Provost so that he does not overhear the Duke's compliment at ll. 86–7, but

returns him in time to answer the Duke's question at ll. 88–9. The Provost's own speech makes it clear that he does not answer the door himself but orders an officer to do so.
86 **seldom-when** rarely (an obsolete adverbial phrase; see *OED seldom* C)
87 **steelèd** hardened (because he is constantly seeing misery and suffering in the prison)
89 **unshifting** unmoving (for discussion of this textual crux see Appendix A)
   postern back- or side-gate, as distinct from the main entrance
91 **he is called up** he (the officer acting as gatekeeper) has been summoned to open the door for the messenger
95 **Happily** haply, perhaps

No countermand; no such example have we.
Besides, upon the very siege of justice
Lord Angelo hath to the public ear
Professed the contrary.
          Enter a Messenger
                                This is his lordship's man.   100

DUKE
And here comes Claudio's pardon.
MESSENGER (*giving Provost a letter*) My lord hath sent you
     this note, and by me this further charge, that you
     swerve not from the smallest article of it, neither in
     time, matter, or other circumstance. Good morrow; for,
     as I take it, it is almost day.
PROVOST I shall obey him.   *Exit Messenger*
DUKE (*aside*)
This is his pardon, purchased by such sin
For which the pardoner himself is in.
Hence hath offence his quick celerity,   110
When it is borne in high authority.
When vice makes mercy, mercy's so extended

---

100 This] RANN; *Duke*. This F   lordship's] ROWE; Lords F   101 DUKE And] RANN; *Pro*. And F
102 *giving ... letter*] WILSON; *not in* F   107 *Exit Messenger*] ROWE; *not in* F

98 **siege of justice** judge's seat (used by Angelo)
100–1 [PROVOST] ... DUKE Most editors reverse the speech-prefixes given in F. The Provost is more likely than the Duke to recognize Angelo's messenger, and l. 101 would sound very odd in his mouth after what he has just said about Angelo's rigour.
100 **lordship's** Compare Induction 2, l. 2, of *The Taming of the Shrew*, where F reads *Wilt please your lord drink a cup of sack*, altered in F2 to *lordship*. As Malone suggested, Shakespeare perhaps used the contraction *Lo.* or *Lord.*, and Crane failed to expand it correctly. If this is the right explanation, it would point to foul papers as the ultimate source for the Folio text of *Measure*.
104 **swerve** deviate
108–9 **such sin ... is in** *In* can mean 'in prison' (*OED in adv.* 6a), as at 4.3.4 below and *2 Henry IV* 5.5.38 ('Doll is in'), but the *pardoner* can only be Angelo, so *in*

must mean 'engaged, entangled in' (*OED* 6b), and the phrase can be glossed as 'sin of a kind which the pardoner himself has become involved in'. If this is what Shakespeare intended, *such sin | For which* is a cumbersome way of putting it, and *pardoner* may be a misreading of *prisoner* (perhaps influenced by *pardon* in the line above). If so, the meaning would be 'sin of the same kind as that for which the prisoner himself is in gaol', and this would bring out the parallelism betwen Claudio and Angelo.
110 **quick celerity** See 3.1.262 n. and compare *swift celerity* at 5.1.395.
111 **borne in** supported by (evil can operate rapidly and easily when it is protected by those in authority)
112 **extended** This could mean 'granted', as in Psalm 109: 12, 'Let there be none to extend mercy unto him' (*OED v.* 9), but it is more likely to have sense 6b, 'enlarged in scope (beyond its proper limits)'.

That for the fault's love is the offender friended.

Now, sir, what news?

PROVOST I told you: Lord Angelo, belike thinking me remiss in mine office, awakens me with this unwonted putting-on, methinks strangely, for he hath not used it before.

DUKE Pray you let's hear.

PROVOST (*reads*) 'Whatsoever you may hear to the con-   120
trary, let Claudio be executed by four of the clock, and in the afternoon Barnardine. For my better satisfaction, let me have Claudio's head sent me by five. Let this be duly performed, with a thought that more depends on it than we must yet deliver. Thus fail not to do your office, as you will answer it at your peril.' What say you to this, sir?

DUKE What is that Barnardine who is to be executed in the afternoon?

PROVOST A Bohemian born, but here nursed up and bred,   130
one that is a prisoner nine years old.

DUKE How came it that the absent Duke had not either delivered him to his liberty or executed him? I have heard it was ever his manner to do so.

PROVOST His friends still wrought reprieves for him, and indeed his fact till now in the government of Lord Angelo came not to an undoubtful proof.

DUKE It is now apparent?

120 PROVOST (*reads*)] ROWE; *The Letter.* F

113 **friended** befriended (by those in authority who love the sin he has committed)
115 **belike** probably, apparently
116 **awakens** arouses, stimulates
116-17 **unwonted putting-on** unusual urging or incitement (see *OED put. v*¹ 47h)
120 PROVOST (*reads*) F gives a heading '*The
Letter.*' but no speech-prefix. Compare
All's Well 3.4.4, where F has '*Letter.*' and
no speech-prefix for the Steward who
reads Helena's letter to the Countess. This
again might point to a foul-papers origin
for *Measure* (see l. 100 n. above). Middleton uses '*the letter*' twice in the autograph
Trinity manuscript of *A Game at Chess* (ed.
R. C. Bald, 1929, 2.1.15 and 3.1.33),
but Crane omits the phrase in his three
transcripts of the play.

125 **must yet deliver** can make known for
the time being
125-6 **Thus fail not … peril** a stock legal
formula; William Lambarde, in his *Eire-
narcha, or of the Office of the Justices of
Peace* (1581, p. 268), quotes a form of
'mittimus' for justices sending prisoners
to gaol, addressed to the gaoler and
ending 'Hereof fail you not, as you will
answer thereunto at your uttermost
peril'.
131 **nine years old** for the last nine years;
compare *Errors* 1.1.44, 'From whom my
absence was not six months old'
135 **wrought** obtained
136 **fact** deed, crime
government rule, administration
137 **undoubtful** undoubted, certain

PROVOST Most manifest, and not denied by himself.

DUKE Hath he borne himself penitently in prison? How   140
seems he to be touched?

PROVOST A man that apprehends death no more dreadfully
but as a drunken sleep, careless, reckless, and fearless of
what's past, present, or to come; insensible of mortality,
and desperately mortal.

DUKE He wants advice.

PROVOST He will hear none. He hath evermore had the
liberty of the prison; give him leave to escape hence, he
would not. Drunk many times a day, if not many days
entirely drunk. We have very oft awaked him, as if to   150
carry him to execution, and showed him a seeming
warrant for it; it hath not moved him at all.

DUKE More of him anon. There is written in your brow,
Provost, honesty and constancy. If I read it not truly,
my ancient skill beguiles me; but in the boldness of my
cunning I will lay myself in hazard. Claudio, whom here
you have warrant to execute, is no greater forfeit to the
law than Angelo who hath sentenced him. To make you
understand this in a manifested effect, I crave but four
days' respite, for the which you are to do me both a   160
present and a dangerous courtesy.

PROVOST Pray, sir, in what?

DUKE In the delaying death.

PROVOST Alack, how may I do it, having the hour limited,
and an express command under penalty to deliver his

---

139 **manifest** clear, obvious

141 **touched** moved, affected (by the near-
ness of his execution)

142 **apprehends** responds to

142–3 **no more dreadfully but as** with no
more terror than if it were

144–5 **insensible ... mortal** incapable of
being moved by the idea of death, and at
the same time irretrievably doomed to die
(*desperately* may also imply 'with no hope
of salvation')

146 **wants** lacks, needs

147 **evermore** always

147–8 **the liberty of the prison** permission to
go anywhere within the limits of the
prison (earliest example of *OED liberty*
4b). For a similar phrase compare Hey-

wood, *A Woman Killed with Kindness*
4.1.12–13, 'He is denied the freedom of
the prison | And in the hole is laid with
men condemned'.

155 **beguiles** deceives

155–6 **in the boldness of my cunning** ?with
full confidence in my skill (as a judge of
character)

156 **lay myself in hazard** put myself in a
dangerous position

159 **manifested** clearly revealed, easily
understood (perhaps the Duke is thinking ahead to the final scene in which
Angelo's trickery will be revealed publicly)

164 **limited** specified

head in the view of Angelo? I may make my case as
Claudio's to cross this in the smallest.

DUKE By the vow of mine order I warrant you. If my
instructions may be your guide, let this Barnardine be
this morning executed, and his head borne to Angelo.   170

PROVOST Angelo hath seen them both, and will discover
the favour.

DUKE O, death's a great disguiser, and you may add to it.
Shave the head, and tie the beard, and say it was the
desire of the penitent to be so bared before his death;
you know the course is common. If anything fall to you
upon this more than thanks and good fortune, by the
saint whom I profess I will plead against it with my life.

PROVOST Pardon me, good father, it is against my oath.

DUKE Were you sworn to the Duke or to the deputy?   180

PROVOST To him and to his substitutes.

DUKE You will think you have made no offence if the Duke
avouch the justice of your dealing?

PROVOST But what likelihood is in that?

DUKE Not a resemblance but a certainty. Yet since I see
you fearful, that neither my coat, integrity, nor persuasion can with ease attempt you, I will go further than I
meant, to pluck all fears out of you. Look you, sir, here
is the hand and seal of the Duke. (*Showing a letter*) You
know the character, I doubt not, and the signet is not   190
strange to you.

PROVOST I know them both.

189 *Showing a letter*] WILSON; *not in* F

167 **to cross** if I thwart, go counter to
168 **warrant you** guarantee your safety
171–2 **discover the favour** recognize the
face
174 **tie the beard** Editors have suggested
various emendations for *tie*, but it may
simply mean what it says, that Barnardine's long and straggling beard should
be tied in a knot or knots so as to make it
less recognizable.
176 **fall** happen
178 **whom I profess** to whose religious order
I have made my vows
179 **Pardon me** often used as a courteous
way of refusing a request
183 **avouch** vouch for, confirm
185 **resemblance** probability

186 **coat** clerical dress
187 **attempt** try to persuade
189 *Showing a letter* F has no stage-direction,
though the text clearly indicates that the
Duke brings out a letter. Some modern
directors have also added stage-business
by the Duke, here or at the end of the
scene, which reveals his true identity to
the Provost (he opens his cloak or produces a ring). But the text is not explicit
on the point, and the Provost continues
to treat him as a friar until the revelation
in Act 5.
190 **character** individual handwriting
signet the Duke's personal seal, used by
him for official documents
191 **strange** unfamiliar

DUKE The contents of this is the return of the Duke. You
    shall anon over-read it at your pleasure, where you
    shall find within these two days he will be here. This is a
    thing that Angelo knows not, for he this very day
    receives letters of strange tenor, perchance of the Duke's
    death, perchance entering into some monastery, but by
    chance nothing of what is writ. Look, the unfolding star
    calls up the shepherd. Put not yourself into amazement   200
    how these things should be; all difficulties are but easy
    when they are known. Call your executioner, and off
    with Barnardine's head. I will give him a present shrift,
    and advise him for a better place. Yet you are amazed,
    but this shall absolutely resolve you. Come away, it is
    almost clear dawn.   *Exeunt*

4.3   *Enter Pompey*

POMPEY I am as well-acquainted here as I was in our
    house of profession. One would think it were Mistress
    Overdone's own house, for here be many of her old
    customers. First, here's young Master Rash, he's in for a
    commodity of brown paper and old ginger, nine score

206 *Exeunt*] F (*Exit.*)

197 **tenor** meaning, substance

198–9 **by chance … writ** As it so happens,
    the Duke will do none of the things
    written in the letters.

199 **the unfolding star** the morning star,
    indicating that it is time to unfold the
    sheep (no other example of *unfolding* in
    this sense is recorded). Commentators
    have praised this vivid touch of pastoral-
    ism; it also hints that the time has come
    for the prisoners to be released.

201–2 **all difficulties … known** This is usu-
    ally seen as equivalent to the proverb,
    'everything is easy after it has been done'
    (Tilley D418), but *known* may mean 'fully
    recognized and understood'; difficulties
    vanish when we face up to them.

204 **a better place** The phrase is used several
    times by Shakespeare, but this is the sole
    instance in which it means 'heaven, the
    next world'.

205 **this** the letter mentioned in ll. 188–91
    absolutely resolve you completely clear
    up your difficulties

4.3.1 **am as well-acquainted** have as good a
    circle of acquaintances

2 **profession** professional activity, though
    in Pompey's mouth it clearly refers to
    prostitution, as it does when used in
    scene 19 of *Pericles*. There may perhaps
    be a link with 2.1.63–4, 'now she pro-
    fesses a hot-house'.

4 **Rash** hasty, impetuous (in making finan-
    cial commitments). In the following cata-
    logue of prisoners they are all given
    allegorical type-names in the manner of
    Langland or Bunyan. They are mostly
    young gallants who have failed disas-
    trously in their attempts to be fashionable
    men-about-town.

5 **commodity** The term refers to a practice
    by which usurers cheated their clients,
    who contracted to pay back a certain sum
    of money, but received part of the loan in
    the form of goods or commodities, which
    they were then supposed to sell. These
    were frequently of poor quality and worth
    only a small fraction of the sum owed for
    them.
    brown paper coarse wrapping-paper, of
    little value; frequently mentioned by Eliz-
    abethan writers as a typical 'commodity'

and seventeen pounds, of which he made five marks
ready money. Marry, then ginger was not much in
request, for the old women were all dead. Then is there
here one Master Caper, at the suit of Master Three-pile
the mercer, for some four suits of peach-coloured satin,   10
which now peaches him a beggar. Then have we here
young Dizzy, and young Master Deep-vow, and Master
Copper-spur, and Master Starve-lackey the rapier and
dagger man, and young Drop-heir that killed lusty
Pudding, and Master Forthright the tilter, and brave
Master Shoe-tie the great traveller, and wild Half-can

4.3.14 Drop-heir] F; Drop-hair OXFORD   15 Forthright] WARBURTON; *Forthlight* F   16 Shoe-
tie] F (*Shootie*)

5 **old** perhaps implying 'stale, poor quality'
5–7 **nine score … ready money** He was
legally responsible for a debt of £197, of
which he received only £3. 6s. 8d. in
actual cash, £3.33 in decimal currency.
(A mark was worth 13s. 4d., two-thirds
of £1.) The discrepancy between the two
figures is deliberately outrageous.

8 **the old women were all dead** Old women
were supposed to love ginger; see *Merchant* 3.1.8–9, 'as lying a gossip … as
ever knapped ginger'. Possibly they were
dead because of the plague of 1603.
9 **Caper** an extravagant leap or jump carried out while dancing
9–10 **suit … suits** an obvious play of
words: (a) law-suit; (b) suits of clothing
Three-pile See 1.2.32 n.
10 **peach-coloured** pale red or deep pink
11 **peaches him a beggar** accuses him of
beggary, brings him to trial as a beggar
(because he cannot pay for his clothes).
The verb is dependent on *suit* in l. 9, and
obviously plays on *peach* in *peach-
coloured*.
12 **Dizzy** giddy, mentally confused
Deep-vow presumably a lover who passionately swears fidelity to his mistress
13 **Copper-spur** OED does not record this
phrase, but under *spur*, *sb*¹ 1c, it gives *gilt*
or *gilded spurs*, 'as the distinctive mark of
a knight', and quotes Marston's *The
Malcontent* 1.8.27–8, 'as your knight
courts your city widow with jingling of
his gilt spurs'. Presumably Master Copper-spur has had his spurs coated with
polished copper in an attempt to pass
them off as gilt spurs.
13 **Starve-lackey** A *lackey* is a footman or

servant; in this case his master is too
mean or penurious to feed him properly.
13–14 **rapier and dagger** Fencing or duel-
ling with a rapier in one hand and a
dagger in the other became fashionable
at the end of the 16th c., replacing the
older use of sword and buckler.
14 **Drop-heir** not discussed in OED or recorded elsewhere. As he is *young* he
probably accompanies and preys upon
rich heirs, but the exact force of *Drop* is
hard to establish. It may mean that he
brings them down to penury, or, in view
of the fact that he has *killed lusty Pudding*,
it may be an early use of OED's sense 18,
and imply that he quarrels with the heirs
and then strikes them down. Leisi suggests a pun on *Drop-hair* (someone whose
hair has fallen out because of syphilis).
14–15 **lusty Pudding** ?a rich young heir,
corpulent because he eats large meals
15 **Forthright** F's *Forthlight* is not recorded
in OED, and cannot be given a satisfactory explanation. *Forthright* has OED's
sense 1 for the adjective, 'going directly
forward', and could be glossed as 'someone who charges boldly at the target'.
tilter Tilting was an aristocratic sport in
which horsemen armed with lances tried
to knock each other from their seats.
(Sometimes the participant attacked a
target made of wood, or tried to seize a
ring suspended in mid-air on the point of
his lance.)
brave 'extravagantly dressed' rather
than 'courageous'
16 **Shoe-tie** shoe-lace (but of a very elaborate
kind made into an ornamental rosette).
Shoe-ties were jeered at as a fashionable
affectation by Ben Jonson in *Every Man*

that stabbed Pots, and I think forty more, all great doers
in our trade, and are now 'for the Lord's sake!'

    Enter Abhorson

ABHORSON Sirrah, bring Barnardine hither.

POMPEY Master Barnardine, you must rise and be hanged,   20
Master Barnardine!

ABHORSON What ho, Barnardine!

BARNARDINE (*within*) A pox o' your throats! Who makes
that noise there? What are you?

POMPEY Your friends, sir, the hangman. You must be so
good, sir, to rise and be put to death.

BARNARDINE (*within*) Away, you rogue, away, I am sleepy.

ABHORSON Tell him he must awake, and that quickly too.

POMPEY Pray, Master Barnardine, awake till you are
executed, and sleep afterwards.   30

ABHORSON Go in to him and fetch him out.

POMPEY He is coming, sir, he is coming. I hear his straw
rustle.

    Enter Barnardine

ABHORSON Is the axe upon the block, sirrah?

POMPEY Very ready, sir.

BARNARDINE How now, Abhorson, what's the news with
you?

---

23 *within* (F has '*Barnardine within.*' *centred after l.* 22)   27 *within*] THEOBALD; *not in* F

Out of His Humour, Induction, l. 112, and
another reference by Jonson, in Epigram
88, l. 4, suggests that they were a French
fashion which the young man referred to
here might have picked up on his travels.

16–17 **wild Half-can that stabbed Pots** *Half-
can* is not recorded in *OED*, and the sense
is not clear. Dover Wilson ingeniously
suggested that 'a half-can was a larger
vessel than a "pot" which it had put out
of fashion among topers', but there seems
to be no evidence clearly establishing the
relation in size between a *can* (a drinking-
vessel of wood or metal) and a *pot* (normally of pewter or earthenware). Both
cans and pots came in various shapes and
sizes; possibly a *half-can* held half a pint,
though there is no support for this in
OED. F has no initial capital for *Pots*, but
in view of *wild* it is probable that he was a
drinking-companion stabbed by Half-can

in a drunken frenzy. A similar phrase,
half-pots, again not recorded in *OED*,
occurs in Middleton and Dekker's *The
Roaring Girl* 1.2.204–5.

17–18 **doers in our trade** frequenters of
prostitutes

18 **for the Lord's sake** the cry of prisoners
begging for food through the prison win-
dows. A fuller version, 'Meat for the
lord's sake!', occurs in Heywood's *A
Woman Killed with Kindness* 3.1.78.

20 **rise** Lever notes the play on words: (*a*) get
up from sleep; (*b*) ascend the scaffold.
  be hanged The phrase is often merely an
oath, as in 'Speak and be hanged', *Timon*
5.2.16, but here it is also gruesomely
literal. Lines 34 and 62 suggest that
Barnardine is to be beheaded with an axe,
not hanged, but Pompey may use the
phrase for the sake of the joke.

ABHORSON Truly, sir, I would desire you to clap into your
    prayers, for look you, the warrant's come.
BARNARDINE You rogue, I have been drinking all night, I   40
    am not fitted for it.
POMPEY O, the better, sir, for he that drinks all night, and
    is hanged betimes in the morning, may sleep the
    sounder all the next day.
        Enter Duke as a Friar
ABHORSON Look you, sir, here comes your ghostly father.
    Do we jest now, think you?
DUKE Sir, induced by my charity, and hearing how hastily
    you are to depart, I am come to advise you, comfort
    you, and pray with you.
BARNARDINE Friar, not I. I have been drinking hard all   50
    night, and I will have more time to prepare me, or they
    shall beat out my brains with billets. I will not consent
    to die this day, that's certain.
DUKE

    O, sir, you must, and therefore I beseech you
    Look forward on the journey you shall go.
BARNARDINE I swear I will not die today for any man's
    persuasion.
DUKE But hear you—
BARNARDINE Not a word. If you have anything to say to
    me, come to my ward, for thence will not I today. *Exit*   60
        Enter Provost
DUKE

    Unfit to live or die; O gravel heart!
PROVOST

    After him, fellows, bring him to the block.
        Exeunt Abhorson and Pompey
    Now, sir, how do you find the prisoner?

44.1 *as a Friar*] ROWE; *not in* F   62 PROVOST After] HANMER; After F   62.1 *Exeunt ... Pompey*]
CAPELL; *not in* F

38–9 **clap into your prayers** start praying
    urgently
43 **betimes** early
45 **ghostly father** father confessor
52 **billets** sticks used for firewood or as a
    weapon
60 **ward** the part of the prison where Barnar-
    dine sleeps (sometimes glossed as 'cell',
    but the word tends to refer to a larger

area, where several prisoners would be
    confined)
61 **gravel heart** not recorded elsewhere;
    equivalent in meaning to such phrases as
    flint-hearted (*Venus* 95), *marble-hearted*
    (*Lear* 1.4.237), and *stony-hearted* (*1
    Henry IV* 2.2.26)
62 **After ... block** F attributes this line to the
    Duke. It might be argued that in his anger

DUKE

A creature unprepared, unmeet for death,
And to transport him in the mind he is
Were damnable.

PROVOST   Here in the prison, father,
There died this morning of a cruel fever
One Ragozine, a most notorious pirate,
A man of Claudio's years, his beard and head
Just of his colour. What if we do omit   70
This reprobate till he were well inclined,
And satisfy the deputy with the visage
Of Ragozine, more like to Claudio?

DUKE

O, 'tis an accident that heaven provides.
Dispatch it presently, the hour draws on
Prefixed by Angelo. See this be done,
And sent according to command, whiles I
Persuade this rude wretch willingly to die.

PROVOST

This shall be done, good father, presently.
But Barnardine must die this afternoon,   80
And how shall we continue Claudio,
To save me from the danger that might come
If he were known alive?

DUKE   Let this be done:
Put them in secret holds, both Barnardine
And Claudio.

---

the Duke forgets that he is a friar who has
no power to issue orders of this kind, but
four lines later he says that it would be
'damnable' to execute Barnardine, and
the line is much more appropriate to the
Provost. In addition, l. 61 is the last line of
page G3 in F, and l. 62 is the first line of
the next page; perhaps the speech-prefixes
became confused during the process of
casting-off copy prior to composition.

64 **unprepared** in the spiritual sense (see
2.1.35 n.)
unmeet unsuitable
65 **transport** remove from this world to
the next, put to death (the only example
of this specific sense in Shakespeare
and *OED*)

68 **Ragozine** presumably a native of Ragusa,
an Adriatic port commercially flourish-
ing in the 16th c., now part of Yugoslavia
(modern Dubrovnik)
70 **omit** disregard, leave aside
71 **reprobate** evil character, villain
well inclined in a suitable frame of mind
(to be executed)
74 **accident** unexpected event, chance happening. The fortunate coincidence of Ragozine's death does seem implausible,
and modern audiences sometimes laugh
at this line.
75 **presently** See 3.1.264 n.
81 **continue** keep alive
84 **in ... holds** *OED hold sb*[1] 4 gives this as a
stock phrase, 'in custody, confinement'.

Ere twice the sun hath made his journal greeting
To yonder generation, you shall find
Your safety manifested.

PROVOST   I am your free dependant.

DUKE

Quick, dispatch, and send the head to Angelo.

Exit Provost

Now will I write letters to Angelo—   90
The Provost, he shall bear them—whose contents
Shall witness to him I am near at home,
And that by great injunctions I am bound
To enter publicly. Him I'll desire
To meet me at the consecrated fount
A league below the city, and from thence,
By cold gradation and well-balanced form,
We shall proceed with Angelo.

Enter Provost with the head of Ragozine

PROVOST

Here is the head, I'll carry it myself.

DUKE

Convenient is it. Make a swift return,   100
For I would commune with you of such things
That want no ear but yours.

87 yonder] ROWE; yond F   89.1 *Exit Provost*] POPE; *Exit.* F (*at l.* 88)   90 Angelo] F; Varrius
NOSWORTHY   97 well-balanced] ROWE; weale-ballanc'd F   98.1 *with ... Ragozine*] DYCE;
not in F

86 **journal** daily
87 **yonder** This emendation of F's *yond* is
based on the assumption that Crane or
the compositor accidentally shortened
the word. Confusion between the two
words could easily occur; in *Othello*
1.2.28, F has *yond* while Q has *yonder*.
generation those who are alive at the
moment; possibly a biblical usage (compare 'this generation' in Matthew 12:
41–2). *Yonder generation* refers to those
outside the prison, who would be able to
observe the passage of the sun.
88 **I am ... dependant** (*a*) I am completely at
your service; (*b*) I put myself entirely
under your protection
90 **letters to Angelo** Possibly *Angelo* is a
compositor's error for *Varrius*, but the F
reading can be defended (see the fuller
discussion in Appendix A).
93 **injunctions** This can only mean 'instruc-

tions' or 'orders' (*OED* 1), but we are not
told of the source from which they origi-
nate. Possibly the Duke is simply making
it clear that he has good reasons for his
public entry, since he might have been
expected to return as quietly and privately as he went away at the end of Act 1.
95 **consecrated fount** holy spring or well
97 **cold gradation** advancing step by step in
a calm and methodical way
well-balanced Attempts to gloss F's *weale-
ballanc'd* as 'balanced as in a good weal it
should be' or 'weighed for the public
good' are strained and unconvincing.
The emended phrase would mean 'judici-
ously poised, showing no overt partial-
ity', and it is earlier than any of the
usages quoted in *OED*.
form legal procedure (*OED* 11)
101 **commune** talk, consult (stressed on the
first syllable)

PROVOST   I'll make all speed.   *Exit*

ISABELLA (*within*)

Peace, ho, be here!

DUKE

The tongue of Isabel—she's come to know

If yet her brother's pardon be come hither.

But I will keep her ignorant of her good,

To make her heavenly comforts of despair

When it is least expected.

    Enter Isabella

ISABELLA

Ho, by your leave!

DUKE

Good morning to you, fair and gracious daughter.   110

ISABELLA

The better, given me by so holy a man.

Hath yet the deputy sent my brother's pardon?

DUKE

He hath released him, Isabel, from the world.

His head is off, and sent to Angelo.

ISABELLA

Nay, but it is not so!

DUKE   It is no other.

Show your wisdom, daughter, in your close patience.

ISABELLA

O, I will to him and pluck out his eyes!

DUKE

You shall not be admitted to his sight.

ISABELLA

Unhappy Claudio, wretched Isabel,

Injurious world, most damnèd Angelo!   120

DUKE

This nor hurts him, nor profits you a jot.

Forbear it therefore, give your cause to heaven.

Mark what I say, which you shall find

By every syllable a faithful verity.

The Duke comes home tomorrow—nay, dry your eyes.

103 *within* (F *has 'Isabell within.' centred after l.* 102)

106–8 These lines are discussed in the Intro-   116 **close** reticent, secretive
duction, pp. 24–5.

One of our convent, and his confessor,
Gives me this instance: already he hath carried
Notice to Escalus and Angelo,
Who do prepare to meet him at the gates,
There to give up their power. If you can pace your
    wisdom 130
In that good path that I would wish it go,
And you shall have your bosom on this wretch,
Grace of the Duke, revenges to your heart,
And general honour.
ISABELLA   I am directed by you.
DUKE
This letter then to Friar Peter give;
'Tis that he sent me of the Duke's return.
Say, by this token I desire his company
At Mariana's house tonight. Her cause and yours
I'll perfect him withal, and he shall bring you
Before the Duke, and to the head of Angelo 140
Accuse him home and home. For my poor self,
I am combinèd by a sacred vow,

130 can ∧] F; can, ROWE

126 **his confessor** The audience might assume, if it still remembers, that this is
Friar Thomas from 1.3, but the rest of
the scene suggests that it is the Friar
Peter who is suddenly introduced into
the play at l. 135. The discrepancy is not
noticed in the theatre, and if F is based
on foul papers it may be due to
Shakespeare's failure to make up his
mind whether or not the two friars were
the same person.

127 **instance** proof, evidence
he It is not clear whether this is the Duke
or someone else, though *him* at l. 129
must be the Duke.

130 **If . . . wisdom** Many editors put a comma
after *can*. This makes the construction
more coherent by modern standards, but
Shakespeare's *If* constructions do not
always develop according to strict grammatical rules (compare 5.1.512, 'If any
woman wronged. . .', *Caesar* 2.1.113–
16, *Othello* 1.1.122 ff., and *All's Well*
5.3.116–18).
pace train (it) to move in a slow and
steady way

132 **your bosom on** what you eagerly desire
inflicted on

133 **to your heart** as ample as your heart
could wish. For a parallel construction
compare 5.1.241, *to your height of pleasure.*

136 **that** the letter
of telling of

139 **perfect** instruct or inform completely
(stress on first syllable)

140 **to the head** to his face, in a directly
personal way. This is *OED*'s first quotation, *head sb.* 38, but the usage occurs
earlier in *Dream* 1.1.106, and *Ado*
5.1.62.

141 **home and home** See 1.3.41 n. The
repetition has an intensifying effect, as in
phrases like *through and through* (*As You
Like It* 2.7.59 and *Winter's Tale* 4.4.112).

142 **combinèd** *OED combine v.* 6 tentatively
suggests that this may mean 'bound'. It
could, however, have the commoner
meaning of 'joined, associated with
someone else' (*OED* 1b), and the whole
line would mean 'I have promised to join
someone else'.

And shall be absent. (*Giving her a letter*) Wend you
    with this letter.
Command these fretting waters from your eyes
With a light heart; trust not my holy order
If I pervert your course. Who's here?
    Enter Lucio
LUCIO Goode'en, friar, where's the Provost?
DUKE Not within, sir.
LUCIO O pretty Isabella, I am pale at mine heart to see
    thine eyes so red; thou must be patient. I am fain to dine   150
    and sup with water and bran; I dare not for my head fill
    my belly, one fruitful meal would set me to't. But they
    say the Duke will be here tomorrow. By my troth,
    Isabel, I loved thy brother; if the old fantastical Duke of
    dark corners had been at home, he had lived.
                                    Exit Isabella
DUKE Sir, the Duke is marvellous little beholding to your
    reports, but the best is, he lives not in them.
LUCIO Friar, thou know'st not the Duke so well as I do.
    He's a better woodman than thou tak'st him for.
DUKE Well, you'll answer this one day. Fare ye well.   160
LUCIO Nay, tarry, I'll go along with thee. I can tell thee
    pretty tales of the Duke.
DUKE You have told me too many of him already, sir, if
    they be true. If not true, none were enough.

143 *Giving . . . letter*] OXFORD; *not in* F   147 Goode'en] This edition; Good'euen F   155.1 *Exit Isabella*] THEOBALD; *not in* F

143 **Wend you** betake yourself, go. The
   Duke seems to take it for granted that she
   knows who Friar Peter is and where he
   lives.
144 **fretting** vexing, painful
146 **pervert your course** deflect you from the
   right course of action
149 **pale at mine heart** frightened; compare
   pale-hearted fear, *Macbeth* 4.1.101
150 **fain** obliged
151 **bran** the coarsest type of bread, with a
   high proportion of wheat-husk
   for my head for fear of losing my head by
   execution
152 **fruitful** abundant, copious (perhaps also
   with a hint of 'fertile, productive of
   offspring')
   set me to't set me to work (in a sexual
   sense)

154 **fantastical** See 3.1.356 n.
154–5 **of dark corners** 'given to lurking in
   secret hiding-places'. The phrase may
   also imply that the Duke makes secret
   assignations with women.
156 **beholding** obliged, indebted
157 **he lives not in them** *Lives* can mean
   'dwells, inhabits' or 'continues to be
   remembered' (*OED live v*[1] 11, frequent in
   Shakespeare's *Sonnets*), and *in* can mean
   'by virtue of', so the whole clause can be
   variously paraphrased: 'he doesn't correspond to your account' or 'his reputation
   doesn't depend on you'.
159 **woodman** one who hunts in a wood or
   forest (and implying that the Duke chases
   after women; compare Falstaff's use of
   the term in *Merry Wives* 5.5.26)

LUCIO I was once before him for getting a wench with
child.

DUKE Did you such a thing?

LUCIO Yes, marry did I; but I was fain to forswear it. They
would else have married me to the rotten medlar.

DUKE Sir, your company is fairer than honest. Rest you   170
well.

LUCIO By my troth, I'll go with thee to the lane's end. If
bawdy talk offend you, we'll have very little of it. Nay,
friar, I am a kind of burr, I shall stick.   *Exeunt*

4.4   *Enter Angelo and Escalus*

ESCALUS Every letter he hath writ hath disvouched other.

ANGELO In most uneven and distracted manner. His actions show much like to madness; pray heaven his
wisdom be not tainted. And why meet him at the gates
and redeliver our authorities there?

ESCALUS I guess not.

ANGELO And why should we proclaim it, in an hour before
his entering, that if any crave redress of injustice, they
should exhibit their petitions in the street?

ESCALUS He shows his reason for that, to have a dispatch   10
of complaints and to deliver us from devices hereafter,
which shall then have no power to stand against us.

ANGELO Well, I beseech you let it be proclaimed betimes i'

4.4.5 redeliver] CAPELL; re-/liuer F

169 **medlar** the fruit of the medlar-tree, not
edible until it has decayed to a soft pulpy
state. The term is applied contemptuously to women in Dekker's *2 Honest
Whore* 1.1.98, 'women are like medlars,
no sooner ripe but rotten'. See also Tilley
M863 and R133.

170 **fairer** more speciously attractive

174 **burr** a prickly seed-head which attaches
itself to clothing. 'To stick like a burr' is
proverbial (Tilley B724).

4.4.1 **disvouched** a form not recorded elsewhere of *disavouched*, 'repudiated, con-
tradicted'
other each preceding one (*OED other
pron.* B2c)

2 **uneven** irregular, inconsistent

4 **tainted** infected (with some kind of mental illness)

5 **redeliver** The word in F is split between
two lines (*re-/liuer*). *OED* quotes it under
reliver v., a legal term meaning 'give up
again, restore', and some editors retain F.
But the other recorded uses of *reliver* and
relivery date from the mid 15th c., and
it is more probable that in splitting
the word the compositor accidentally
omitted a syllable.

7 **in an hour before** Lever glosses as 'leaving a clear hour', but *OED in* 22e gives it
as exemplifying an obsolete usage in
which *in* is redundant, so that the phrase
simply means 'an hour before'.

9 **exhibit** hold out

10 **dispatch** prompt settlement

11 **devices** plots, intrigues

13–15 **Well … him** Some editors rearrange
these lines as verse. But it is better to have

the morn. I'll call you at your house. Give notice to such
men of sort and suit as are to meet him.

ESCALUS I shall, sir. Fare you well.

ANGELO Good night.   *Exit Escalus*

This deed unshapes me quite, makes me unpregnant
And dull to all proceedings. A deflowered maid,
And by an eminent body that enforced   20
The law against it! But that her tender shame
Will not proclaim against her maiden loss,
How might she tongue me! Yet reason dares her no,
For my authority bears so credent bulk
That no particular scandal once can touch
But it confounds the breather. He should have lived,
Save that his riotous youth with dangerous sense

---

17 *Exit Escalus*] CAPELL; *Exit* F (*after l.* 16)   24 so] DYCE; of a F; off a F4

the dialogue consistently in prose, with Angelo shifting to verse when he begins his soliloquy.

14 **call** call on, meet
15 **of sort and suit** of high rank and with a retinue of servants
18 **unshapes me quite** totally destroys my self-possession
   unpregnant slow-witted, lacking in resourcefulness
19 **dull to all proceedings** unresponsive to all that is happening
20 **eminent body** important public figure
   enforced put into force, compelled others to obey
22 **maiden loss** loss of virginity
23 **tongue** reproach
   reason dares her no *No* is used in the 16th and 17th cs., in a way apparently unrecorded in *OED*, to mean 'not to do so', as in the anonymous morality play *Wealth and Health*, 1557 (MSR, 1907, l. 658), 'if thou dost, thou were as good no', where the last clause means 'you would have been better off not doing it', and Beaumont and Fletcher, *A Wife for a Month* 4.3.124, 'I charged him no' (meaning 'I ordered him not to'). But 'reason dares her not to do it' hardly fits the context, and it must mean something like 'reason tells her she dare not do it (because of the risk involved)'.
24 **bears so** F's *bears of a* is altered in F4 to *bears off a*, but none of the senses of *bears*

off recorded in *OED* fits the context, and in that form the line is rhythmically very clumsy. The emendation accepted here gives a construction similar to that in *1 Henry IV* 5.1.62–3, where Worcester tells the king that his power 'Grew by our feeding to so great a bulk | That even our love durst not come near your sight'.
   credent inspiring respect and belief
25 **particular** personal (aimed at Angelo himself)
26 **confounds** with a mixture of senses: (*a*) destroys, ruins; (*b*) confutes (in a debate or argument); (*c*) throws into confusion
   breather person uttering the scandal
   should This may simply be the conditional, equivalent to 'would': 'I would have pardoned him, were it not for the fact that . . .'. This gives us a hypocritical Angelo, pretending to himself that he really meant to spare Claudio, but was obliged not to. On the other hand, *should* can mean 'ought to', which would display some pangs of conscience in Angelo: 'I ought to have pardoned him, but I do have an excuse for not doing so'. Both meanings may be present.
27 **riotous youth** youthful wildness
   with dangerous sense probably meaning 'full of sensuality leading to disastrous consequences', though *dangerous* can mean 'ready to meet danger, venturesome', as in Tourneur's *The Atheist's Tragedy* 4.2.38, 'His spirit is so boldly dangerous'.

Might in the times to come have ta'en revenge
By so receiving a dishonoured life
With ransom of such shame. Would yet he had lived!   30
Alack, when once our grace we have forgot,
Nothing goes right; we would, and we would not. *Exit*

4.5   *Enter Duke as himself and Friar Peter*
DUKE (*giving him letters*)
    These letters at fit time deliver me.
    The Provost knows our purpose and our plot.
    The matter being afoot, keep your instruction,
    And hold you ever to our special drift,
    Though sometimes you do blench from this to that
    As cause doth minister. Go call at Flavius' house,
    And tell him where I stay. Give the like notice
    To Valentius, Rowland, and to Crassus,
    And bid them bring the trumpets to the gate.
    But send me Flavius first.
FRIAR PETER   It shall be speeded well.   *Exit*   10
        Enter Varrius
DUKE
    I thank thee, Varrius, thou hast made good haste.

4.5.0.1 *as himself*] ROWE; *not in* F   1 *giving him letters*] JOHNSON; *not in* F   6 Flavius'] POPE;
Flauia's F; Flavio's EVANS   10 *Exit*] THEOBALD; *not in* F

28 **revenge** The implication seems to be that
    Claudio's sensual nature would have
    revenged itself for the shameful pardon
    granted him by further misconduct,
    though it is hard not to see a hint of fear
    on Angelo's part that Claudio would
    have tried to take revenge on him.
29–30 **By so … shame** by accepting in a
    rebellious and wanton manner a life
    which had been dishonoured by the
    shameful way in which it had been
    purchased
31 **grace** See 3.1.185 n.
32 **we would, and we would not** echoing
    Romans 7: 19, 'For I do not the good
    thing, which I would, but the evil, which
    I would not, that I do'
4.5.1 **me** for me, on my behalf
    3 **afoot** in operation

3 **keep your instruction** follow your in-
    structions
4 **special** See 1.1.18 n. and 1.2.118 n.;
    their plot is aimed specifically at Angelo.
    drift (*a*) purpose, intention; (*b*) scheme or
    plot
5 **blench** start aside, swerve (*OED* 2); in
    giving his evidence Peter may need to
    make rapid shifts of argument, in order to
    disconcert Angelo
6 **minister** prompt, suggest
    Flavius The names here and in l. 8 are an
    odd mixture, but they are there solely to
    create an atmosphere of bustle, and it is
    pointless to look for specific sources for
    the more classical-sounding names.
9 **trumpets** trumpeters
10 **speeded** (*a*) hastened; (*b*) brought to a
    successful conclusion

Come, we will walk. There's other of our friends
Will greet us here anon. My gentle Varrius! *Exeunt*

4.6 *Enter Isabella and Mariana*

ISABELLA

To speak so indirectly I am loath.
I would say the truth, but to accuse him so,
That is your part. Yet I am advised to do it,
He says, to veil full purpose.

MARIANA   Be ruled by him.

ISABELLA

Besides, he tells me that if peradventure
He speak against me on the adverse side,
I should not think it strange, for 'tis a physic
That's bitter to sweet end.

MARIANA   I would Friar Peter—

Enter Friar Peter

ISABELLA

O peace, the friar is come.

FRIAR PETER

Come, I have found you out a stand most fit,   10
Where you may have such vantage on the Duke
He shall not pass you. Twice have the trumpets
    sounded.
The generous and gravest citizens
Have hent the gates, and very near upon
The Duke is entering, therefore hence, away!   *Exeunt*

4.6.8.1 *Enter ... Peter*] F (*centred under first part of l.* 8, 'That's ... end')

4.6.1 **indirectly** quoted in *OED* under 1c,
'not to the point, evasively', but the
stronger meaning, 1b, 'wrongfully, dis-
honestly' is perhaps more appropriate:
Isabella is reluctant to tell what she
knows are lies
2 **him** Angelo
  so truthfully
4 **He** the Duke
  veil conceal, disguise
7 **physic** medicine
8 **bitter to sweet end** unpleasant to swallow
but having a good effect. For similar
proverbial formulations see Tilley M558
and P327.

10 **stand** place at which to stand
11 **vantage on** a favourable position in respect to
12 **Twice ... sounded** Compare *2 Henry IV*
5.5.2, 'The trumpets have sounded
twice'; they sound a third time when
King Henry V enters.
13 **generous** equivalent to 'most generous,
of highest birth'; the superlative inflec-
tion of *gravest* also modifies *generous*
(Abbott 398)
14 **hent** reached, occupied
  very near upon very shortly, in a few
moments

5.1 *Flourish. Enter Duke as himself, Varrius, Provost,*
Officers, Lords, Angelo, Escalus, Lucio, and Citizens at
several doors

DUKE (*to Angelo*)

My very worthy cousin, fairly met.

(*To Escalus*) Our old and faithful friend, we are glad to
see you.

ANGELO *and* ESCALUS

Happy return be to your royal grace.

DUKE

Many and hearty thankings to you both.

We have made enquiry of you, and we hear

Such goodness of your justice that our soul

Cannot but yield you forth to public thanks,

Forerunning more requital.

ANGELO

You make my bonds still greater.

DUKE

O, your desert speaks loud, and I should wrong it   10

To lock it in the wards of covert bosom,

When it deserves with characters of brass

A forted residence 'gainst the tooth of time

And rasure of oblivion. Give me your hand,

5.1.0.1 *Flourish*] EVANS; *not in* F   *as himself*] LEVER; *not in* F   0.1–2 *Provost, Officers,*] CAPELL;
not in F   14 me] F3; we F

5.1.1 **cousin** used elsewhere in Shakespeare
as a courtesy form of address from a ruler
to a nobleman who is not necessarily
related to him. As applied to Angelo the
term appears to be highly complimen-
tary, but it is part of the Duke's strategy to
lure Angelo into a false sense of security.

6 **goodness** a way of combining two meanings: 'good reports concerning the excellence'

7 **yield ... thanks** This seems a slightly
cumbersome way of saying 'thank you in
public', but the formality may be deliberate: their merit is so great that he is
compelled to make a public affirmation
although it may embarrass their modesty.

8 **Forerunning more requital** preceding a
greater reward to be made later

9 **bonds** probably in the sense of 'ties of

duty'; the favours being shown to him
will oblige him to carry out his obliga-
tions to the Duke even more conscien-
tiously than before

11 **wards of covert bosom** secret recesses of
my heart

12 **characters of brass** bronze letters (of the
sort found on a tomb or monument)

13 **forted** fortified
tooth destructive effects

14 **rasure of oblivion** erasure or loss of
reputation brought about because the
person concerned is no longer remembered. In ll. 12–14 the Duke echoes the
language of Renaissance poets who
promise to immortalize their subjects (see
Sonnets 19 and 55). The lines are addressed specifically to Angelo, and are
heavily ironic.

And let the subject see, to make them know
That outward courtesies would fain proclaim
Favours that keep within. Come, Escalus,
You must walk by us on our other hand,
And good supporters are you.
  Enter Friar Peter and Isabella
FRIAR PETER (*to Isabella*)
Now is your time. Speak loud, and kneel before him.   20
ISABELLA
Justice, O royal Duke! Vail your regard
Upon a wronged—I would fain have said, a maid.
O worthy prince, dishonour not your eye
By throwing it on any other object
Till you have heard me in my true complaint,
And given me justice, justice, justice, justice!
DUKE
Relate your wrongs. In what, by whom? Be brief.
Here is Lord Angelo shall give you justice;
Reveal yourself to him.
ISABELLA   O worthy Duke,
You bid me seek redemption of the devil.   30
Hear me yourself, for that which I must speak
Must either punish me, not being believed,
Or wring redress from you. Hear me, O hear me, here!
ANGELO
My lord, her wits I fear me are not firm.
She hath been a suitor to me for her brother
Cut off by course of justice—

19.1 Friar] *not in* F

15 **subject** the Duke's subjects or citizens, seen both as a collective singular (compare 3.1.398 and *Hamlet* 1.1.71 and 1.2.33) and as plural (hence *them* in the second half of the line)
17 **keep within** remain concealed
19 **supporters** with a double meaning: (*a*) attendants in a procession (*OED* 5); (*b*) assistants, helpers
20 **kneel** If Isabella obeys the Friar's instruction all her speeches up to l. 120 should be delivered kneeling. But directors rarely make her do so, perhaps because they think it will lessen the dramatic impact of her kneeling at l. 444.

21 **Vail** lower or cast down
29 **Reveal yourself** *OED* quotes this under 3b, 'show yourself', but it also has the implication of 'explain yourself, let him know your problem'.
32 **punish ... believed** cause me to be punished as a slanderer if it is not believed
33 **here** Some editors emend to *hear*, and Lever regards F's *here* as a 'weak conclusion'. But F never confuses the two words elsewhere in the play, and in fact *here* is emphatic: 'here and now, on the spot'.
36 **Cut off** This is used of someone who dies or is killed prematurely (*OED cut v.* 55d), but it does not necessarily indicate execu-

ISABELLA   By course of justice!

ANGELO

And she will speak most bitterly and strange.

ISABELLA

Most strange, but yet most truly will I speak.
That Angelo's forsworn, is it not strange?
That Angelo's a murderer, is't not strange?   40
That Angelo is an adulterous thief,
An hypocrite, a virgin-violator,
Is it not strange and strange?

DUKE   Nay, it is ten times strange.

ISABELLA

It is not truer he is Angelo
Than this is all as true as it is strange.
Nay, it is ten times true, for truth is truth
To the end of reckoning.

DUKE   Away with her. Poor soul,
She speaks this in the infirmity of sense.

ISABELLA

O prince, I conjure thee, as thou believ'st
There is another comfort than this world,   50
That thou neglect me not with that opinion
That I am touched with madness. Make not impossible
That which but seems unlike. 'Tis not impossible
But one the wicked'st caitiff on the ground

tion by beheading, as is clear from *Hamlet*
1.5.76.

37 **bitterly** angrily, violently
strange equivalent to *strangely* (see Abbott 397). Angelo hints that Isabella is crazed with hatred towards him because of his execution of Claudio.
38 Isabella hits back with the stock antithesis, *strange but true* (see Tilley S914).
41 **adulterous** Isabella already regards Angelo as Mariana's husband because of what she has heard at 3.1.224 and 4.1.70.
thief The word has a shock-effect in branding Angelo as a common criminal; what he has stolen is a woman's virginity.
43 **strange and strange** Compare 4.3.141 n.
ten times See 2.4.80 n.
46 **truth is truth** proverbial (Tilley T581)
47 **To the end of reckoning** (*a*) to the end of

time, perhaps with a hint of the 'last reckoning', the day of judgement (*OED*, 4c); (*b*) no matter how far we push our calculations on the matter
48 **in the infirmity of sense** because her mind is diseased
49 **conjure** entreat, implore
50 **comfort** support, strength deriving from religious faith
51 **neglect ... opinion** do not disregard my complaint because you believe
52 **touched** tainted
53 **unlike** unlikely, improbable
54 **one the wicked'st caitiff** equivalent to 'one who is the wickedest caitiff'; an archaic construction common in Chaucer ('oon the beste knyght', *Troilus and Criseyde*, 1.1081) and paralleled in *Cymbeline* 1.6.166–7, 'he is one | The truest mannered ...'. See *OED one* 26.
caitiff villain

May seem as shy, as grave, as just, as absolute,
As Angelo. Even so may Angelo,
In all his dressings, caracts, titles, forms,
Be an arch-villain. Believe it, royal prince.
If he be less, he's nothing; but he's more,
Had I more name for badness.

DUKE   By mine honesty,   60
If she be mad, as I believe no other,
Her madness hath the oddest frame of sense,
Such a dependency of thing on thing,
As e'er I heard in madness.

ISABELLA   O gracious Duke,
Harp not on that, nor do not banish reason
For inequality, but let your reason serve
To make the truth appear where it seems hid,
And hide the false seems true.

DUKE   Many that are not mad
Have sure more lack of reason. What would you say?

ISABELLA
I am the sister of one Claudio,   70
Condemned upon the act of fornication
To lose his head, condemned by Angelo.

---

55 **absolute** faultless, perfect

57 The four nouns in this line describe
external attributes which give Angelo
dignity and impressiveness, and to some
extent overlap. *Dressings* probably refers
to uniforms or robes which indicate his
status; *caracts*, quoted in *OED* under
sense 1, 'mark, sign, or character', may
be symbols of office or badges of rank;
titles are dignities and official positions;
and *forms* are probably ceremonies or
formal procedures which Angelo strictly
adheres to.

59–60 **If he … badness** If he is less evil than I
have shown him to be, then his crimes
are insignificant, but I could prove him to
be far worse if I had a larger vocabulary
to describe evil

62 **oddest** *OED* quotes this under sense 10a
of *odd*, 'unusual, strange', but it is surely
in sense 7, 'unique, remarkable'; the
Duke is not saying that Isabella's arguments are odd, but the opposite, that they
are strikingly logical for someone who
appears to be mad.

62 **frame of sense** coherence of meaning

63 **dependency of thing on thing** logical
connection between one thing and
another

65 **Harp not on that** do not keep on talking
about that (her presumed madness)

65–6 **banish reason | For inequality** reject a
rational argument because it does not
correspond to the normal view (of Angelo). Some editors regard *inequality*, not
used elsewhere by Shakespeare, as referring to the disparity of rank between
Isabella and Angelo, but the Duke has
said nothing about this, and it is less
appropriate to the context.

68 **hide** As Dover Wilson suggests, *hide*
probably depends on *truth* rather than
reason in l. 66; when the truth emerges
from hiding it will obliterate Angelo's
plausible lie.
seems that seems

71 **act** either (*a*) legal act, statute, as at
1.2.168 and 1.4.64, or (*b*) deed, sin, as at
2.3.26 and l. 452 below

I, in probation of a sisterhood,
Was sent to by my brother; one Lucio
As then the messenger—
LUCIO   That's I, an't like your grace.
I came to her from Claudio, and desired her
To try her gracious fortune with Lord Angelo
For her poor brother's pardon.
ISABELLA   That's he indeed.
DUKE (*to Lucio*)
You were not bid to speak.
LUCIO   No, my good lord,
Nor wished to hold my peace.
DUKE   I wish you now then.   80
Pray you take note of it, and when you have
A business for yourself, pray heaven you then
Be perfect.
LUCIO   I warrant your honour.
DUKE
The warrant's for yourself, take heed to't.
ISABELLA
This gentleman told somewhat of my tale.
LUCIO Right.
DUKE
It may be right, but you are i' the wrong
To speak before your time. (*To Isabella*) Proceed.
ISABELLA   I went
To this pernicious caitiff deputy—
DUKE
That's somewhat madly spoken.
ISABELLA   Pardon it;   90
The phrase is to the matter.
DUKE
Mended again. The matter; proceed.

---

73 **probation** a period of testing for candidates to a religious order
75 **As then** at that particular time (*OED as* 34a). Possibly Isabella wishes to indicate that she does not normally have any connection with Lucio.
77 **gracious** happy, prosperous (*OED* 7)
82 **for yourself** that concerns yourself
83 **perfect** able to play your part perfectly

83–4 **warrant … warrant** playing on *warrant* as a verb, meaning 'assure', and a noun, meaning 'legal document to summon or arrest someone'
91 **to** relevant, appropriate to
92 **Mended again** Once more Isabella has justified herself, corrected what appeared to be an error.
The matter See 2.2.33 n.

ISABELLA

In brief, to set the needless process by—
How I persuaded, how I prayed and kneeled,
How he refelled me, and how I replied,
For this was of much length—the vile conclusion
I now begin with grief and shame to utter.
He would not but by gift of my chaste body
To his concupiscible intemperate lust
Release my brother; and after much debatement,   100
My sisterly remorse confutes mine honour,
And I did yield to him. But the next morn betimes,
His purpose surfeiting, he sends a warrant
For my poor brother's head.

DUKE   This is most likely!

ISABELLA

O that it were as like as it is true.

DUKE

By heaven, fond wretch, thou know'st not what thou
         speak'st,
Or else thou art suborned against his honour
In hateful practice. First, his integrity
Stands without blemish; next, it imports no reason
That with such vehemency he should pursue   110
Faults proper to himself. If he had so offended,
He would have weighed thy brother by himself,
And not have cut him off. Someone hath set you on.
Confess the truth, and say by whose advice
Thou cam'st here to complain.

ISABELLA   And is this all?

Then, O you blessèd ministers above,

---

93 **set ... by** set aside, disregard
    needless either (*a*) 'useless, producing no
    result' or (*b*) 'which need not be described
    in full'
    process argument, discussion (*OED* 4)
94 **persuaded** urged, pleaded
95 **refelled** rejected, refused
99 **concupiscible** intense, burning with de-
    sire
101 **remorse** See 2.2.54 n.
    confutes defeats in argument, overcomes
103 **purpose** plan to free Claudio (though it
    could possibly refer to his lust for Isabella)

103 **surfeiting** growing sick because of his
    over-indulgence in sexuality
105 **like** likely, probable
107 **suborned** induced by someone else to
    make false accusations
108 **practice** conspiracy
109 **imports no reason** means nothing rea-
    sonable, does not make sense
110 **pursue** follow in order to punish
113 **set ... on** incited, prompted
116 **ministers** angels, particularly those
    who intervene in human affairs

Keep me in patience, and with ripened time
Unfold the evil which is here wrapped up
In countenance! Heaven shield your grace from woe,
As I, thus wronged, hence unbelievèd go.   120
DUKE
I know you'd fain be gone. An officer!
To prison with her.
        Isabella is arrested
                            Shall we thus permit
A blasting and a scandalous breath to fall
On him so near us? This needs must be a practice.
Who knew of your intent and coming hither?
ISABELLA
One that I would were here, Friar Lodowick.
                        ⌈*Exit with Officers*⌉
DUKE
A ghostly father, belike. Who knows that Lodowick?
LUCIO
My lord, I know him, 'tis a meddling friar.
I do not like the man; had he been lay, my lord,
For certain words he spake against your grace   130
In your retirement, I had swinged him soundly.
DUKE
Words against me? This' a good friar belike.
And to set on this wretched woman here
Against our substitute! Let this friar be found.

122 *Isabella ... arrested*] WILSON; *not in* F   126.1 *Exit ... Officers*] LEVER; *not in* F

117–19 **and with ... countenance** These
        lines may echo such proverbs as 'Time
        brings the truth to light' (Tilley T324)
        and 'Time reveals (discloses) all things'
        (T333).
118 **Unfold** open up, disclose
        wrapped up concealed
119 **countenance** The primary meaning is
        'patronage, favour' (*OED* 8); the Duke's
        obstinate support for Angelo is helping to
        conceal the truth. Other senses given in
        OED could be present, all of which would
        refer to Angelo and his behaviour: 1
        bearing, demeanour, 2b outward show,
        4 facial expression, 6 composure, confi-
        dence of manner, and 9 worldly reputa-
        tion.

120 If she has been kneeling Isabella should
        rise to her feet and turn as though to exit.
122 **To prison with her** The problem of
        Isabella's exit is discussed in Appendix A.
123 **blasting** blighting, defaming
126 **Lodowick** It might seem rather late in
        the play to learn the Duke's name when
        in disguise, but the presence of Friar Peter
        makes it necessary to distinguish be-
        tween the two friars.
128 **meddling** fond of intrigue
131 **retirement** absence from public life
        had would have
        swinged beaten, thrashed
132 **This'** equivalent to 'this is', a contrac-
        tion found several times in Shakespeare
        (Abbott 461)

LUCIO

But yesternight, my lord, she and that friar,
I saw them at the prison; a saucy friar,
A very scurvy fellow.

FRIAR PETER   Blessed be your royal grace!

I have stood by, my lord, and I have heard
Your royal ear abused. First, hath this woman
Most wrongfully accused your substitute,   140
Who is as free from touch or soil with her
As she from one ungot.

DUKE   We did believe no less.

Know you that Friar Lodowick that she speaks of?

FRIAR PETER

I know him for a man divine and holy,
Not scurvy, nor a temporary meddler,
As he's reported by this gentleman,
And on my trust a man that never yet
Did, as he vouches, misreport your grace.

LUCIO

My lord, most villainously, believe it.

FRIAR PETER

Well, he in time may come to clear himself,   150
But at this instant he is sick, my lord,
Of a strange fever. Upon his mere request,
Being come to knowledge that there was complaint
Intended 'gainst Lord Angelo, came I hither,
To speak as from his mouth what he doth know
Is true and false, and what he with his oath
And all probation will make up full clear
Whensoever he's convented. First, for this woman,

---

136 **saucy** insolent
137 **scurvy** worthless, contemptible
139 **abused** imposed upon, deceived
141 **touch or soil** Both words can mean
  'sexual contact' and 'moral stain or
  taint'; possibly *touch* has more of the first
  meaning, *soil* more of the second.
142 **ungot** not yet begotten
145 **temporary meddler** *OED*, *temporary* 2,
  glosses as 'a meddler with temporal or
  secular affairs'; he is not the kind of priest
  who loves to intrigue in politics or
  worldly matters.

148 **misreport** slander
152 **strange** This could be in *OED*'s sense 8,
  'rare, unusual', or 9, 'exceptionally
  severe'.
  mere sole (perhaps intended to emphasize
  that the two friars are not part of some
  larger conspiracy)
157 **probation** proof
  make up full clear establish clearly as the
  complete truth
158 **convented** summoned to appear (stress
  on the second syllable)

To justify this worthy nobleman
So vulgarly and personally accused,   160
Her shall you hear disprovèd to her eyes,
Till she herself confess it.
DUKE   Good Friar, let's hear it.
                                        Exit Friar Peter
Do you not smile at this, Lord Angelo?
O heaven, the vanity of wretched fools!
Give us some seats.
          Two seats are brought in
                          Come, cousin Angelo,
In this I'll be impartial: be you judge
Of your own cause.
          The Duke and Angelo sit
          Enter Friar Peter with Mariana veiled
                          Is this the witness, friar?
First let her show her face, and after speak.
MARIANA
Pardon, my lord, I will not show my face
Until my husband bid me.   170
DUKE What, are you married?
MARIANA No, my lord.
DUKE Are you a maid?

162.1 *Exit ... Peter*] OXFORD; *not in* F   165 *Two ... in*] WILSON; *not in* F   167 *The Duke ... sit*]
OXFORD; *not in* F   *Enter ... veiled*] OXFORD; *Enter Mariana* F (*at end of line*)   168 her face] F2;
your face F

---

160 **vulgarly** publicly, in the eyes of the
world (*OED* 3)
161 **to her eyes** This seems to mean 'to her
face, in a defiant or challenging manner'
(see *OED to* 5b, quoting *2 Henry IV*
3.1.59–60, 'even to the eyes of
Richard | Gave him defiance'). The phrase
suggests that at this point Shakespeare
envisaged a direct confrontation between
Mariana and Isabella.
164 **vanity** futility (a powerful irony: the
Duke pretends to regard Isabella's accusations as a sordid plot which cannot
possibly succeed, but the line is really
directed at Angelo himself)
166 **impartial** Many editors gloss as 'unin-
volved, not taking part' rather than
'unbiased', but there is no support for this
in *OED*, and Shakespeare's uses of the
word elsewhere have the normal modern

meaning. Possibly the term is a double
irony: he appears to be *partial* to Angelo,
who will therefore hope to escape detection, but he is really *impartial* in that he
will make Angelo expose his hypocrisy to
the full.
166–7 **be you judge | Of your own cause** This
echoes Olivia's words to Malvolio in
Twelfth Night 5.1.351–2, 'Thou shalt be
both the plaintiff and the judge | Of thine
own cause'. Angelo is intended to assume
that the Duke sees him as somewhat like
Malvolio, the innocent victim of a cruel
trick who has the moral right to judge his
persecutors. At the same time the audience should be aware of the common
proverb, 'No man ought to be judge in his
own cause' (Tilley M341)
168 **First ... speak** a curiously close echo of
1.4.12–13

MARIANA No, my lord.

DUKE A widow then?

MARIANA Neither, my lord.

DUKE Why, you are nothing then: neither maid, widow,
    nor wife?

LUCIO My lord, she may be a punk, for many of them are
    neither maid, widow, nor wife.   180

DUKE Silence that fellow. I would he had some cause to
    prattle for himself.

LUCIO Well, my lord.

MARIANA

    My lord, I do confess I ne'er was married,
    And I confess besides I am no maid.
    I have known my husband, yet my husband
    Knows not that ever he knew me.

LUCIO He was drunk then, my lord, it can be no better.

DUKE For the benefit of silence, would thou wert so too.

LUCIO Well, my lord.   190

DUKE

    This is no witness for Lord Angelo.

MARIANA

    Now I come to't, my lord.
    She that accuses him of fornication
    In self-same manner doth accuse my husband,
    And charges him, my lord, with such a time
    When I'll depose I had him in mine arms
    With all the effect of love.

ANGELO

    Charges she mo than me?

MARIANA

    Not that I know.

DUKE

    No? You say your husband.   200

177–8 **neither maid, widow, nor wife** a
    stock riddle (Tilley M26), and the answer
    was frequently, though not invariably,
    the same as Lucio's
179 **punk** prostitute
181–2 **had ... himself** needed to defend
    himself against an accusation
186 **known** had intercourse with

189 **For ... too** I wish you were drunk, if it
    made you keep quiet
197 **all ... love** full sexual union
198 **Charges ... me?** Angelo is bewildered:
    not recognizing himself as the *husband* in
    question, he asks whether Isabella has
    accused other men of having had illicit
    relations with her.

MARIANA

Why, just, my lord, and that is Angelo,
Who thinks he knows that he ne'er knew my body,
But knows, he thinks, that he knows Isabel's.

ANGELO

This is a strange abuse. Let's see thy face.

MARIANA

My husband bids me, now I will unmask.
    She unveils
This is that face, thou cruel Angelo,
Which once thou swor'st was worth the looking on;
This is the hand, which with a vowed contract
Was fast belocked in thine; this is the body
That took away the match from Isabel,   210
And did supply thee at thy garden-house
In her imagined person.

DUKE (*to Angelo*)

Know you this woman?

LUCIO

Carnally, she says.

DUKE

Sirrah, no more!

LUCIO

Enough, my lord.

ANGELO

My lord, I must confess I know this woman,
And five years since there was some speech of
    marriage
Betwixt myself and her, which was broke off,
Partly for that her promisèd proportions   220
Came short of composition, but in chief

205.1 *She unveils*] ROWE; *not in* F

201 **just** just so, exactly
204 **abuse** imposture, deceit (*OED* 4)
209 **belocked** the only example in *OED* of
    belock v., an intensive form of *lock*. It
    might possibly be a rare survival of the
    Middle English verb *belouke*, 'shut, en-
    close', found as late as 1430.
210 **match** basically in *OED*'s sense 11,
    'agreement, appointment', but the term
    can also refer to a sexual encounter

211 **supply thee** satisfy your desire
    garden-house Wealthier Elizabethans
    often built summer-houses or banquet-
    ing-houses in their gardens, which could
    be elaborate structures with several
    rooms and galleries. They were notorious
    as places of assignation.
220 **proportions** portion, dowry
221 **composition** what had been agreed
    upon

For that her reputation was disvalued
In levity. Since which time of five years
I never spake with her, saw her, nor heard from her,
Upon my faith and honour.

MARIANA (*kneeling*)   Noble prince,
As there comes light from heaven, and words from
        breath,
As there is sense in truth, and truth in virtue,
I am affianced this man's wife as strongly
As words could make up vows; and, my good lord,
But Tuesday night last gone, in's garden-house,   230
He knew me as a wife. As this is true,
Let me in safety raise me from my knees,
Or else for ever be confixèd here
A marble monument.

ANGELO   I did but smile till now.
Now, good my lord, give me the scope of justice.
My patience here is touched; I do perceive
These poor informal women are no more
But instruments of some more mightier member
That sets them on. Let me have way, my lord,
To find this practice out.

DUKE (*rising*)   Ay, with my heart,   240
And punish them to your height of pleasure.
Thou foolish friar, and thou pernicious woman,

---

225 *kneeling*] COLLIER (*ed. of* 1858); *not in* F   240 *rising*] WILSON; *not in* F

222 **disvalued** made valueless, destroyed
223 **In** because of, by means of
    levity *OED* glosses the term when applied
    to women as 'unbecoming freedom of
    conduct' (3c); Angelo appears to be
    accusing her of sexual promiscuity (compare the Duke's remarks at 3.1.228–9).
226–9 **As there comes ... vows** The logic of
    the passage is that just as one thing issues
    from, or is contained in, or implied by,
    another thing (with a series of examples),
    so her status as his wife is guaranteed by
    the vows he made in the past.
227 **sense** what is wise or reasonable (*OED*
    28)
233 **confixèd** fixed firmly, fastened
234 **I did but smile** with a range of implications: 'I regarded these accusations with

a contemptuous smile'; 'I did not get
angry'; 'I had no wish to punish anybody'. Angelo may be answering the
Duke's 'Do you not smile at this' at
l. 163.
235 **scope** full and unfettered use
236 **touched** wounded, irritated
237 **informal** This is Shakespeare's only use
    of the word, and its meaning is not fully
    clear. *OED* gives it as the sole example of
    sense 2, 'disordered in mind', but it may
    be closer to sense 1 and mean 'behaving
    in a strange or disorderly manner'.
238 **member** member of the community,
    person
241 **to your height of pleasure** as severely as
    you wish (for the construction see
    1.4.70 n.)

Compact with her that's gone, think'st thou thy oaths,
Though they would swear down each particular saint,
Were testimonies against his worth and credit
That's sealed in approbation? You, Lord Escalus,
Sit with my cousin, lend him your kind pains
To find out this abuse, whence 'tis derived.
There is another friar that set them on;
Let him be sent for.   250

FRIAR PETER
Would he were here, my lord, for he indeed
Hath set the women on to this complaint.
Your provost knows the place where he abides,
And he may fetch him.

DUKE   Go, do it instantly.   *Exit Provost*
And you, my noble and well-warranted cousin,
Whom it concerns to hear this matter forth,
Do with your injuries as seems you best
In any chastisement. I for a while
Will leave you, but stir not you till you have
Well determined upon these slanderers.   260

ESCALUS
My lord, we'll do it throughly.   *Exit Duke*
    Escalus sits in the Duke's place
Signor Lucio, did not you say you knew that Friar
Lodowick to be a dishonest person?

LUCIO *Cucullus non facit monachum.* Honest in nothing but
in his clothes, and one that hath spoke most villainous
speeches of the Duke.

254 *Exit Provost*] CAPELL; *not in* F   261 *Exit Duke*] *Exit.* F, *at l.* 260   261.1 *Escalus ... place*]
CAPELL; *not in* F

243 **Compact** joined together (in a conspir-
    acy)
244 **each particular** every individual (they
    are imagined as going through the whole
    canon of saints, swearing by each one
    separately)
246 **That's sealed in approbation** whose
    official approval has been confirmed as if
    it were a document that has had a seal
    applied to it. This may refer back to the
    Duke's public endorsement of Angelo at
    the opening of the scene.
255 **well-warranted** fully authorized and ap-

proved by your superiors
256 **forth** through to the end
257 **injuries** (*a*) wrongs (*OED* 1); (*b*) calum-
    nies (*OED* 2)
259 **stir not you** do not move, or go away
260 **Well determined** made a careful and
    thorough judgement
263 **dishonest** disreputable
264 *Cucullus ... monachum* literally, 'the
    hood does not make the monk', i.e.
    someone wearing a monk's clothing is
    not necessarily a monk. A widely used
    proverb (Tilley H586).

ESCALUS We shall entreat you to abide here till he come,
    and enforce them against him. We shall find this friar a
    notable fellow.

LUCIO As any in Vienna, on my word.   270

ESCALUS Call that same Isabel here once again, I would
    speak with her.   *Exit an Officer*
    Pray you, my lord, give me leave to question. You shall
    see how I'll handle her.

LUCIO (*aside*) Not better than he, by her own report.

ESCALUS Say you?

LUCIO Marry, sir, I think if you handled her privately she
    would sooner confess; perchance publicly she'll be
    ashamed.

    ᷓ *Enter Isabella with an Officer*

ESCALUS I will go darkly to work with her.   280

LUCIO That's the way, for women are light at midnight.

ESCALUS Come on, mistress, here's a gentlewoman denies
    all that you have said.

        Enter Duke as a Friar with Provost

LUCIO My lord, here comes the rascal I spoke of, here with
    the provost!

ESCALUS In very good time. Speak not you to him, till we
    call upon you.

LUCIO Mum.

ESCALUS (*to the Duke*) Come, sir, did you set these women
    on to slander Lord Angelo? They have confessed you   290
    did.

DUKE 'Tis false.

272 *Exit an Officer*] DYCE; *not in* F   279.1 *Enter ... Officer*] OXFORD; *Enter Duke, Prouost, Isabella.* F
283.1 *Enter ... Provost*] OXFORD; *for* F *see previous note*

268 **enforce ... him** make powerful use of his
    slanderous speeches as evidence against
    him
269 **notable** notorious (compare 'a most
    notable coward', *All's Well* 3.6.10, and
    'O notable strumpet', *Othello* 5.1.79)
274 **handle** deal with (but Lucio plays upon
    it as meaning something like 'fondle,
    caress')
276 **Say you?** What do you say? (a stock
    phrase)
280 **I ... with her** I will begin questioning

her in a cryptic and puzzling way (which
will throw her off her guard). Lucio
however interprets *darkly* as 'secretly, in
the dark', as though Escalus was about to
make love to her.
281 **light** (*a*) bright, illuminating; (*b*) lascivi-
ous. Lever gives several examples of this
stock joke.
282–3 **here's a gentlewoman ... said** This
clearly indicates that Isabella has not
been present during Mariana's speeches
(contrast l. 161 n. above).

ESCALUS How! Know you where you are?

DUKE

    Respect to your great place, and let the devil

    Be sometime honoured for his burning throne.

    Where is the Duke? 'Tis he should hear me speak.

ESCALUS

    The Duke's in us, and we will hear you speak.

    Look you speak justly.

DUKE

    Boldly, at least. But O, poor souls,

    Come you to seek the lamb here of the fox?   300

    Good night to your redress! Is the Duke gone?

    Then is your cause gone too. The Duke's unjust

    Thus to retort your manifest appeal,

    And put your trial in the villain's mouth

    Which here you come to accuse.

LUCIO

    This is the rascal, this is he I spoke of!

ESCALUS

    Why, thou unreverent and unhallowed friar,

    Is't not enough thou hast suborned these women

    To accuse this worthy man, but in foul mouth,

    And in the witness of his proper ear,   310

    To call him villain, and then to glance from him

    To the Duke himself, to tax him with injustice?

---

294 **Respect** elliptical for 'let respect be shown'

295 **for** Leisi suggests that *for* should be read as *fore* (i.e. before), and compares *All's Well* 4.4.3, where the Folio reading of *for whose throne* is always interpreted as *fore*. But *honoured for* is a normal construction (compare *1 Henry VI* 1.8.5, 'How shall I honour thee for this success?'), and makes perfectly acceptable sense, with *for* meaning 'because of, in respect of': 'let us occasionally honour the devil because after all he is the king of hell (though in other respects he deserves no honour at all)'. Angelo must be respected only for his high position, not his personal character.

300 **lamb ... fox** a variant on the proverb 'give not the wolf the sheep to keep' (Tilley W602). Shakespeare, apparently uniquely, prefers 'fox' to 'wolf'; compare *Two Gentlemen* 4.4.89–90 and *First Part of the Contention* (*2 Henry VI*) 3.1.252–9.

301 **Good night to your redress** bid farewell to any hope of justice

302 **gone** lost, ruined

303 **retort** throw back against you, reject
    manifest obviously based on truth

307 **unreverent** irreverent, impertinent
    unhallowed unholy

309 **in foul mouth** in violently abusive language

310 **in ... ear** in such a way that he himself heard and can testify to what you said

311 **glance** said of a weapon that slides off one target to hit another; implying *OED*'s sense 3, 'allude to in passing in a critical or sarcastic fashion'

312 **tax him with** accuse him of

Take him hence. To the rack with him! We'll touse
    you
Joint by joint, but we will know his purpose.
What! Unjust?
DUKE   Be not so hot. The Duke
Dare no more stretch this finger of mine than he
Dare rack his own. His subject am I not,
Nor here provincial. My business in this state
Made me a looker-on here in Vienna,
Where I have seen corruption boil and bubble   320
Till it o'errun the stew: laws for all faults,
But faults so countenanced that the strong statutes
Stand like the forfeits in a barber's shop,
As much in mock as mark.
ESCALUS Slander to the state! Away with him to prison.
ANGELO What can you vouch against him, Signor Lucio?
Is this the man that you did tell us of?
LUCIO 'Tis he, my lord. Come hither, goodman baldpate.
Do you know me?
DUKE I remember you, sir, by the sound of your voice. I   330
met you at the prison, in the absence of the Duke.

313 **touse** pull apart

313–14 **him ... you ... his** The shifts of pronoun need no emendation; in his excitement Escalus first shouts a command at the officers, then threatens the Duke in disguise to his face, and then distances himself from the criminal by reverting to the third person.

318 **Nor ... provincial** he is not a member of the ecclesiastical province in which Vienna is situated, and is not subject to its discipline

321 **o'errun the stew** a play on words based on the double meaning of *stew* as 'stew-pot, cooking vessel' and 'brothel': (*a*) boil over the side of the pot; (*b*) spread outwards from the brothel

322 **countenanced** supported (by those in authority)

323 **forfeits** *OED*'s earliest example of sense 3, 'trivial penalty for a minor misdemeanour'; the word can of course refer to graver punishments, as at l. 523 below
in a barber's shop It appears that Elizabethan barbers put up lists of penalties for swearing and other kinds of misbehaviour by customers awaiting attention;

compare Richard Harvey, *Plain Percival* (1590, p. 11), 'speak a bloody word in a barber's shop, you make a forfeit' and Thomas Fuller, *The Holy State and the Prophane State* (1642, p. 395), 'No more than the forfeits in a barber's shop, where a gentleman's pleasure is all the obligation to pay, and none are bound except they will bind themselves'.

324 **As much in mock as mark** as much an object of derision as a warning to be heeded

328 **goodman** often used as a form of address to men at the social level of yeomen or farmers; Lucio, the 'gentleman', is patronizing the supposed friar
baldpate As a true friar the Duke would have a tonsure or shaven head, but as he consistently wears a hood when in disguise his hair is not visible. Compare Marlowe's *Doctor Faustus*, A version only, l. 870, 'a troupe of baldpate friars'.

330 **I remember ... voice** As Lever notes, the Duke's hood may make it difficult for him to see other people; there may also be a jibe at Lucio's loquacity.

LUCIO O, did you so? And do you remember what you said
    of the Duke?

DUKE Most notedly, sir.

LUCIO Do you so, sir? And was the Duke a fleshmonger, a
    fool, and a coward, as you then reported him to be?

DUKE You must, sir, change persons with me, ere you
    make that my report. You indeed spoke so of him, and
    much more, much worse.

LUCIO O thou damnable fellow, did not I pluck thee by the   340
    nose for thy speeches?

DUKE I protest I love the Duke as I love myself.

ANGELO Hark how the villain would close now, after his
    treasonable abuses.

ESCALUS Such a fellow is not to be talked withal. Away
    with him to prison. Where is the Provost? Away with
    him to prison! Lay bolts enough upon him; let him
    speak no more. Away with those giglets too, and with
    the other confederate companion.

> *Mariana is brought to her feet and arrested*
> *The Provost lays hands on the Duke*

DUKE Stay, sir, stay a while.   350

ANGELO What, resists he? Help him, Lucio.

LUCIO Come, sir, come, sir, come, sir! Faugh, sir! Why,
    you bald-pated, lying rascal, you must be hooded, must
    you? Show your knave's visage, with a pox to you.

349.1 *Mariana ... arrested*] OXFORD; *not in* F   349.2 *The Provost ... Duke*] JOHNSON; *not in* F

334 **notedly** especially, particularly

335 **fleshmonger** fornicator, pander (*OED* 2;
     earliest quotation in this sense)

336 **coward** Some earlier editors were wor-
     ried by the fact that cowardice is not
     mentioned in previous exchanges be-
     tween the Duke and Lucio, and devised
     ingenious explanations for the discrep-
     ancy. The simplest answer is surely that
     Lucio is an inveterate liar and irrespon-
     sibly fabricates accusations against the
     'friar' just as he had done against the
     Duke.

338 **make ... report** attribute those remarks
     to me

343 **close** *OED* gives this as the earliest use of
     sense 14a, 'come to terms or agreement',
     but it could simply be sense 8a, 'con-
     clude, finish': after a series of slanderous
     and treasonable accusations the 'friar'
     ends up by swearing that he truly loves
     the Duke.

344 **abuses** insulting speeches

347 **bolts** leg-irons, fetters

348 **giglets** lewd women, wenches

349 **confederate companion** i.e. Friar Peter,
     their other accomplice. *Companion* often
     has a contemptuous flavour, as in *2
     Henry IV* 2.4.119–20, 'I scorn you,
     scurvy companion'.

Show your sheep-biting face, and be hanged an hour.
Will't not off?

> *He pulls off the Friar's hood and reveals the Duke*
> *Angelo and Escalus rise*

DUKE

Thou art the first knave that e'er mad'st a duke.
First, Provost, let me bail these gentle three.
(*To Lucio*) Sneak not away, sir, for the friar and you
Must have a word anon. Lay hold on him.   360

> *Lucio is arrested*

LUCIO (*aside*)

This may prove worse than hanging.

DUKE (*to Escalus*)

What you have spoke I pardon; sit you down.
We'll borrow place of him. (*To Angelo*) Sir, by your
      leave.

> *He takes Angelo's seat*

Hast thou or word or wit or impudence
That yet can do thee office? If thou hast,
Rely upon it till my tale be heard,
And hold no longer out.

ANGELO   O my dread lord,
I should be guiltier than my guiltiness
To think I can be undiscernible,
When I perceive your grace, like power divine,   370
Hath looked upon my passes. Then, good prince,

356.1 *He … Duke*] ROWE; *not in* F   356.2 *Angelo … rise*] OXFORD; *not in* F   360.1 *Lucio is arrested*] WILSON; *not in* F   363.1 *He … seat*] CAPELL; *not in* F

355 **sheep-biting** said of a dog that bites or
   worries sheep; figuratively, 'thieving,
   sneaking'. A second implication may be
   present: *OED*'s sense 4 of *sheep-biter* is
   'one who runs after "mutton", a whoremonger'.
   hanged dogs that worried sheep were
   hanged; see Fletcher's *Rule a Wife and
   Have a Wife* 5.4.8–10, 'How like a sheep-
   biting rogue, taken i' the manner | And
   ready for the halter, dost thou look
   now! | Thou hast a hanging look, thou
   scurvy thing!'
   an hour The exact implication is not
   clear; it may mean 'for a little while' and
   be facetious, as Leisi argues, though 'it
   Lever asserts (Introduction, p. xv) that 'it

was customary for an hour's interval to
elapse between the time of execution and
the official pronouncement of death'.
357 **mad'st** created (normally done by a
   monarch, not a rogue like Lucio)
358 **three** Isabella, Mariana, and Friar Peter
363–4 **your … thou** To address someone as
   thou could be insulting in Elizabethan
   English ('the Duke begins with ironical
   politeness, but passes into open contempt', Abbott 233).
365 **do thee office** be of service, help you
367 **hold no longer out** give up resistance
   and admit the truth
369 **undiscernible** imperceptible
371 **passes** As a noun *pass* has a wide range
   of meanings, including 'event, result of

No longer session hold upon my shame,
But let my trial be mine own confession.
Immediate sentence, then, and sequent death
Is all the grace I beg.

DUKE   Come hither, Mariana.
(*To Angelo*) Say, wast thou e'er contracted to this
        woman?

ANGELO

I was, my lord.

DUKE

Go take her hence, and marry her instantly.
Do you the office, friar, which consummate,
Return him here again. Go with him, Provost.   380
        *Exeunt Angelo and Mariana with Friar Peter and
        Provost*

ESCALUS

My lord, I am more amazed at his dishonour
Than at the strangeness of it.

DUKE   Come hither, Isabel.
Your friar is now your prince. As I was then
Advertising and holy to your business,
Not changing heart with habit, I am still
Attorneyed at your service.

ISABELLA   O give me pardon
That I, your vassal, have employed and pained
Your unknown sovereignty.

DUKE   You are pardoned, Isabel.
And now, dear maid, be you as free to us.

380.1–2 *Exeunt ... Provost*] POPE; *Exit.* F

one's actions', 'crisis, predicament',
'thrust made in fencing', and 'trick', and
it is hard to determine how far these are
relevant in this context. *OED*, *sb.*², rather
diffidently gives it as the sole example of
sense 2, '(?) course of action', which
could be an extension of sense 1, 'passages, movements from place to place'.

374 **sequent** consequent (and also implying
    'following on without delay')
379 **consummate** completed
381–2 **I am ... of it** the mere fact that he has
    carried out this evil deed is more amazing
    to me than the strange form it has taken

384 **Advertising** heedful, attentive (stress on
    second syllable)
    holy presumably in *OED*'s sense 1, 'dedi-
    cated, devoted'
386 **Attorneyed** acting as an agent
387 **vassal** humble servant
    pained ?put to trouble, caused you to
    take pains on my behalf (this sense does
    not seem to be recorded in *OED* or used
    elsewhere in Shakespeare)
388 **Your unknown sovereignty** you as
    ruler, unrecognized by me
389 **free** generous (in pardoning him for not
    having rescued Claudio)

Your brother's death, I know, sits at your heart,   390
And you may marvel why I obscured myself,
Labouring to save his life, and would not rather
Make rash remonstrance of my hidden power
Than let him so be lost. O most kind maid,
It was the swift celerity of his death,
Which I did think with slower foot came on,
That brained my purpose; but peace be with him.
That life is better life, past fearing death,
Than that which lives to fear. Make it your comfort,
So happy is your brother.

ISABELLA   I do, my lord.   400

    Enter Angelo and Mariana with Friar Peter and
    Provost

DUKE

For this new-married man approaching here,
Whose salt imagination yet hath wronged
Your well-defended honour, you must pardon
For Mariana's sake; but as he adjudged your brother,
Being criminal in double violation
Of sacred chastity and of promise-breach
Thereon dependent for your brother's life,
The very mercy of the law cries out
Most audible, even from his proper tongue,
'An Angelo for Claudio, death for death;   410

400.1 *Mariana*] ROWE; *Maria* F (*Enter Angelo, Maria, Peter, Prouost.*)

390 **sits at your heart** affects you deeply (a stock phrase, *OED sit* 14a)
393 **rash** hasty, reckless
    remonstrance demonstration, manifestation
397 **brained** a figurative use of *OED*'s sense 1, to kill by dashing out the brains
400 **So ... brother** that your brother has the happiness to be no longer afraid of death
402 **salt** lecherous (Angelo has sexually wronged Isabella in imagination even if not in reality)
404 **adjudged** condemned
406 **sacred chastity** The Duke is clearly addressing Isabella, and the phrase must refer to her chastity as a postulant, not to Mariana's; but he has just shown that the 'violation' was only in imagination. Possibly the language is exaggerated because

he wants to test Isabella's reaction to the death-sentence he is about to pronounce.
    of promise-breach We can hardly avoid reading this as dependent on *violation*, which produces an awkward tautology (*violation ... of promise-breach*).
408 **very mercy** even the most merciful aspects of the law, which would normally plead for pardon
410–12 F does not use quotation-marks, and it is not clear whether the voice of mercy speaks only l. 410 or 410–12. The fact that all three are in the same balanced style, and lead to a climax in the play's title, suggests the latter interpretation.
410 **death for death** proverbial (Tilley/Dent D139.1, and Whiting D91)

Haste still pays haste, and leisure answers leisure;
Like doth quit like, and Measure still for Measure'.
Then, Angelo, thy fault's thus manifested,
Which, though thou wouldst deny, denies thee
          vantage.
We do condemn thee to the very block
Where Claudio stooped to death, and with like haste.
Away with him.

MARIANA   O my most gracious lord,
I hope you will not mock me with a husband.

DUKE

It is your husband mocked you with a husband.
Consenting to the safeguard of your honour,   420
I thought your marriage fit; else imputation,
For that he knew you, might reproach your life,
And choke your good to come. For his possessions,
Although by confiscation they are ours,
We do instate and widow you with all,
To buy you a better husband.

MARIANA   O my dear lord,
I crave no other nor no better man.

---

424 confiscation] F2; confutation F

411 **pays ... answers** These verbs are roughly equivalent: 'repays, provides a satisfactory equivalent for'. The general implication of the line is that Angelo will be given the same kind of summary justice that he gave to Claudio (*with like haste*, l. 416).

412 **Like ... like** proverbial (Tilley/Dent L282.1)
quit requite
Measure still for Measure In this specific context *measure* must have *OED*'s sense 15, 'punishment, retribution'. The word clearly has this meaning in *Richard Duke of York* (*3 Henry VI*) 2.6.55, 'Measure for measure must be answered', and in *A Warning for Fair Women*, 1599, G3, 'Measure for measure, and lost blood for blood'. The Duke is here advocating an Old Testament morality of an eye for an eye and a tooth for a tooth. The phrase is proverbial (Tilley M800).

414 **though thou wouldst deny** At ll. 374–5 Angelo begged for an immediate death-

sentence, so ll. 413–14 presumably mean 'Your evil is so clearly evident that even if you did wish to put in a plea for yourself you could not expect to benefit from that plea'.

415 **the very block** This little touch is not found in Cinthio or any of the English sources. In Pontus Heuter (see Introduction, p. 15) the equivalent of Angelo is executed in the same cell as his victim.

418 **mock** delude, tantalize

421–2 **imputation, |For that he knew you** the accusation that she had had illicit relations with Angelo

423 **choke your good to come** destroy your future benefit (presumably re-marriage after the death of Angelo; see l. 426)

425 **instate** endow, invest with
widow grant to you as a widow's portion
with all This could simply be *withal*, equivalent to 'with', but F's *with all*, 'with everything, all his possessions', gives a stronger reading.

DUKE

Never crave him, we are definitive.

MARIANA (*kneeling*)

Gentle my liege—

DUKE   You do but lose your labour.

Away with him to death. (*To Lucio*) Now, sir, to you.   430

MARIANA

O my good lord! Sweet Isabel, take my part:

Lend me your knees, and all my life to come

I'll lend you all my life to do you service.

DUKE

Against all sense you do importune her.

Should she kneel down in mercy of this fact,

Her brother's ghost his pavèd bed would break

And take her hence in horror.

MARIANA   Isabel,

Sweet Isabel, do yet but kneel by me.

Hold up your hands, say nothing; I'll speak all.

They say best men are moulded out of faults,   440

And for the most become much more the better

For being a little bad. So may my husband.

O Isabel, will you not lend a knee?

DUKE

He dies for Claudio's death.

ISABELLA (*kneeling*)   Most bounteous sir,

Look, if it please you, on this man condemned

As if my brother lived. I partly think

A due sincerity governed his deeds

Till he did look on me; since it is so,

Let him not die. My brother had but justice,

In that he did the thing for which he died.   450

For Angelo,

---

429 *kneeling*] JOHNSON; *not in* F   444 *kneeling*] ROWE; *not in* F

428 **are definitive** have made the final, unal-
terable judgement
429 **lose your labour** waste your efforts
434 **Against all sense** completely unreason-
ably
436 **pavèd bed** grave covered with stone
slabs. Editors speculate on the kind of
burial Claudio would have received if he
had been executed, but the main point is

surely to suggest a heavy restraint which
would not be able to prevent Claudio's
indignant ghost from breaking free.
440 **They say** The formula suggests a
proverbial saying, but no comparable
proverb has been identified.
moulded created, formed
441 **the most** the most part
446 **I partly think** I am willing to believe

His act did not o'ertake his bad intent,
And must be buried but as an intent
That perished by the way. Thoughts are no subjects,
Intents but merely thoughts.

MARIANA   Merely, my lord.

DUKE

Your suit's unprofitable. Stand up, I say.
        Mariana and Isabella rise
I have bethought me of another fault.
Provost, how came it Claudio was beheaded
At an unusual hour?

PROVOST   It was commanded so.

DUKE

Had you a special warrant for the deed?   460

PROVOST

No, my good lord, it was by private message.

DUKE

For which I do discharge you of your office.
Give up your keys.

PROVOST   Pardon me, noble lord.
I thought it was a fault, but knew it not,
Yet did repent me after more advice.
For testimony whereof, one in the prison
That should by private order else have died
I have reserved alive.

DUKE

What's he?

PROVOST

His name is Barnardine.   470

456.1 *Mariana . . . rise*] OXFORD; *not in* F

---

453 **buried** hidden away, forgotten
454 **subjects** *OED* gives this a specialized
   philosophical sense (6b), 'things having
   real independent existence', but has no
   other example of the usage, and the word
   may have the more usual sense of 'those
   under the dominion of a king or prince',
   so that *thoughts are no subjects* would
   mean 'we cannot control our thoughts
   in the way a king rules over his subjects'. Compare Donne's use of a similar

phrase in a letter to Goodyer, 1609,
quoted in R. C. Bald, *John Donne: A Life*
(Oxford, 1970), p. 216: 'they profess
that clergymen, though traitors, are no
subjects'. The idea may be a variation on
the proverbial 'thought is free' (Tilley
T244).
460 **special** See 1.1.18 n. and 1.2.118 n.
464 **knew it not** was not certain of it
465 **advice** reflection, deliberation

DUKE

I would thou hadst done so by Claudio.
Go fetch him hither, let me look upon him.

Exit Provost

ESCALUS

I am sorry one so learned and so wise
As you, Lord Angelo, have still appeared,
Should slip so grossly, both in the heat of blood
And lack of tempered judgement afterward.

ANGELO

I am sorry that such sorrow I procure,
And so deep sticks it in my penitent heart
That I crave death more willingly than mercy.
'Tis my deserving, and I do entreat it.   480

*Enter Provost with Barnardine, Claudio muffled, and
Julietta*

DUKE

Which is that Barnardine?

PROVOST   This, my lord.

DUKE

There was a friar told me of this man.
Sirrah, thou art said to have a stubborn soul
That apprehends no further than this world,
And squar'st thy life according. Thou'rt condemned;
But, for those earthly faults, I quit them all,
And pray thee take this mercy to provide
For better times to come. Friar, advise him;
I leave him to your hand. What muffled fellow's that?

PROVOST

This is another prisoner that I saved,   490

472.1 *Exit Provost*] HANMER; *not in* F   480.1 *muffled*] CAPELL; *not in* F (*Enter Barnardine and
Prouost, Claudio, Iulietta.*)

---

475 **slip** See 2.2.65 n.
   blood sexual appetite
476 **tempered** balanced, controlled
480.1 *muffled* with the face concealed by
   clothing (see also l. 489 below). The
   word can mean 'blindfolded', as in *All's
   Well* 4.3.119, but there is no reason to
   blindfold Claudio; the essential thing is

that other people should not recognize
him.
484 **apprehends ... world** cannot see beyond the present life, has no conception
   of a life after death
485 **squar'st** frame, arrange (dependent on
   thou in l. 483)
486 **quit** acquit, pardon

Who should have died when Claudio lost his head,
As like almost to Claudio as himself.
　　He reveals Claudio
DUKE (*to Isabella*)
If he be like your brother, for his sake
Is he pardoned, and for your lovely sake,
Give me your hand and say you will be mine,
He is my brother too—but fitter time for that.
By this Lord Angelo perceives he's safe;
Methinks I see a quickening in his eye.
Well, Angelo, your evil quits you well.
Look that you love your wife, her worth worth yours.　　500
I find an apt remission in myself,
And yet here's one in place I cannot pardon.
(*To Lucio*) You, sirrah, that knew me for a fool, a
　　coward,
One all of luxury, an ass, a madman,
Wherein have I so deserved of you
That you extol me thus?
LUCIO Faith, my lord, I spoke it but according to the trick.
If you will hang me for it, you may, but I had rather it
would please you I might be whipped.
DUKE
Whipped first, sir, and hanged after.　　510
Proclaim it, Provost, round about the city:

492.1 *He ... Claudio*] HANMER; *not in* F

492.1 *He reveals Claudio* F has no stage-
directions here, and gives no indication
whatever of Isabella's response to her
discovery that Claudio is still alive. However, the Duke's *fitter time for that* at
l. 496 suggests that brother and sister are
intensely reacting to each other in a way
which makes it inappropriate for the
Duke to begin proposing to Isabella at this
point.
495 **Give** The imperative is here used as a
conditional ('if you give me your hand,
Claudio will then become my brother
also').
497 **By this** by this time, by now
498 **quickening** revival, greater intensity of
expression
499 **your evil quits you well** your evil has
been well repaid (by marriage to Mariana
instead of punishment)

500 **her worth worth yours** her worth is
fully equal to yours. Some recent editors
treat the second *worth* as a verb, and
gloss the phrase as 'let your worth become equal to hers', but this is very
strained. The Duke is not defending
Mariana, but being sarcastic at Angelo's
expense ('you've no reason to feel superior to her').
501 **apt remission** willing forgiveness
502 **in place** present, among us
504 **all of luxury** full of lechery
507 **trick** This may be in *OED*'s sense 2,
'prank, frolic' (i.e. 'it was only a joke'), or
2b, 'whim, caprice' (i.e. 'it was a
thoughtless remark on the spur of the
moment, not a considered judgement'),
or 7, 'habit, custom' (i.e. 'it was just my
way of talking').

If any woman wronged by this lewd fellow—
As I have heard him swear himself there's one
Whom he begot with child—let her appear,
And he shall marry her. The nuptial finished,
Let him be whipped and hanged.

LUCIO I beseech your highness, do not marry me to a
   whore. Your highness said even now, I made you a
   duke; good my lord, do not recompense me in making
   me a cuckold.   520

DUKE

Upon mine honour thou shalt marry her.
Thy slanders I forgive, and therewithal
Remit thy other forfeits. Take him to prison,
And see our pleasure herein executed.

LUCIO Marrying a punk, my lord, is pressing to death,
   whipping, and hanging.

DUKE

Slandering a prince deserves it.

                              Exeunt Officers with Lucio
She, Claudio, that you wronged, look you restore.
Joy to you, Mariana. Love her, Angelo;
I have confessed her, and I know her virtue.   530
Thanks, good friend Escalus, for thy much goodness;
There's more behind that is more gratulate.
Thanks, Provost, for thy care and secrecy;
We shall employ thee in a worthier place.
Forgive him, Angelo, that brought you home
The head of Ragozine for Claudio's;
The offence pardons itself. Dear Isabel,

527.1 *Exeunt ... Lucio*] DYCE; *not in* F

512 **If any woman wronged** This could be
   made more grammatical by modern standards by emending *woman* to *woman's*
   (compare *that's* for F *that* at l. 542 below), but the intrusive parenthesis at
   ll. 513–14 may have modified the construction. See 4.3.130 n.
522 **therewithal** in addition
523 **Remit thy other forfeits** cancel your
   other punishments (Lucio will not be
   whipped or hanged)
525 **pressing to death** See *OED* under *peine*,
   'a form of punishment formerly inflicted
   on persons arraigned for felony who

refused to plead, in which the prisoner's
body was pressed with heavy weights
until he pleaded or died'.
528 **She** equivalent to 'Her' (see 3.1.215 n.)
532 **behind** yet to come (in the way of
   reward)
   gratulate *OED* quotes this as the sole
   example of *gratulate* as an adjective,
   meaning 'pleasing, gratifying'. But it
   may be equivalent to sense 2 of *gratula-
   tory* and mean 'expressive of my gratitude to you' (the Duke will give him
   something more substantial than
   thanks).

I have a motion much imports your good,
Whereto if you'll a willing ear incline,
What's mine is yours, and what is yours is mine.   540
So bring us to our palace, where we'll show
What's yet behind, that's meet you all should know.

Exeunt

542 that's] F2; that F   542.1 *Exeunt*] ROWE; *not in* F

538 **motion** proposal, suggestion
much imports your good which will
involve a great benefit to you

540 **What's mine ... mine** proverbial (Tilley
M980)

LONGER TEXTUAL NOTES

1.1.7–10

> My ſtrength can giue you : Then no more remaines
> But that, to your ſufficiency,as your worth is able,
> And let them worke : The nature of our People,

MANY attempts have been made, none of them fully convincing, to make sense of these lines by re-punctuation and minor emendation. One problem is to know whether *that* in line 8 is a pronoun or conjunction. However, *that* is used as a pronoun in line 6, and a repetition would be clumsy; it seems probable that Shakespeare was using a construction of a type found in *As You Like It* 1.1.162–3, 'Nothing remains but that I kindle the boy thither, which now I'll go about'. F's long line (*But that ... able*) is strikingly clumsy and hypermetrical, and the most probable explanation is that compositorial eye-skip resulted in the omission of the end of one line and the beginning of another:

> But that, to your sufficiency ...
>   ... as your worth is able,
> And let them work.

The many conjectural attempts to fill the gap are recorded in Eccles, pp. 297–8. It might have been something like:

> But that to your sufficiency you add
> A power as ample as your worth is able ...

Escalus plainly has 'sufficiency' (ability, competence for the job); all he needs is full authority from the Duke to get on with his work.

1.3.20

Many earlier editors found the metaphorical shift from horses to weeds too violent, and emended *weeds* to *steeds* or *jades*. But *weed* can refer in Elizabethan English to an evil person who has no useful function in society, as in *OED weed sb.*[1] 4, which quotes from 1598, 'Justices, to disburden their shire of corrupt weeds, as they term it, do pick out the scum of their country for the wars'. In *Promos and Cassandra*, Part 1, Act 2, scene 3, Promos refers to 'swarms of unthrifts' that live 'by rapine, spoil, and theft' and comments, 'So that the way is by severity | Such wicked weeds even by the roots to tear' (Bullough, *Sources*, p. 452). Weeds of this kind would be active and energetic, and would need a powerful restraint. G. K. Hunter (*SQ* xv, 1964, 167) notes that in *2 Henry IV* 'weeds' at 4.3.54 is followed by 'headstrong' and 'curb' at line 62. Elsewhere in Shakespeare curbs or bridles are linked with 'headstrong' human beings; compare *Errors* 2.1.13–15, *Shrew* 4.1.195, and *Troilus* 3.2.119–20.

2.1.37–40

> *Eſc.* Well: heauen forgiue him; and forgiue vs all:
> *Some riſe by ſinne, and ſome by vertue fall:*
> Some run from brakes of Ice, and anſwere none,
> And ſome condemned for a fault alone.

The problem here is to explain or emend *brakes of ice* in line 39. The best way to approach the phrase is to set it in its context. Lines 37 and 38 establish a pattern of balance and antithesis (*forgive him . . . forgive us*; *some rise . . . some fall*) which in line 38 is intensified by paradox (*rise by sin . . . by virtue fall*). The repetition of *Some . . . And some* indicates that lines 39–40 are using on a larger scale the pattern of line 38, and we must therefore consider the final couplet of Escalus's speech as a unit. I propose to look at the other words first and then to examine *brakes of ice*. In line 39 *run from* seems to have its usual Shakespearian sense of 'run away, escape, flee from', and *answer* is in *OED*'s sense 6b, 'suffer the consequences of, atone for'. In line 40 *condemned* has its strongest sense, 'condemned to death', while the placing of *alone* at the end of the line emphasizes the implications of *for a fault alone*, 'for one single fault'. The general sense of the couplet would thus seem to be, 'some people escape after committing multiple sins without paying for any of them, while others are executed for a solitary offence'.

As it stands *brakes of ice* does not seem to make satisfactory sense. Elsewhere in Shakespeare *brake* always means 'thicket', and attempts to give it some of the rare and specialized meanings recorded in *OED* are unconvincing. Some editors emend *brakes* to *breaks*, glossing *breaks of ice* as 'violations of chastity'. A parallel for this usage occurs in *The Revenger's Tragedy* 4.4.78–80, 'she first begins with one | Who afterward to thousand proves a whore: | Break ice in one place, it will crack in more'. This presupposes a misreading at some stage of *break* as *brake*, but it would be strange for a common word to be misread as a rarer word, and *break*, as noun or verb, is always spelt *breake* elsewhere in the play. Those works by Shakespeare which contain multiple uses of both words (*Venus* and *Dream*) consistently make a spelling-distinction between *brake(s)* on one hand and *break* or *breake(s)* on the other. Furthermore, *brake* as 'thicket' often implies a place full of thorny plants and undergrowth which is difficult and painful to go through or escape from; compare 'Through bog, through bush, through brake, through briar', *Dream* 3.1.102, with *All is True (Henry VIII)* 1.2.76–7, ''Tis but the fate of place, and the rough brake | That virtue must go through', and with a passage in Davenant's *The Law against Lovers*, Act v, 'Love has led thee a dance | Through a brake of thorns and briars' (*Works*, 1673, p. 326). I have therefore allowed *brakes* to stand and have adopted the earliest emendation made to the passage, Rowe's *vice* for *ice*. A possible explanation for the mistake in F would be that the compositor made an auditory error while setting up the lines, mishearing *of vice* in his mind as *of ice*.

2.2.97

F's *now* is hard to interpret, and the common emendation to *new* is not self-evidently an improvement. *Either . . . or* implies a distinct pair of alternatives, but if *new* in *new-conceived* means 'recently', as it clearly does in *Kinsmen* 4.2.129, it is difficult to think of a satisfactory alternative. It is just possible that *new* means 'anew, afresh' (*OED new adv.* 5), rather than 'recently', and that an antithesis is intended between *now-conceived*, 'which has already reached the stage of conception' (compare *now-born* in *All's Well* 2.3.180), and *new-conceived*, 'conceived afresh in the future because of official negligence'. But this interpretation, which would require the addition of a hyphen after *now*, is distinctly clumsy for the actor to speak.

2.4.16–17

These lines have long been regarded as problematic, and emendation of *not* to *now* or *yet* has been suggested, but it may be possible to make sense of the passage as it stands. In medieval chivalry, and the heraldry deriving from it, a crest was a visual emblem worn by a knight on the top of his helmet as an identifying device, and the term clearly refers back to *horn* in the preceding line. The horn can of course be the emblem of a cuckold (compare *As You Like It* 4.2.13–14, 'Take thou no scorn to wear the horn; | It was a crest ere thou wast born'), but here it obviously identifies the devil (compare Tilley D252, 'The devil is known by his horns'). Angelo has discovered with horror that his angelic appearance ('angel on the outward side', 3.1.526) masks a devilish nature, and suggests, with grim irony, that we should charitably assume in the case of the devil that inner and outer do not necessarily correspond: let us attach a label saying 'good angel' to his horn, because we can no longer take for granted that it indicates a devilish presence.

2.4.88–90

> *Ang.* Admit no other way to faue his life
> (As I fubfcribe not that, nor any other,
> But in the loffe of queftion) that you, his Sifter,

If F's parenthesis is correct, the lines are very difficult to explain. R. J. C. Watt (*RES*, NS 38, 1987, 230–2) suggests that the parenthesis should stop at *other*, which makes *But ... that you* follow on much more logically from line 88. Watt notes that *question* can have a legal and philosophical sense ('argument, topic of debate') and glosses *in the loss of question* as 'when or assuming you have lost the argument (about your brother's death)'. He interprets the general sense of Angelo's speech down to line 98 as 'Suppose that there were no other way to save your brother's life (not that I concede that this *is* a way of doing so, nor that there is any such way) but (having lost your case) that you ... submit your chastity to a certain person. What would you do?' This gives a more logical and coherent meaning to the speech than any previous interpretation.

3.1.95–8

F's *prenzie* at 3.1.95 and 98 is the most puzzling crux in the play. There are two main arguments for emendation. One is that the word is not recorded elsewhere and its meaning has to be inferred from the context. The second is that whoever prepared the text for the Second Folio of 1632 found the word unsatisfactory and emended it to *princely*. (It might be noticed that such forms as *prence*, *prense*, 'prince', and *prencelie*, 'princely', are fairly common in 16th-c. Scots; see vol. 6 of *A Dictionary of the Older Scottish Tongue*, ed. A. J. Aitken and J. Stevenson. But it is difficult to explain how and at what stage such a form might have found its way into the text.) On the other hand, the word occurs twice, which makes it seem less likely to be an accidental blunder. Crane used the *-zie* form in words like *lazie*, *drowzie*, and *greazie*; the letters are very clearly formed and could hardly be misread by a compositor. Any mistake must have occurred while Crane was copying from his original, but though Crane sometimes made errors he did not write gibberish. The most favoured emendation among modern editors is *precise*, in the same sense as at 1.3.50; while this would fit line 95, it would be inappropriate as applied to clothing in line 98. Furthermore, it is hard to see why a relatively common word, used three times earlier in the play in its normal spelling, should suddenly be twice misread in such an odd way. Numerous conjectural emendations have been put forward, but none is wholly satisfactory, and it is best to let the F reading stand.

3.1.515–36

Many earlier commentators disliked this passage of gnomic couplets, and considered it a reviser's interpolation. But it is hard to see why a reviser would want to add something of this kind, and though the writing is sometimes so compressed as to be obscure (as in line 518), and a couplet may have dropped out between lines 528 and 529, all modern editors accept it as authentic. As Lever notes (pp. 93–4), the speech falls into four parts; if a couplet is missing, each section was originally six lines long. Lines 515–20 generalize about the behaviour expected from a ruler, and lines 521–6 rebuke Angelo for failing to live up to this pattern. Lines 527–30 are puzzling (see the separate discussion below), but seem to be a return to generalization. In the final section the Duke reverts to the predicament in front of him, and justifies his method of dealing with Angelo.

3.1.527–30

> How may likenesse made in crimes,
> Making practise on the Times,
> To draw with ydle Spiders strings
> Most ponderous and substantiall things?

There has been much editorial tinkering with these lines, but no emendation is fully convincing, and if a couplet has dropped out we shall never recover the complete sense. The separate parts can be given some meaning: *likeness made in crimes* seems to mean 'a resemblance caused by having committed the same crime as someone else' (apparently referring to Angelo and Claudio); *Making practice on the times* means 'practising deceit on those around him' (the repetition of *made* and *Making* is somewhat clumsy); and the final couplet means literally 'to pull along heavy weights with a cobweb' and figuratively 'to use flimsy and spurious devices to produce momentous consequences'. It is impossible, however, to put all this together in a coherent and logical unity.

4.2.41–4

Most editors emend F by transferring this passage to Abhorson. There may have been a compositorial confusion of speech-prefixes; the passage occurs in the left-hand column of G2ᵛ of F, page 76, the whole of which was set by compositor B, and in the right-hand column (TLN 1964–5, 4.2.100–1 of the present edition) occurs what most editors regard as an error in speech attribution. There may be another error of this type by compositor B on G3ᵛ (see 4.3.62 n.). But it could be that Abhorson rather ponderously launches into his syllogism, only to have it snatched from his mouth by the quick-witted Pompey.

4.2.89

F's *unsisting* is not recorded elsewhere. If it derives from the Latin verb *sistere* it would mean 'unresting'. This could be applied to a door, but this particular door is obviously refusing to move. F4's *insisting* could be defended as a derivative of the Latin verb *insistere*, in the sense of 'standing firm', though *OED* quotes no comparable usage. Although *unshifting* is not recorded in *OED* before 1811, it seems to give the best sense; Shakespeare uses *shifting* three times elsewhere, and likes coinages with the *un*-prefix.

4.3.90

Dover Wilson ingeniously argued that *Angelo* should read *Varrius*, and that the compositor had accidentally repeated the phrase 'to Angelo' from the preceding line. If F is right, 'him' in lines 92 and 94 must also refer to Angelo, but at lines 128–9 below it is made clear that Angelo is supposed to meet the Duke 'at the gates', not 'at the consecrated fount', and the 'gates' are referred to again at 4.4.4 and 4.6.14. If we emend to *Varrius* the Duke meets Varrius at the fount and then moves on to the city gates to meet Angelo.

This is tidy and plausible. It means that 4.5, where the Duke meets Varrius, must take place at the consecrated fount, though no editor except Dover Wilson has located it there (Rowe set it in *The Fields without the Town*, Lever in *A Friar's Cell*, presumably because the scene opens with the Duke talking to Friar Peter). It is doubtful, though, whether such a systematic approach is obligatory. With the unlocalized settings used in Jacobean (and often in 20th-c.) productions it simply does not matter where 4.5 takes place. The Duke's letters to Angelo are intended to confuse and demoralize him; clearly they affirm things which turn out not to be true (see 4.2.196–9) and contradict each other (4.4.1), so much so that Angelo wonders whether the Duke has become insane. Even if they are illogical, the 'letters to Angelo' of 4.3.90 may be part of this psychological warfare, and the Duke sends out a final batch of unspecified letters as late as 4.5.1, apparently only minutes before his public entry to the city.

5.1.126

In most cases where F fails to provide a character with an exit direction, there is no difficulty in deciding where it should be placed. Isabella's exit in the earlier part of Act 5 is not so clear-cut. Line 120 shows that she intends to go out by herself, but two lines later the Duke orders her to be arrested and taken to prison. He continues to interrogate her, however, and she replies at line 126, though she does not speak again until line 386. The references to 'this wretched woman here' (l. 133) and 'this woman' (ll. 139 and 158) suggest that she is still present, and 'to her eyes' appears to mean 'to her face, in her presence' (see commentary on l. 161), as though Shakespeare's original intention was to arrange a kind of confrontation between Isabella and Mariana. But at line 243 the Duke refers to Isabella as 'her that's gone'; Escalus orders her to be brought back again, and F provides her with an entrance after line 279. Escalus's speech to her at lines 282–3 indicates that she has not been present while Mariana has been speaking. Possibly Shakespeare changed his mind in the course of composition, and decided that if Mariana was going to beg Isabella to plead for Angelo's life it would be unwise to make the two women appear to quarrel earlier in the scene.

There is no point in the text at which an exit for Isabella will resolve this contradiction. Theobald placed her exit immediately before Mariana's entrance at line 167; Capell, followed by the great majority of subsequent editors, put it at the end of line 162. Dover Wilson, however, pointed out the absurdity of sending her off immediately after Friar Peter has claimed that she will be 'disprovèd to her eyes, | Till she herself confess it'. It seems best to follow Lever in sending her off after her reply to the Duke in line 126; the longer she stays the less plausible her exit becomes, and she plays no part in the action.

ALTERATIONS TO LINEATION

1.1.8–9	But ... able] This edition; *one line in* F
1.2.43–5	Behold ... to] POPE; *three lines, dividing after* comes *and* roof F
140	One ... you] POPE; *two lines, dividing after* friend F
141–2	A ... after] POPE; *two lines, dividing after* hundred F
1.4.30–1	'Tis ... sin] CAPELL; *one line in* F
75–6	Alas ... good] HANMER; *two lines, dividing after* poor F
2.1.57–8	Go ... Elbow] POPE; *three lines, dividing after* is *and* name F
243–4	Whip ... trade] ROWE; *prose in* F
2.2.63–4	As ... he] CAPELL; *one line in* F
84	Tomorrow ... him] POPE; *two lines, dividing after* sudden F
115–16	Would ... heaven] CAPELL; *two lines, dividing after* for thunder F
143–4	She ... well] STEEVENS; *two lines, dividing after* such sense F
2.4.119	To ... mean] ROWE; *two lines, dividing after* would have F
3.1.3–4	But ... die] CAPELL; *prose in* F
295–6	Indeed ... prove] POPE; *two lines, dividing after* sort, sir F
341	Adieu ... friar] POPE; *two lines, dividing after* Pompey F
488–9	One ... himself] CAPELL; *two lines, dividing after* strifes F
510–12	If ... himself] POPE; *four lines, dividing after* life, proceeding, *and* fail F
4.1.32–4	There ... him] CLARK; *two lines, dividing after* upon the F
4.2.3–5	If ... head] POPE; *three lines, dividing after* can *and* wife's head F
102–6	My ... day] POPE; *five lines, dividing after* note, charge, it, *and* circumstance F
115–18	I ... before] POPE; *five lines, dividing after* you, remiss, awakens me, *and* strangely F
168–70	By ... Angelo] POPE; *four lines, dividing after* you, guide, *and* executed F
171–2	Angelo ... favour] POPE; *two lines, dividing after* both F
4.3.25–6	Your ... death] POPE; *two lines, dividing after* hangman F
28	Tell ... too] POPE; *two lines, dividing after* awake F
36–7	How ... you] POPE; *two lines, dividing after* Abhorson F
84–5	Put ... Claudio] NEILSON; *one line in* F
147	Goode'en ... Provost] DYCE; *two lines, dividing after* Goode'en F
161–2	Nay ... Duke] POPE; *two lines, dividing after* thee F
4.6.12	He ... sounded] POPE; *two lines, dividing after* you F
15	The ... away] POPE; *two lines, dividing after* entering F
5.1.20	Now ... him] POPE; *two lines, dividing after* time F
27	Relate ... brief] POPE; *two lines, dividing after* wrongs F
33	Or ... here] POPE; *two lines, dividing after* you F
69	Have ... say] HANMER; *two lines, dividing after* reason F
127	A ... Lodowick] HANMER; *two lines, dividing after* belike F
282–3	Come ... said] F2; *two lines, dividing after* gentlewoman F
284–5	My ... provost] POPE; *two lines, dividing after* of F
315–16	The Duke | Dare no] HANMER; The Duke dare | No F
325	Slander ... prison] POPE; *two lines, dividing after* state F
451–2	For ... intent] JOHNSON; *one line in* F

JOHN WILSON'S SETTING OF 'TAKE, O TAKE'

By John Caldwell

JOHN WILSON cannot have composed this song for the earliest recorded production of *Measure for Measure* in 1604, as he was born only in 1595. It is also quite evidently a setting of the two-stanza version found in *Rollo* and other sources (see *Introduction*, pp. 69–70). Wilson may have written the song for performance in *Rollo*, but it is the only closely contemporary setting of a text almost identical to that of the First Folio, and it has long been associated with performances of Shakespeare's play.

This transcription has been made from John Wilson's song-book in the Bodleian Library, MS Mus.b.1, f. 19ᵛ. Several other manuscript and printed versions exist, but they are not collated here: a critical edition appears in *English Songs 1625–1660*, ed. Ian Spink (London, 1971, = *Musica Britannica*, xxxiii), No. 21.[1] The verbal text has been modernized to conform to that of the present edition. Apart from the details of spelling and punctuation, no changes were necessary: the repetitions in lines 5 and 6 of the song cannot be accommodated in the musical setting, and the manuscript reading 'though' in the last line, which in any case fits the music better than the First Folio's 'but', has been adopted in this text of the play itself. The second stanza is of course omitted.

The music has been transposed down a tone to make performance more practicable for the majority of singers: this is indeed the key in which it appears in two early manuscripts. The original is for voice and bass, the upper stave of the accompaniment being a purely editorial realization. The accompaniment may be played on a harpsichord or, ideally, a small chamber organ. There is contemporary evidence, in the plays of Edwards and Marston,[2] for the use of the regal to accompany songs; the term usually referred to a small organ with a reed stop, though it could also mean an organ with a reed stop only. Another possibility is for the accompaniment to be played on a lute or theorbo-lute: the given accompaniment may be intabulated as it stands or as transposed back to the original key (the lute itself being tuned to any convenient pitch). It would be idiomatic in such a version to double the bass line with a viol, but this might be obtrusive on the stage, even if the singer himself (or herself) were to play the lute. The contemporary use of the regal was probably intended to solve the problem of song-accompaniment in plays by means of a reasonably powerful instrument behind the scenes; boys did not normally play the lute, and the appearance of accompanists on stage would often be inappropriate.

[1] See also J. P. Cutts, *Musique de la troupe de Shakespeare* (Paris, 1959), Nos. 1, 1a.

[2] I am grateful to Peter Holman for drawing my attention to the evidence from Marston's plays.

INDEX

An asterisk indicates that the note supplements information given in *OED*. Biblical allusions and proverbs and proverbial phrases are grouped together.

Index